TREASURE IN THE CELLAR

TREASURE IN THE CELLAR

A TALE OF GOLD IN DEPRESSION-ERA BALTIMORE

LEONARD AUGSBURGER

MARYLAND HISTORICAL SOCIETY
BALTIMORE, MD
2008

Maryland Historical Society
201 W. Monument Street
Baltimore, Maryland 21201
www.mdhs.org

Publication of this work was made possible by the generous support
of the Friends of the Press of the Maryland Historical Society.

ISBN 0-938420-97-6

CIP Data Pending

Manufactured in the United States of America.
The paper used in this book meets the minimum requirements of the
American National Standard for Information Sciences Permanence of Paper
for Printed Library Materials ANSI Z39.48-1984.

This book is printed on acid-free paper.

For my wife, my treasure
Debra Kurtz

CONTENTS

CONTENTS

PREFACE

I began collecting coins, as many children do, by plugging Lincoln cents into penny boards and watching the holes disappear one by one. Today's generation finds the same fascination with the State Quarters. Teenage years brought the twin distractions of fast cars and awkward romantic endeavors, and coin collecting activities were put off until I established a professional career in the emerging world of software. A good coin collection demands a good library, and the literature of the coin collector is surprisingly broad, encompassing auction catalogs, periodicals, and an ever expanding array of books. This is fueled in part by the explosion of electronic resources which allow authors to conduct research at a remarkable pace. One also finds a diversity of topics, ranging from technical discussions about minute differences in coins, to historical essays related to images depicted on coins, to personal stories of collectors and collecting. It was the latter to which I was most drawn when I began to write articles for a number of hobby periodicals.

The story of the Baltimore gold hoard of 1934 was one that was known to collectors. There had been an auction sale in 1935, and copies of the auction sale catalog had long been prized as collector's items. Even better was to own a coin from the hoard itself. In reading various accounts of the hoard, I was surprised at the questions that were *not* answered. Everyone seemed to know the basic facts: two boys playing in a cellar had dug up a fortune in gold, and an important auction sale was held the following year. It was further known that one of the boys had died young, and that the other had gotten into a bit of trouble with the law. But at that point, no one seemed to know a whole lot more. To my mind, this was not at all satisfying. What really happened to the kids? What happened to the gold? And who buried the gold there in the first place?

What we had here was a *National Treasure* situation, except in reverse. In the *National Treasure* films we watch a group of characters follow a series of clues, engaged along the way in many enterprising exploits, such as kidnapping the President of the United States. Eventually the clues lead to a fantastic treasure. They are highly entertaining tales, but the Baltimore hoard did not follow the same arc. Instead, the Baltimore story started out with the treasure, and then asked researchers to use the treasure in order to uncover the clues. This I set out to do, determined to uncover every shred of information related to the hoard, and this quest turned into something of a treasure hunt itself.

I knew, of course, that there would be much information in the newspapers of the 1930s, and a number of research trips, traveling from Chicago to Baltimore, were focused on searching newspapers on microfilm at the Enoch Pratt Free Library. Along the way a helpful librarian pointed me towards the card file index at the *Baltimore Sun,* which was invaluable for finding the right dates to search. It was clear from the newspapers that there was a substantial legal trail as well, and Robert Barnes at the Maryland State Archives performed the initial searches for case material from Baltimore City Circuit Court #2, where the legal drama unfolded. Eventually I located the Maryland State Appeals Court material at the Archives as well; this contained its own treasure—photographs of the cellar, and a partial inventory of the hoard heretofore unknown to coin collectors. From the press and legal records, I also knew that Secret Service records were somewhere out there. That they were accessible to the public rather surprised me—after all, aren't they supposed to be "secret?" And yet, these were all waiting at the United States National Archives in College Park, Maryland, gathering dust for seventy years, until a researcher called for them.

Perhaps the most intriguing search was for one of the boys. As far as I knew, Theodore Jones might still be living. The family had adopted an alias when they moved to Baltimore in 1934, and but for a marriage certificate signed by Theodore's mother in 1935 with her true name, probably never would have been found. The marriage certificate led me to Edward Sines, one of Theodore's children, who most graciously welcomed me into his home and shared his recollections of the hoard. This story is richer for his willingness to talk to a stranger about something that had caused his family much trouble. Family members of other hoard principals were located by all manner of resources: vital records at the Maryland State Archives, United States Census records, Baltimore City directories, newspaper obituaries, and quite a bit of cold calling on my part. Most of the people I contacted were fascinated with the story, even if they ended up having no connection to it, as was often the case.

I did not envision this as a book when I started the project, rather it seemed like the sort of article I would like to write, and indeed an initial article was published in November 2002. At the time, I had not yet located the family of Theodore Jones, and the idea that he might still be out there compelled me to keep chasing leads. As I kept digging and finding new source material, it became obvious that a book was necessary to do justice to the story. Here, then, is the story of these two boys, Theodore and Henry, and I hope you enjoy reading it as much I enjoyed the "treasure hunt" of researching and writing it.

Leonard Augsburger
February 20, 2008

ACKNOWLEDGMENTS

This story was initially suggested by Ken Lowe, a dealer in numismatic literature, who prepared a brief chronology of the hoard in his house organ *Out on a Limb* in April 1988. By that time little was known of the hoard beyond what had appeared in several hobby periodicals in the 1930s. Lowe summarized these accounts but suspected there was much left untold. "There are some loose ends to this story," he thought. Lowe's work was continued by this writer in *Rare Coin Review #150*, November, 2002. This article pulled in new sources, most notably contemporary Baltimore newspaper accounts and legal material from the Maryland State Archives. Still, many of the descendants of the hoard principals had not yet been located.

The participation of these families was invaluable. Robert Levin and Harriet Berkis provided background on Harry O. Levin. Robert Levin lent the Harry O. Levin scrapbook, assembled by the Levin family in the 1920s. Edward Sines gave information on his father, Theodore. Henry Grob's relatives, John Grob Jr. and Chris Hoerner, were equally forthcoming. Sally Foster, a great-granddaughter of Andrew J. Saulsbury, shared much family ephemera. Descendants of Harry Chenven, Norman and Jesse Chenven, contributed family stories and genealogical research. Craig D. Lowry provided genealogical research on James Lowry Donaldson. Chuck and Michael Merrill gave information on their fathers, Eli and Yale Merrill, respectively. Joan Pitstick shared research on the Sines family in Ohio. Priscilla Menzies and Wade Fuller provided information on Perry Fuller. George Ross French offered history on the Findlay and French families.

Others without family connections to the characters also took interest. Herbert Trenchard of the Baltimore Philatelic Society did research on Perry Fuller. Robert Eagen, current owner of 132 S. Eden, gave much time and offered a tour of the property. Lee Augsburger, brother of the author, supplied helpful advice on legal research and practice. John Kleeberg, attorney and former curator at the American Numismatic Society, provided a thoughtful and thorough review of the manuscript and contributed a number of improvements. Joel Orosz, Q. David Bowers, Roger Burdette, Alison Frankel, and David Tripp, all numismatic authors extraordinaire, offered encouragement and research suggestions.

Internet databases were helpful, particularly www.ancestry.com for census images, www.lexis.com for legal research, and the Harry Bass Numismatic Indexes Project at www.harrybassfoundation.org/search-numlitasp. For access to period articles in the *Washington Post* and the *New York Times* I used www.ProQuest.com. Information at www.books. Google.com added previously undiscovered tidbits to the narrative. Other non-electronic indexes were also useful, especially those to the *Baltimore Sun* and the *Maryland Historical Magazine*.

National and state archives contained much useful information. The Secret Service case file was accessed at the National Archives in College Park, Maryland. The most important source material, the Baltimore City Circuit Court and Maryland State appellate court records, which spanned from 1934 to 1939, were accessed at the Maryland State Archives in Annapolis, MD. Independent researchers Robert Barnes and Trish Surles also performed genealogical searches at the Maryland State Archives. Contemporary newspaper accounts from the *Baltimore Sun, Baltimore Evening Sun, Baltimore News and Post, Baltimore American, the Daily Record,* and *the Jewish Times* were referenced at the Enoch Pratt Free Library in Baltimore. Staff at the Maryland Historical Society, Jewish Museum of Maryland, Star-Spangled Banner Flag House, Enoch Pratt Free Library, and Legislative Reference at City Hall, all in Baltimore, responded to numerous research requests. The author is especially grateful to Laura Cleary at the University of Maryland for locating photographs in the *Baltimore News American* Archive.

PART I

THE DISCOVERY

The entrance to the 132 S. Eden St. cellar,
facing the front building of the property.
(Maryland State Archives)

CHAPTER 1

THE HOUSE AT 132 SOUTH EDEN STREET
"CHOPPING WOOD WITH A CANDLE"

Rose Smulovitz, a Russian Jewish widow of about seventy, lived on the third floor of a run-down rooming house in east Baltimore. She had been in the United States twenty years, perhaps thirty, depending on which way you wanted to spell the name and which scanty records you felt were accurate enough to believe. The census taker who visited the residence at 132 S. Eden Street on April 10, 1930, would have needed fluency in Russian, Yiddish, Polish, German, and Italian in order to easily converse with everyone he interviewed. "An English word falls upon the ear almost with a sense of shock, as something unexpected and strange," wrote Jacob Riis, a chronicler of tenement life. Rose herself spoke Yiddish, and her front window overlooked the City Springs Square, where children of all ethnicities gathered and began the process of American integration.

The census taker recorded that Rose paid four dollars a month in rent, and that she was not working. A son, whose name is indecipherable, shows up in an earlier census and was probably her only means of support. The son worked in a "clothing factory," a euphemism for a sweatshop, where waves of immigrants gave their best years in hopes for the next generation. He did well for a garment worker, being enumerated as a cutter in the federal census. The cutters were entrusted to cut the patterns from raw fabric, a resource far more valued than the laborers themselves. They encountered a jigsaw puzzle in every piece of fabric, playing the patterns to preserve every last thread. The workers down the line got the worst of it. "I doubt if the human system can stand the pace they've set," thought a Baltimore work relief administrator. "They are simply making nervous wrecks out of their workmen. It's not at all uncommon for a girl operating a machine in one of these garment factories to throw up her arms and scream . . ."

There were no side windows in this block of row houses where Rose lived, leaving little ventilation in the summer. The winter was equally unaccommodating, with no electric service on the third floor and only a wood-burning stove for warmth. Wood was retrieved from the cellar underneath the back part of the house. More of a crawl space, even a small person had to bend over and awkwardly carry the fuel back upstairs to the fire. A resident of the second floor related the situation a few years later.

Q. You saw Mrs. Smulovitz chopping wood there?
A. Yes, sir; many times.
Q. What kind of light was back there?
A. No light.
Q. She was chopping in the dark, was she?
A. Well, with a candle.
Q. Did she lean over and stoop to get in there?
A. Yes, she had to bend down.
Q. And you saw her every day down there?
A. Every day.
Q. In the back part where she had to stoop over, chopping wood with a candle?
A. Yes, sir.

Harry Fleischer was under oath. Clarence Goetz, the court stenographer, dutifully noted the proceedings for posterity. History would not normally record the story of a poor widow struggling against the cold. There were millions before who had equally suffered, and millions more to come. But this was no ordinary cellar. Every swing of Rose's ax threatened to uncover a treasure. Every stooped step, every aching back, every chilled bone, hung on a single stroke of the ax. Twelve inches away she was, just a few handfuls of dirt and oyster shells, waiting to liberate her miserable existence in a strange land. But it would not be her fate to unearth this fortune. Two fatherless children, equally unlucky in life, were destined to come after Rose. To them would lay the spoils of a copper jug filled with thousands of gold coins.

BENJAMIN KALIS, PROPERTY OWNER

Benjamin Kalis visited 132 S. Eden Street for the first time on November 15, 1933. The three-story house sat long neglected amid a block of row houses on the west side of Eden, facing a park on the opposite side of the street. Kalis sized up the property quickly. He was from Russia himself, like many of residents on this block, and had worked his way out of the kind of squalid dwelling that now stared him in the face. Kalis came to America in 1912. In eight industrious years, he took his turn in the sweatshops, became active in the labor movement, married, purchased his own home, and had established himself in the property management business. If that wasn't enough to complete the American dream, Kalis topped it off by becoming an American citizen in 1919. His wife, Ida, was productive in her own way, bearing two children by the age of twenty-two and taking in immigrant boarders, a constant reminder of where they had come from.

Kalis inspected the property and came up with the figure of six hundred dollars. "The property was in a terrible condition," he said later, "everything was open, that is, the windows, [the] doors." Most of the window sashes were missing. Six hundred dollars was his estimate to get the property back into a rentable, if not entirely livable condition. Kalis looked around for anyone already living in the building. He found Rose Smulovitz in the third-floor front apartment. There were probably squatters as well, one of whom we shall hear from later. After finding no one else on the premises, he conferred with the owner, who authorized the work to begin. Six hundred dollars represented about six months' wages for a working class man, but Kalis had risen above that. By now, Kalis was a capable manager, no stranger to hard work, but no longer getting his own hands dirty. A team of ten workers was dispatched to resuscitate the dilapidated structure, and the ever-productive Kalis managed to execute the repairs and fill the building with tenants in a few short weeks, by January 1934.

Kalis could deal with the house well enough, but the City Springs Square on the other side of Eden Street was beyond his control. It was inhabited, one reporter wrote, by "bums, panhandlers, and smoke hounds [winos]." "It wasn't wise for women or children to walk in the square," he added. Benches and surrounding street lights were in disrepair, smashed by vandals with loose bricks pried out of the park walks. Compounding the blight was the Baltimore Bureau of Street Cleaning, which weekly cleaned out the alleys behind the area row houses and dumped its collection smack dab in the middle of Eden Street, right beside the acre-and-a-half square. From there it was collected by a truck. How fast the truck arrived depended on who you talked to. The engineer at City Hall claimed it always arrived within an hour, while the park custodian suggested it was more like the greater part of a day.

The house at 132 S. Eden, facing City Springs Square, was really two buildings, connected by a passage bordering the north side of the property. The smaller back building, facing an alley to the west, was stacked up like blocks, with the higher floors having successively less space than the lower floors. Stove pipes extended from the lower floors through the ceilings, adjacent to the rooms on the upper floors. Thus, the third-floor apartment in the back building was the least desirable at 132 S. Eden, being not only the smallest space, but also the residence most inundated with exhaust from the lower apartments. A cellar ran underneath the building, with the portion of the cellar underneath the rear building being lower in height than the front portion. Descending steps, entered from an outside hatchway that extended from the back of the front building, were the only means of access into the cellar. Kalis naturally divided the property into six units, one for each floor in the front building and one for each floor in the back.

The rush renovation of the building in November 1933 failed to completely solve certain structural problems. In August 1934, the kitchen floor in the first-floor rear apartment caved in. Charles Fleetwood, a carpenter in the employ of Benjamin Kalis, hoisted the joists in the rear part of the cellar, and covered up the hole from the first floor that peered into the dark void. Fleetwood braced the basement rafters as well as he could against the dirt floor. At the same time, a plumber, Robert King, was called in to repair water pipes running through the same part of the cellar. It was not the first repair job on the pipes, which had frozen at least twice during the early winter months of 1934. Fleetwood had been working on the house ever since Kalis had taken over, and later admitted the ongoing nature of the renovation. According to Fleetwood, "we were backwards and forwards, hanging a door today or putting a hinge on a door," and later, "off and on maybe two or three weeks I would go there to put a hinge on a door or fix a stove." King agreed, saying, "we go to that property often." Kalis himself had to look over things at least once a week.

Fleetwood and King were now joined in history with Smulovitz, the old widow in the third-floor front apartment. The trio worked in the back portion of cellar, moving the earth, tantalizingly close to a fortune, but in the end leaving the cellar with nothing more than another day's labor in their wake. Two teenaged boys had watched the workers coming and going through the back portion of the cellar, and an idea came into their heads.

VERITABLE CHILDREN OF WANT

If the structure on 132 S. Eden wasn't creaky enough, the land underneath it had an equally shaky history. This particular piece of real estate was subject to a "ground rent," a concept employed in various cities, including Philadelphia, St. Louis, and Baltimore. The ground rent system was, and remains, especially popular in Baltimore, and required the homeowner to pay annual rent on the land itself to the holder of the ground rent. In essence, the ownership of the land was separate from the ownership of anything actually built on the land. The advantage to the homeowner was that one never had to pay in full for the land underneath the house. For landowners, ground rents served as a convenient store of wealth, with regular income being produced with little management. Real estate developers built and sold new homes at cost, with anticipation of making their profits on future ground rents. The system worked well, unless the homeowners didn't pay the annual ground rent. In 1933, that is exactly what happened at 132 S. Eden.

Oscar and Ida Schapiro, Russian immigrants like many of their neighbors, had purchased the house on 132 S. Eden in 1919, and repeatedly mortgaged the property over the next few years. Ida died a widow in 1931, and the estate now had a white elephant on its hands. The house was nearly uninhabitable; a judge later described it as "in a run down condition, decaying; doubtless an unwanted asset." He further portrayed the tenants as "people of the humblest sort of means; veritable children of want." Still, the house had brought in thirty-eight dollars a month in rent the previous year, and the Schapiro estate gamely hung on until September 1932, when their last ground rent payment, sixty dollars a year, was made to the landowners. In 1933, the situation apparently deteriorated, and the ground rent payment was missed in September. The Schapiro estate had essentially walked away from the property and left the holders of the ground rent to do whatever they wished. It would be not be long before the Schapiro heirs realized that they had made an enormous mistake.

The ground rent at 132 S. Eden was owned by two elderly sisters, Elizabeth French, a widow, and Mary Pillar Boyd Findlay. Unlike the immigrant newcomers in the Eden Street neighborhood, the two sisters had family history in the Baltimore area. Indeed, this particular ground rent had been in their family since 1851. The sisters' father, Charles Findlay, was born in nearby Washington, on "the night the British burned the capital," as Mary Findlay put it in her application for membership in the Maryland Historical Society, referring to the War of 1812. The two women lived together in the fashionable Bolton Hill neighborhood in Baltimore, situated about three miles northwest of 132 S. Eden. The three miles represented the difference between single- and triple-digit rents. A room at 132 S. Eden might cost eight dollars a month; the two sisters paid nearly one hundred a month for theirs. Many of their Bolton Street neighbors employed servants, and Elizabeth and Mary were no exception, with two African-American servants listed at their address in the 1930 census.

The two sisters seemed to have entrusted their business affairs to the only child between them, Elizabeth's son Henry Findlay French. Findlay, as he was usually known, was born into a naval tradition. His father, a graduate of the Naval Academy, was born at Fort McHenry, where his father in turn had served before the Civil War. Findlay's father died young, of tuberculosis, leaving him as the only man in the family. Henry earned his law degree from the University of Maryland, and shortly thereafter took his own turn in the military, serving in the army in World War I and reaching the rank of major. Although trained as an attorney, he spent most of his professional career leading various Baltimore commerce associations, working to attract large companies to the Baltimore area. By 1933, French had not practiced law in a long time, but he was well connected to many who did, and so it was that C. Arthur Eby came to be associated with the goings-on at 132 S. Eden Street.

Eby had his own opinions about real estate, particularly in his own Baltimore neighborhood. Like many urbanites in the 1920s, he was not pleased with the fact that blacks were integrating themselves into white neighborhoods. President of the Maryland Avenue Association in north Baltimore, Eby noted that "his association was keeping a vigilant lookout for any movement of negroes into the association's territory." Similar neighborhood associations sprung up around Baltimore, all with the same charter. Their legal basis was shaky, but that did not stop them from erecting walls of litigation around any African-American trying to buy a home in their section. House deeds contained restrictions preventing sale to non-Caucasians, perhaps not enforceable, but still a great barrier to anyone who would have to fight through a court system that might not be entirely sympathetic. If that failed to work, these neighborhood associations could resort to "moral suasion," as in the case of the Civic Improvement and Protective Association, another north Baltimore group that managed to prevent African-Americans from renting some small houses in their neighborhood.

French's problem wasn't integration on Eden Street, which was already a melting pot. But after failing to receive the ground rent payment due in September 1933, he consulted with Eby, his attorney, and decided the best course of action would be to file an ejectment proceeding against the Schapiro estate. French probably inspected the property personally and found a very sorry state of affairs. He waited until November, giving the Schapiro bunch every bit of leeway to jump back into the fray, but on November 8, his patience was exhausted and an ejectment suit was finally brought in the Baltimore City Superior Court. Not surprisingly, the Schapiro representatives ignored the summons, having already decided to abandon the property. This made for a rather routine affair, and on December 12, Judge Samuel K. Dennis awarded French's mother and aunt title to the house at 132 S. Eden, one cent in damages, and twenty-four dollars in court costs. French jumped the gun by authorizing Benjamin Kalis to begin repairs before the proceedings were technically complete. The defendants had been served and ordered to report to the court by November 13. When none showed, French apparently felt comfortable to go ahead and dispatch Kalis to the property, which he did two days later. On December 13, the sheriff officially delivered the property to French, possibly by accompanying French to the site. By this time, Kalis had already repaired and rented the house. French was likely pleased with the progress of the reconstruction, and pleased that he had turned a non-paying ground rent into an income-producing situation for his aged mother and her sister.

CHAPTER 2

BESSIE SINES AND THEODORE JONES

Some time around 1932, Bessie Sines and her twelve-year-old son, Theo-dore, moved from Pittsburgh to Baltimore. Pittsburgh, the one-time gate-way to the West, had already lost its luster as an industrial powerhouse before the onset of the Depression. Economic vitality remaining or not, the bellowing steel mills still created enough haze that it was sometimes necessary to operate street lights during the day. There, Bessie worked in a glass factory, supporting three children. The glass industry sprang up in Pittsburgh in the nineteenth century, eventually supplying a sizable por-tion of the American demand for cut and engraved glass, not to mention more workmanlike uses, like the street light globes that guided Pittsburgh residents through the smoke screen of American industrial progress.

Bessie adopted a different last name in Baltimore. The exact reasons for this, and the whereabouts of her husband, are lost to history. It can only be assumed that Bessie, who was divorced, had reasons for not wanting to be found. Theodore did not often talk of such things, and such questions were not to be asked. "If my Dad opened his mouth," a son said, "it was usually to yell at us kids." Theodore would mellow in his old age, but this would not come until long after he and his mother were known as Theodore and Bessie Jones. Theodore's true age was also a mystery. He was probably born in 1920, but from time to time he used other dates as suited his purposes. The motivation for shifting the birth date was more obvious than the matter of his last name, and we shall learn why later. As for the father, Theodore once told a newspaper reporter that he thought he was dead and hadn't seen him since he was a young child.

Bessie may have been temporarily hiding, but there were still trips back and forth between Pittsburgh and the anonymity of Baltimore. Theo-dore made the trip at least once by hitchhiking. It was a distance of about two hundred and fifty miles, short enough to ease his mother's worry, but long enough in those pre-interstate days to immerse Theodore in the language of the road. Hitchhiking is rarely a nonstop affair, and Theodore probably moved in fits and starts across the Cumberland, through Appalachia, and coal-mining country, driver and passenger sizing each other up, sharing a ride along with the stories of other rides. Sometimes it was necessary to go backwards to a larger city to improve one's chances of getting a hitch in the right direction. Waiting on the side of a road one day, Theodore saw something on the ground. He picked up a cross, and wrapped it around his neck. This was the moment, he related months later, when his luck started to change.

Bessie and Theodore came to live on 132 S. Eden Street in Baltimore shortly after New Year's Day, 1934. There was fresh wallpaper covering the entire apartment, but like the New Year's Day festivities this mere decoration was simply a feeble attempt to hide the misery of the past. Bessie took in laundry, which she did by hand, to keep Theodore fed. Their rent was set at eight dollars a month, but even this small amount was not always paid. As Bessie put it, "Well, that is what we rented it for but we are under the Welfare, and, of course, he don't get the full amount." Kalis, the landlord, accepted whatever he got and allowed Bessie and her son to remain in the second-floor rear apartment. Kalis even put the electric bill under his company name, because Bessie could not afford the five dollar deposit to initiate service. Kalis was clearly versed in desperation long before the depth of the Depression overwhelmed the rest of his fellow citizenry; without doubt he had other tenants in other buildings in similar or worse conditions. Bessie and Theodore might have had Kalis' empathy, but they still had to live underneath a crazy old man's apartment.

THE SQUATTER HARRY CHENVEN

Harry Chenven lived in the one-room, third-floor apartment in the rear portion of 132 S. Eden, just above Bessie and Theodore. An old description of the property more accurately described Harry's apartment as an attic, but he stayed there just the same. By 1934 the building was aged and "easy of entry," as one newspaper diplomatically put it. Chenven kept a padlock on the outside of his door, apparently not wanting anyone invading his room when he was out, but willing to protect his castle himself when present. Chenven had moved into the ramshackle building in 1927, the last place he would live, bringing his own tattered past to rest in an equally decrepit dwelling. His was the least desirable space in the building, lacking even a functional toilet. Chenven had to take matters into his own hands when nature called. "He used to keep a vessel at night and dump it out over my windows," Bessie Jones recalled. "My mother hollered up at him," Theodore added, "he had a habit of dumping it out the window at night." Theodore was forced to explain the soiled windows to a friend at least once.

What Theodore couldn't explain was how a young jeweler in Russia turned into an old man in Baltimore whose chamber pot seemed to get slippery whenever he was near a window. Harry Gamerman, a friend of Chenven, couldn't explain it either, and if anyone should have known, it was Gamerman. He had met Chenven in the old country, Russia, where both worked as jewelers. When Chenven stepped off the boat onto the streets of Baltimore in 1908, he knew at least one person who had sailed for America in front of him, and that was Gamerman. The two did business together, and Chenven was quickly prosperous, building an inventory of fourteen thousand dollars in his jewelry store at 247 S. Broadway by 1914. Chenven specialized in buying old gold and sending it to the U.S. mint in Philadelphia, where it was melted down and converted into gold coins. A son, Isaac Zachary Chenven, was born in 1913. All signs seemingly pointed to another chapter in the history of immigrant American success stories. But it would be up to Zachary, the son as he was known, to finish the story that his father had begun with such great promise.

Somehow, in 1915, Harry Chenven crashed. From Gamerman's viewpoint, Chenven "took sick" and lost his memory. The Chenven family disagreed, stating that Chenven simply abandoned his wife and child. The U.S. Secret Service might have doubted Gamerman's credibility as well, because they suspected Gamerman of passing counterfeit currency. Whatever really happened, Harry Chenven spent the next year in a sanitarium, and did not reunite with his family when he was released. "He came out and never remembered what business he was in or what he did," said Gamerman, and after that Chenven sold newspapers to make a living. "But he had to be helped out to a certain extent," Gamerman added. Chenven's sister in New York sent Gamerman a hundred dollars a year, which he distributed to Harry as needed, and also took care of paying Harry's rent. The question of Chenven's own money was a mystery. "Sometimes he says he has got it and sometimes he says he don't know where it is," Gamerman said. If Harry did have money, he never used it to escape living in the broken-down building at 132 S. Eden.

Benjamin Kalis, the landlord, hadn't found Chenven there when he first visited the property in November 1933. Gamerman, a genuine friend, was intimately acquainted with Chenven's situation, and knew very well where Chenven was living. Gamerman had dealt with at least three of Chenven's landlords at 132 S. Eden, and in the months leading up to the Schapiro estate's abandonment of the house, it seems likely that the property wasn't managed at all. Indeed, so little attention was paid to this shack of woe that neighbors later thought the house had actually been vacant prior to its renovation in late 1933. Gamerman didn't go out of his way to find an absentee landlord, and Chenven stayed on as a squatter after the Schapiro estate gave up on the property. Gamerman resumed paying Chenven's rent to Kalis, for about eight months, until Harry Chenven died of a stroke, alone in his third-floor room on August 19, 1934.

ROOSEVELT'S GOLD RECALL

Franklin D. Roosevelt became president on March 5, 1933, uttering in his inauguration address the timeless admonition, "the only thing we have to fear is fear itself." Over the previous few months, the American public and bankers worldwide had feared greatly for the soundness of the American banking system. At this time, the United States was on a gold standard, meaning that gold coins circulated freely, and paper money was backed by gold. It was thus possible to redeem currency for its equivalent in actual gold, and in the early months of 1933, this is exactly what many foreign banks began doing. Gold was now flowing freely out of the country, while within its own borders American citizens were busily withdrawing gold coins from banks and personally hoarding them. Roosevelt's first act in office was to shut down the banks and stem the tide.

On March 6, Roosevelt declared a bank holiday, effectively closing banks to the public, with the stated intention of eliminating hoarding and stopping the outward flow of gold. On March 9, the Federal Reserve Bank ordered member banks to furnish names of gold hoarders, those who had taken gold out of banks after February 1st and had not returned it by March 13th. The mere threat of exposure was enough to entice many to redeposit their hidden caches of the yellow metal. Over the next few days the public lined up at banks to redeposit gold, just as they had lined up to withdraw it a few weeks earlier. Somewhat of a patriotic fervor arose to return gold, or at least, to not be identified as a hoarder. An Italian-American girl wrote to the President, "Yes, Mr. President. I found out that I was a hoarder. The five-dollar gold piece which I was keeping for the last two years for the sake of sentimental value represented part of the gold that is needed to keep the currency sound and restore, if not prosperity, at least normalcy." Inside the letter was the five-dollar coin. A Syracuse woman read this account and was equally moved to write Roosevelt, saying, "when I read her letter I realized I too was a hoarder. . . . I am enclosing my only gold piece. . . .Through depression I have lost home and all—now late in life I must start again."

The gold recall was codified and made official by President Roosevelt's

Executive Order 6102, on April 5, 1933, ordering all gold to be turned in by May 1st. By this time much of the hoarded gold had already been returned into the banking system, and the public was far more excited about its first taste of Prohibition repeal. On April 7, Congress authorized the shipping of 3.2% beer, an event heralded by full-page newspaper ads from the beer companies, and accompanied by much reporter fanfare. The Abner Brewing Company generated some good publicity for itself by having company officials personally deliver two cases to the White House promptly at 12:05 A.M. on the 7th. Winking an eye at his profession, one reporter noted that "the President and his secretary, Stephen T. Early, arranged to have the brew delivered to the National Press Club, where it will be quaffed with due ceremony by newspaper men who probably will not be hard pressed to recall the taste of such liquid."

Breweries quickly ramped up to twenty-four hour shifts to meet demand, while the newspapers expended much ink analyzing all details of beer distribution and vending, comparing, for example, the price of various quantities of beer before and after the Prohibition repeal. There was some debate about the extra "kick" in certain brands of beer. A federal chemist tested samples ranging anywhere from 2.5% alcohol upwards to the legal limit of 3.2%, much to the chagrin of those manufacturers who did not quite "measure up" to the allowed limit. French vintners held their noses and planned to ship 3.2% light wines, perhaps in the name of commerce but certainly not in keeping with any tradition of Gallic winemaking.

Lost in the excitement of legalized beer were certain exceptions to the gold recall, which would have implications for anyone coming into a large quantity of gold. Each American citizen was allowed to keep one-hundred dollars in gold coins, giving reasonable allowance to anyone who had a few stray coins and didn't want to feel unpatriotic. Gold for "legitimate and customary use" in industry was excepted. Gold coins "having a recognized special value to collectors of rare and unusual coins" were also permitted. The last clause was particularly important to collectors of gold coins, who until this time weren't entirely sure whether they were supposed to turn in their coin collections or not. Such technicalities were lost on the majority of the public, many of whom were disinterested to begin with. "We were supposed to turn in our gold, but we didn't have any to turn in," observed this author's grandmother. Violators of the gold recall were subject to a maximum fine of ten thousand dollars, and up to ten years' imprisonment, but for many even being in the position to commit such an offense was merely an idle daydream.

There were, of course, "gold bugs" who distrusted the government's scheme to separate citizens from their gold. Peter Kaminsky, of Queens, New York, was one of those who were leery of federal currency and much preferred to keep his wealth in hard metal. Charged with hoarding six thousand dollars in gold in January 1934, he explained himself to the court. "That money represents the savings of three generations. Part of it was left to my father, who added to it with his savings and left what he had to me. I have saved all my life against a rainy day and that money is all I have to protect me in case I lose my job." Kaminsky, married with one young child, was a one-legged Russian immigrant who worked as a machinist in a tin foil plant. He had been in America for twenty years and had undoubtedly worked most diligently over many years to preserve such a nest egg. Weighing on him further was the accumulated history of his ancestors, probably Russian Jews who paid an equally dear price to build this family fortune. Kaminsky's fate is unknown, but similar situations were typically dealt with by "redeeming" the gold for its face value in currency, particularly if the offender was merely hoarding and not trafficking.

The Fort Knox Bullion Depository, completed in 1936, was built to house U.S. gold reserves and the immense quantities of gold that came back into the banking system. Rumor had it that some of the gold was melted and used to gild the White House china. Once Roosevelt had the gold in hand, it never went back to the public. Citizens essentially swapped their hard metal for newly issued currency, which was no longer redeemable for gold. The only thing backing the currency now was faith in the president and the federal government. The public was left with the impression that holding any gold was illegal, and that the feds would hunt down and prosecute hoarders. Within his first month in office, Roosevelt had taken away the nation's gold and replaced it with low-alcohol beer.

The contrast was not lost upon Louis Eliasberg, a Baltimore financier and prominent coin collector. "A story which I once read," he recalled, "was about two men who, in 1932, walked through the streets of Baltimore, one carrying a pint of whiskey on his hip and the other carrying in his pocket six twenty-dollar gold pieces. In 1932 the man who carried the whiskey was violating the Prohibition law, and the man carrying the [gold] was within the law. Consider their plight when two years later, in 1934, the man carrying the gold pieces was violating the law, and the man with the pint of whisky was within the law." Eliasberg himself had accumulated fifty thousand dollars in gold coins in early 1933, anticipating like everyone else that the government was going to outlaw private possession of the precious metal. He stored it in his office safe, and like most of his fellow citizens returned it upon Roosevelt's proclamation. A hard-money man, Eliasberg decided the best revenge would be to take full advantage of the "rare and unusual coins" clause of the Gold Act, and these he systematically began to acquire.

CHAPTER 3

HENRY GROB

Theodore Jones didn't have much luck finding friends after moving with his mother into 132 S. Eden in Baltimore. Theodore thought his "Pittsburgh manner" might have rubbed people the wrong way. He had not yet met Henry Grob, living a block east at 227 E. Caroline, but this came soon. "I had just moved to Maryland," Theodore said, "and the gang in the neighborhood City Springs Park initiated me by beating me up. Henry, when I was getting much the worse of it, helped me out, and that started the friendship. " The two found they had some things in common, and bonded quickly. In a melting pot neighborhood, they were both of German descent. They were both fatherless and pitifully poor, and they both had many hours in the day to fill. "We always went around together," Theodore said, and according to Henry, "I used to go there [Theodore's house] every day." Theodore was the larger of the two boys, five feet eight inches tall in 1934, carrying a full head of hair atop a somewhat narrow face, and looking much older than his age of fourteen. Grob, a year older, was shorter and stout, with a visage betraying his Teutonic origin perhaps a bit more than Theodore's. Henry's father was a blue-eyed blond, of medium height and the same stoutness that his son inherited.

Henry, born May 12, 1919, never knew his father, who had died the previous October, a victim of the Spanish influenza pandemic. The Spanish flu came quickly and violently, in the fall of 1918, in such a way that a twenty-first-century American is incapable of framing an emotional connection to what actually happened. Almost one per cent of the population of the large eastern cities, including Baltimore, died in the space of a few weeks. Every household was affected, or knew someone who was. One out of a hundred was only the death rate, while the number of those taken ill with the flu, or worse, pneumonia, was far greater. The sick related that they felt as if they had "been beaten all over with a club." Schools, churches, and public gathering places shut down, streets emptied, while the public focused on caring for the sick and interring the corpses. Unlike previous influenza outbreaks, the Spanish flu took its greatest toll on those in their twenties and thirties, perversely the same portion of the populace most equipped to render assistance in this time of crisis. Henry's father died in his prime at 28, leaving his wife Ruth and three children, with Henry on the way. The plague left as quickly as it came. In Philadelphia, twelve thousand died from influenza or pneumonia in October. The next month the number dropped to a thousand. The average flu patient made a full recovery, leaving memories of the epidemic permanent only in the broken families. A children's rhyme, used to jump rope, arose from the epidemic. Perhaps chanted in the playground facing 132 S. Eden in Baltimore, it was heard in Boston and New York as well.

> I had a little bird
> And its name was Enza.
> I opened the window
> And in-flew-Enza.

Henry's mother quickly remarried, or at least that's what was reported in the 1920 census. In reality Ruth was now unmarried and living with a philanderer named Leo Stockman in the Highlandtown section of Baltimore, about two miles southeast of 132 S. Eden. Stockman was probably a friend of the family, an acquaintance of Ruth's first husband, John Grob. In 1917, the two men had registered for the World War I draft on the same day at the same office, were registered by the same officer, and were separated in line by no more than a few places, judging by the index numbers on their registration cards. Considering that over one hundred thousand men in Baltimore registered for the draft, the coincidence is difficult to ignore.

Stockman worked as a theatre projectionist, a comfortable if not lucrative profession in the heyday of the American movie palace. To be sure, the occupation wasn't entirely safe, with fires often breaking out in projection booths due to the highly flammable film. But business was good for the theatre owners in the 1920s. At the beginning of the decade the average American already attended the movies twenty times a year. In this pre-television era, the figure nearly doubled by 1930, spurred on by the advent of the "talkie" in 1926. Stockman made as much as fifty-eight dollars a week, a decent salary, working at a characteristic art deco theatre in Baltimore called the Bridge.

But friend of the family or not, Stockman was a womanizer of the worst sort, who loved and left any number of women in his short life. At the time Leo moved in with Ruth and her children, he was still married to his first wife, who he had abandoned and left with a young child several years prior. The relationship between Ruth and Leo, not surprisingly, deteriorated in short order. Stockman eventually finalized his divorce to his first wife, and then remarried yet another woman by 1925. Ruth was now on her own, and with four young children. The two girls were sent to be raised by relatives, while Ruth kept Henry and his older brother, John.

Ruth's relationship with Stockman, documented as marriage but not, was conversely followed by an episode of the opposite flavor. Ruth described it later. "I was a widow for two years and then married one Joe Fisher in Baltimore, Maryland, on Dallas Street, on a day in August, 1921, when I was drinking, at 8:00 P.M., and I left him at 9:00 P.M. This marriage has never been annulled, and there has never been a divorce." Ruth then took up with one Joseph Dragon but continued to use the Fisher name. Dragon at least provided a measure of stability to the widow and her two sons. The couple ran a tavern beneath their residence at 227 S. Caroline into the 1930s. "About October, 1921," Ruth recalled, "I went as a housekeeper for Joseph Dragon, a Hebrew, who promised to marry me, but never did, and the latter part of July, 1934, he left me, and he told me that he was going to marry a 19 year old girl, and he left me with the tavern business. We were at that location for twelve years, and our trade was mostly negroes." Proper taverns being illegal during most of this period, the business was described as a "lunch counter" in the 1930 census, and probably operated as such.

After Dragon left, Ruth operated the business as "Ruth's Tavern," apparently a non-lucrative situation, as she closed down about a year later, then picked vegetables in the fields and worked any other odd jobs she could find to support the family. Many weeks she traveled from Baltimore to the city of Choptank, Maryland, a couple hours removed from Baltimore by train, working there for ten dollars a week plus room and board. There was a large canning industry there, in particular for tomatoes. It was as good a situation as one could reasonably hope for. A Baltimore relief social worker noted that most of her cases getting seasonal work were employed only a few weeks at a time and at wages as low as two dollars a week. While in Baltimore, Ruth took care of her two sons and her brother besides. The brother would travel with her to Choptank, "to keep him from drinking," she said.

THE CELLAR CLUBHOUSE

Theodore and Henry had a lot of free time in the summer of 1934. Theodore hadn't been in school anyway, having only a second-grade education.

He was once asked to spell the name of his good friend Henry Grob and could not give an answer. He had worked from time to time, once driving a milk wagon, a position lost upon returning from a trip to Pittsburgh. But even with a proper education, there were few opportunities for young men living in a poor section of Baltimore. The two boys were thus starved for any diversion, and the cave-in of the kitchen floor in August, in the first-floor apartment underneath Theodore's, had no doubt attracted a good deal of their attention.

In their idle hours on the afternoon of Friday, August 31, 1934, Theodore and Henry hatched the idea of forming a boys' club, which they planned to call the "Rinky-Dinky-Doos." The name recalled a children's ditty made up of nonsense words, the kind of inane tune that is hard to get out of one's head.

> Skinny marinky dinky dink
> Skinny marinky doo
> I love you
> Skinny marinky dinky dink
> Skinny marinky doo
> I love you

The "clubhouse" of the newly instituted society was intended to be the rear portion of the cellar at 132 S. Eden. The two were no strangers to the cellar, and had in fact been playing in the front portion almost daily for most of the summer, perhaps to get some relief from the ninety-degree days, which were in abundance that year. The rear portion of the cellar, however, had been largely unexplored by the pair until recently. The water pipes and rafters in the rear cellar had been repaired between August 7 and August 27. Henry and Theodore evidently felt compelled to play building inspector and had entered the back part of the basement several times before the 31st. To get to the back, the boys had to pass through a door that separated the two parts of the cellar. Eventually there would be a great debate about whether this partition remained regularly locked, and whether or not Kalis, the landlord, ever intended any of the tenants to be back there. For now, it was simply a passageway to a novel part of the building with which Henry and Theodore were not familiar.

It was supposed that each member would contribute a nickel in dues to this boys' club, though nothing was ever actually collected. Nor was the exact purpose of the club ever established, though Henry offered that it might be for playing cards. Out of this scheme to keep themselves and perhaps a few of their friends occupied, Henry and Theodore now made the decisions that would define much of their existence for the next few years. It was Henry's idea that the dues, when collected, ought to be buried in a safe place. And it was Theodore who chose the spot where they should be buried. The two boys thus took a cigar box and proceeded to do a "test burial" in the cellar underneath the back building of 132 S. Eden Street, where Theodore lived with his mother.

With that, the boys entered the 132 S. Eden cellar, and proceeded to the back. The boys carried with them an axe, a corn knife, and a flashlight. The corn knife, with a broad blade about eighteen inches long, wasn't the best tool for digging. The boys likely didn't have much choice and used whatever was on hand. Theodore wielded the axe and the flashlight while Henry carried the corn knife. It seems that Theodore was the leader. He would be the one to mark the spot where the axe would strike first, while Henry, the dutiful worker bee, would scrape away whatever soil Theodore broke up. And if Henry needed to see what he was doing in the dark cellar, he would have to depend on Theodore to share the flashlight, the only source of light beyond a small window that lay under the steps at the entrance to the back side of the rear building.

The boys crept through the narrow way that separated the two parts of the cellar, opening up into the back area, which was about ten feet wide and twenty feet long. There was refuse back there, including an old mattress, the detritus of poverty in this run-down edifice. Theodore, wearing the cross he had found on the side of the road while hitchhiking, picked only one spot to dig. Entering the back cellar from the connecting passageway, he turned to his left, chose a spot next to the brick wall, and the two began to dig. The decision to dig next to a wall was a conscious one, made probably to help fix a location when retrieving whatever was buried. Other than that, the boys had nothing more than dumb luck working for them, or perhaps the law of averages requiring that unexpected events are inevitable. Someone, many years before, had decided to bury something at that exact spot, and the boys were about to make a visceral connection to the one who had gone before them. There was not a whole lot that fate had done to prepare the boys for what happened after that.

CHAPTER 4

TREASURE IN THE CELLAR

Henry and Theodore placed their cigar box on the dirt and eyed the size of the hole they would have to dig. Their chore was eased by digging next to the foundation, as one would only have to dig out on three sides of the box instead of four. They quickly hit a layer of oyster shells, discarded long ago in the same area. Oyster shells made for good ground cover and this was a natural place to dispose of them. The boys used their tools as best they could to remove the earth and shells, but it was necessary to use their hands as well. About a foot down, after a few minutes of excavation, Theodore took the swing that hit pay dirt. The ax fell, and Theodore noticed something jump up out of the earth, which both he and Henry thought was just another oyster shell. It was, in fact, a darkly colored twenty-dollar gold piece, but for the moment neither of the boys took much notice of it. As Henry put it, "Well, he hit something [that] sounded . . . tinny to me, I didn't know what it was, and I thought it was probably just another oyster shell and I never paid any attention, and he kept digging and he kept digging and he felt it and we are digging around it and we saw it was a can." They dug around the can, or pot, about five minutes more, until they could liberate it from the earth that had cradled it for many years. There was an old boot, split lengthwise, awkwardly wrapped around the gallon-sized container, and this last bit of protection was pulled out by the boys, uncovering the prize.

The pot was heavy. The newspapers reported its weight as seventy pounds, though exactly what and how much was in the pot at the moment it was extracted from the earth would become a decidedly controversial subject. Theodore, the stronger of the two boys, lifted it out and set it on the old mattress that lay in the back cellar. It was about nine inches tall and fifteen inches wide, the size of can one might use to pack tomatoes, Henry would say later. The copper pot was green, corroded, and nearly falling apart. Someone later noticed the imprint of a gold coin on the exterior of the pot, as if the copper had disintegrated around the shapes of the coins

The front portion of the cellar, facing north. The entrance to the rear cellar is at the back left. (Maryland State Archives)

directly in contact with it. Theodore struck it with a hammer, and the pot heaved its last breath, disgorging thousands of gold coins onto the soiled mattress that lay in the dirt underneath this hovel of poverty. The boys did not immediately realize what was in front of them. The coins toward the outside of the pot were green and appeared to be corroded, and many of the coins were so stuck together that they could not be pried apart by hand. Theodore picked up a green colored coin and did not recognize it, thinking perhaps it was some kind of medal. Henry scraped it with his knife and identified the twenty-dollar gold piece. The game was afoot.

There would be many mistakes made in dealing with this pot of gold, and the boys made the first one quickly. In the next few minutes, Henry and Theodore inflicted untold damage on the coins, probably to the extent of a million dollars in today's money. It was an understandable misstep; probably not one boy in a thousand would have known to do any different. Gold is a soft metal, and coin collectors are fussy about even the slightest marks on the surfaces of a coin. What is a trifle to a casual observer can mean thousands of dollars more or less to a serious numismatist. There was no way for Henry and Theodore to know this, no way two children of their station in life could possibly have respect for the delicate surfaces of coins that appeared to them already corroded and damaged. In actuality, gold is highly resistant to corrosion, and can be remarkably conserved to its original appearance, even after being hidden in the earth or swallowed up in a long-forgotten shipwreck. Henry and Theodore had a more pressing objective, which was to divide up this kettle of treasure between the two of them.

The two used a hammer, and probably the other tools as well, to begin clawing apart the coins. The hammer, ax, and knife, with every blow and scratch to the clumps of coins, chipped away at the boys' fortune. Eventually the larger coins were sufficiently loose to begin the process of distribution. The United States government had minted gold coins beginning in 1795, using denominations of ten, five, and two-and-a-half dollars. With the advent of gold discoveries in the West, one-dollar and twenty-dollar pieces were added to the lineup in 1849. The twenty-dollar gold piece was roughly the size of a silver dollar, with the other denominations proportioned in size to their value. Henry summed up the division of coins, "First we started giving twenties, then tens and fives, then we got tired of it and just took our hands." There were a few hundred of the larger coins, an easy enough chore to divide, but the several thousand one-dollar gold pieces were problematic. They were small and thin, about two-thirds the size of a penny, stuck together, and hard to separate with the boys' large tools. The small coins were thus split by alternating handfuls.

With the cache divided in two, Henry and Theodore "sat on the dirt floor and dreamed dreams of what they would do with the wealth," as one reporter described it. Whatever happened next, one had to look back at this point in time, when it was just two boys and a pot of gold, sitting in a cellar and talking about the events that were about to unfold, and maybe even doing some advance planning. Neither ever went on record about that conversation, and its content can only be surmised from the storm that was about to break in Baltimore. The two boys may have been from the lowest part of society, they may not have had the benefit of education, but they knew hunger and need, and they knew their mothers had suffered intensely on their behalf. Whatever schemes the two boys hatched that late afternoon on August 31, 1934, Theodore's son put it this way: "Henry and my Dad weren't dumb."

PART 2

WHOSE GOLD?

Theodore Jones, Lieutenant Daniel Pfenning, Henry Grob,
and Sergeant Gustav Lample. Photograph taken at the Baltimore
Eastern Police Station. Notice the pot in front of Grob.
Baltimore News & Post, *September 1, 1934*

CHAPTER 5

LAYING CLAIM

Henry gathered his share of the gold and packed it into his shoes as best he could. He had small feet for a fifteen year old, size five and a half, and was forced to use his pants pockets as well. Walking barefoot across the pavement baked in the Baltimore summer sun, Henry made his way home to 227 S. Caroline Street, a block and a half away. To escape the warm streets, he probably cut across the grass-covered City Springs Square facing 132 S. Eden. Passersby must have considered it rather odd, a boy carrying two shoes filled with some greenish encrusted metal, pockets bulging and slung low. Henry arrived at home without incident.

Henry laid the coins on a table and proudly announced to his mother Ruth, "Mother, I always said I'd be a millionaire. And now I'm a millionaire." Ruth Grob's first reaction was fear. "Take it out of here," she yelled at her son. Henry took the coins up to his sister's apartment, in the same building. Gertrude Grob Eberhart, similarly excited, called up her husband, Paul, a soldier at Fort Hoyle, to sort out the matter. The family regained their composure and began to deliberate as to the best course of action while Henry, full of himself, paraded around the pile of gold with a .22 caliber rifle, probably a U.S. army issue in the custody of his brother-in-law.

Henry and Theodore's first thought had been that the gold could be turned in at a bank and redeemed for its equivalent value in greenbacks. Henry's brother-in-law, Paul, quashed this line of reasoning, suggesting that taking the gold coins to a bank would probably result in their arrest. This was unlikely, as the government would obviously have to make reasonable allowances for hoards discovered after the gold recall. Certainly no one was going to be incarcerated for accidentally stumbling upon a cache of gold. Indeed, a United States district attorney was quoted in the press several days later, indicating that there would not be any trouble taking the coins to a bank. Eberhart was instead reacting out of a general impression that the government was quite interested in pursuing hoarders. The best thing to do, he felt, was to take the coins to the Baltimore police. Paul's advice was significant, because it meant that the coins would ultimately be in the hands of local law enforcement rather than the federal government. In time this lucky decision would prove to be the right one, but at the moment Henry was a bit crestfallen. "He done his best to turn it over to the police, which he did," he said ruefully about his brother-in-law.

The boys' instinct to take the coins to a bank was understandable. After all, hadn't the public lined up outside the banks the last year to turn in all their gold coins? An Ohio gentleman found himself in a similar situation and thought the exact same thing. Robert Perry, of Bradford, Ohio, was excavating his basement and in the course of the dig came upon a tin box full of gold coins that fell apart when it was picked up. Perry immediately turned the coins into a nearby bank, where the gold, six hundred and seventy dollars face value, was exchanged for its equivalent in currency. Perry's gold was now safely in the hands of the federal government, and he had essentially cheated himself of the opportunity to sell it to collectors at a premium over its face value. Henry and Theodore's gold, bound for the Baltimore judicial system, would take a much different route.

Henry and his brother-in-law, Paul, collected Theodore and headed to the Eastern Police Station, a few blocks removed from the Grob apartment. Theodore had been trying to clean up his share of the gold by letting it soak in a bucket filled with water. Fortunately this didn't harm the gold coins; on the other hand, it didn't do much to improve their greenish appearance either. This part of the salvage operation would have to wait until later. There was also the matter of separating the coins, especially the smaller ones, still stuck together in bunches of four and five pieces. At the station, the group first approached Sergeant Harry R. Hill. "We've got about $7,000 in gold pieces here," they said. "We want to give it to you." Even for a policeman, Hill was taken aback. Hill summoned Lieutenant Daniel W. Pfenning and Sergeant Gustav C. Lample to help count the pile of several thousand coins, which represented a face value of $7,882. The gold was placed in the station safe, and Theodore and Henry were assured that they would get the money back "after the legal tangles were ironed out."

The group headed back to Theodore's for further investigation, where the boys turned over an additional $3,542 worth of the yellow metal to the astonished policemen. The boys were rather forthcoming about their motivation, explaining, "We didn't know what would happen, so we decided to hold out a little. We need it. We had planned to give it to our mothers, but when you told us that we would get it back we decided to turn it all in." The *Baltimore Sun* reported that the boys were "quite cheerful" about this part of it, and "had decided that honesty was the best policy."

The word around Baltimore burst forth quickly, just like the thousands of coins separated from the copper jug when struck by Theodore's hammer. By the time the boys and police came back to the station to count the second batch of coins, reporters and photographers were waiting. The first person to cash in on the hoard was a tipster to the *Baltimore News*, who was awarded, several days later, fifty dollars in their weekly "News Tip" contest. At the station, the boys made their first statements to the media, which naturally covered their plans to spend the fortune. Henry said, "Well, the first thing that I had thought of was to buy a house for my mother. After that, if there is anything left, I would start a bank account for her so that she would have some money. I hadn't planned to get anything for myself. There isn't anything that I need especially and mother has been working hard for me all her life. She ought to have it." For his part, Theodore remarked, "Mother has been wanting a washing machine for years. I would get her one first thing. Then maybe I would buy myself a new suit—it's been so long since I had one. After I got mother the washing machine and myself the suit, she could have everything that was left. She would know what to do with it. She had needed money long enough." Theodore thought of his mother first, and many years later thought of his children, who were always given new clothes for holidays. Theodore also gave some consideration to the cross around his neck, the one he had found hitchhiking between Baltimore and Pittsburgh. "It's a funny thing," Theodore remarked the following day. "I was wearing this yesterday when Henry and I started digging in the cellar. I wonder now . . . ?"

I SHOULD BE IRISH?

The Grob and Jones families understood immediately that they needed legal representation. The two mothers enlisted a prominent local attorney, Harry O. Levin, to protect their interests in the gold hoard. Levin, popularly known as "Harry O.," was a natural choice, a well-known defender of the disenfranchised in Baltimore, especially of Catholics and African-Americans. A child of Russian Jewish immigrant parents, Levin had gained his share of the American dream early in life. He was a successful attorney who worked for himself, and was also active on the political scene, serving as a Maryland state senator in the 1920s, several state boards and commissions in the 1930s, and later, in 1940 as a delegate to the Republican National Convention. Levin was hired on contingency, most likely on the morning of September 1, 1934, with the agreement to split the hoard proceeds three ways, one share for each family and one for Levin. The local police, who were counseling all concerned parties to contact attorneys, may have initially referred the two families to Levin. The families must have been delighted to engage a powerful and well-connected attorney at no up-front cost. The final chapter of their relationship would not be so amicable.

Levin was well aware of the rough and tumble that was ahead of him. He was, in some ways, playing the character of a gunslinger, as if taking his part in the scene of a western movie picture set amid gambling, desert towns, saloons, and of course vast quantities of gold waiting to be found in secret places. Levin understood exactly who he would be competing against in this legal marathon, even if he did not know their names yet, and taking this case on contingency was his bet that he could take on whatever the opposition had to offer and come out on top. A courtroom was not nearly as romantic as the image of a few cowboys playing cards in a dusty saloon, but that was no concern of Levin's, even if he was gambling just the same. There would be more attorneys to enter this scene, but it was Levin's role to be first on stage.

No stranger to the public eye, Levin had represented a northern district of Baltimore in the Maryland state legislature in the terms of 1924 and 1927. He was the only Republican in the Baltimore delegation, and if that wasn't remarkable enough, he was a Jew representing a district where the majority of the voters were African-American. Hardly sixty years removed from the Emancipation Proclamation, Republicans proudly carried the banner of Lincoln, the "man who freed the slaves." Until the New Deal politics of Roosevelt held full sway, a Republican could reasonably expect to build support within the African-American electorate, and Levin wasn't afraid to capitalize on history. A Levin endorsement appearing in a local black newspaper, signed by a General Felix Agnus, carried the headline, "Civil War veteran, who battled for freedom with Lincoln, praises senatorial candidate," and further added that "[Levin's] friendship for the colored people is well known and his practice as a lawyer has included the successful handling of many cases involving their interest and welfare."

Levin's campaigns of the 1920s were hard-nosed affairs that turned greatly on the issue of race. Levin's Democratic opponent in 1924, William G. Menchine, was on record as having advocated, at one time, race restricted living areas in Baltimore. The *Afro-American* newspaper in Baltimore identified Menchine as a supporter of one such proposal in 1912. "Where do you propose to house this increasing Negro population," he was quoted as saying.

I say house them on 'mixed streets' where property is depreciated, never again to appreciate and house your increasing white population on exclusively white streets—on new streets, if you choose—where property valuations will remain stable for years to come and thus accomplish true segregation. There is still another reason why 'mixed streets' should be allowed to work out their own salvation, which, in my humble opinion, means to be wholly colored. It is a well known fact that a very large percentage of the colored race suffers from tuberculoses. For this reason, if no other, we should not encourage the occupance by a white family of a residence formerly occupied by a colored family. Yet this is exactly what the law at present does. It compels the owner of a house on the 'mixed street,' where the majority of the houses are occupied by white persons, to rent a house formerly occupied by a Negro to a white person and none other.

The tone of the political engagement in Levin's 1927 campaign was not markedly improved, and the local press seemed to greatly enjoy the fact that Levin was running against his relative, Democrat E. Milton Altfeld, a first cousin. The *Post* was quite open about that part of it, admitting that, "The fight between these two has been the only city fight with any life in it." Nor was the *Post* afraid to lend space in any attempt to sustain controversy, printing Altfeld's rather laughable accusation that Harry O. Levin was distributing campaign literature in Irish neighborhoods using the altered name "Harry O'Levin." Levin delivered a clever retort in the *Baltimore Sun* several days later, "Yes, with a district where the voters are 60% colored, 25% Jewish, and the remaining 15% largely German—I should be Irish?" It was all amusing enough, but later accusations of hate mail, physical intimidation, and use of the so-called "N-word" cast a shadow over the campaign that Levin won by a small margin.

Levin's actual service in the state legislature was more constructive. He fought against patronage, endorsed funds for public defenders, and strongly advocated a new hospital for Maryland blacks, a measure which was passed by the legislature but vetoed by the governor, a bitter pill for Levin, who seems to have made it a pet cause. His name was mentioned as a possible candidate for Congress, but Levin had had enough. "The big corporate interests are firmly entrenched," he wrote about legislative politics. "Their officers are always in evidence, their legislative friends legion, and opposition is generally futile." Levin decided to leave electoral politics in 1930 to settle back into private practice in Baltimore, perhaps to an environment where his skill as an attorney would have better odds against the local competition.

CHAPTER 6

THE BALTIMORE GOLD RUSH

Following the stunning revelation delivered by Henry and Theodore on the evening of August 31, the police investigated what little they could. A special guard was placed at 132 S. Eden, while the police conducted their own "dig" in the cellar, which uncovered nothing. The police also had a look at Harry Chenvin's empty apartment on the third floor of the rear building. Harry had passed away August 19, and there was nothing interesting in there, either. A few officers seemed more anxious to indulge in a bit of reminiscing, engaging hungry reporters in speculation about how the gold had gotten there in the first place. A seemingly plausible theory was advanced by Patrolman Edward Horner, 54, who recalled, "I was born down there, and as a boy played with others of the neighborhood in the 100 block [the 100 south block of Eden Street]. There was an old retired captain, his last name was Donaldson, who lived in the house at 132 with his two sisters. It has been forty years since the last of them died—and they all died in that house. Donaldson operated his own clipper ship in Baltimore and South American ports, carrying general cargo. He was reputed to be a wealthy man, and retired to the house with his two sisters. They lived there for years. First Captain Donaldson died, and several years later both of his sisters died. The money might have been buried by the captain, and he might have died without revealing its hiding place to his sisters. Or they might have left it there after his death, and died themselves before they were in need of it, and without telling anyone else where it was." Horner recalled that Donaldson was involved in the Brazilian coffee trade. A colleague, Sergeant Herman Bruns, 72, chimed in, adding, "The entire neighborhood was used years ago as the center for retired and active seamen. They formed their clubs and lived in the section, while they were active and when they retired. There were many of them living in the neighborhood."

Horner's tale of the seafaring captain was romantic enough, but it didn't hold water. The policeman, ostensibly a professional witness by trade, did not have the facts quite straight. The family he had in mind was actually named Wilson, not Donaldson, and furthermore the Wilson family hadn't lived in 132 S. Eden, but at the neighboring house to the north, 130 S. Eden. Horner's childhood recollections squared with the rest of it. Captain Wilson really was a Brazilian coffee importer who lived with two elderly women, and the family had indeed occupied the house for many years. The true facts would come out later, but in the meantime the ears of a certain Donaldson family percolated.

In between reporters, the officers at the Eastern Police Station dealt with numerous visitors inquiring as to how they could lay claim to the gold, all of whom were instructed to consult with attorneys. Among the interested parties was a woman who would not give her name to a reporter, but offered that she was a niece of Ida Schapiro, a former owner of the house at 132 S. Eden. It was, in all likelihood, the same person who had made the decision to walk away from 132 S. Eden in 1933, failing to pay the ground rent and leaving the broken-down property for the sisters Findlay and French to deal with. Her name was Jennie Zimmerman, and she intended to enter the inevitable litigation, failed ground rent or not. Other area residents who could not divine similar connections to the 132 S. Eden property conducted their own cellar excavations, in "practically every house," according to one account. None were successful. The only recourse now was to the courts, where "scores of claimants are expected to appear," the *Baltimore Sun* predicted.

Theodore Jones and Henry Grob

Henry and Theodore had much to take in, and the first night was understandably anxious. The *Sun* reported that Henry "had a series of dreams in which gold was the central character," while Theodore couldn't fall asleep until five in the morning. Theodore had already lied about his age to the newspapers, saying that he was sixteen when he was really fourteen, and perhaps some thought was given to making sure that this story could hold its own. Theodore also tipped his hand on something which rang more true, when a reporter apparently asked him if he had a girlfriend. "She hasn't got a name, you know," Theodore said, being a bit coy. "But she lives in Salisbury [a town in southeastern Maryland] and I wouldn't mind sending her a paper with my picture in it. Maybe her aunt won't object to me so much now." Theodore's mother was dreamy and reflective. "Just to think," she said, "Here we've been living here all this time, being supported by the Family Welfare, and all that money buried right in the cellar."

The press hit its own gold strike the first few days following the find. There were photographs of Henry and Theodore, Henry and Theodore with the gold, Henry and Theodore in the basement, Henry and Theodore with the police, and of course their mothers as well. Reporters encouraged local residents to wonder what they would do with the money, had they had been so fortunate to find it themselves. A banker said, "I guess there is a great deal of speculation on this subject today, and it is one thing bankers better stay out of," perhaps an oblique reference to the fact that bankers were supposed to be handling greenbacks and not gold. Robert F. Stanton, a Baltimore judge said, "A judge never sees that much money, but if such a stroke of luck occurred, I believe I would turn it over for something extra for the pensioned widows and orphaned children." It was Stanton's first encounter with the hoard, and it would not be his last.

A PITY TO MELT UP SUCH COINS

The gold coins were soon taken from the Eastern Police Station to the Central Police Station in Baltimore, but not before the patrolmen at the Eastern Station had finished the "curating" job that Theodore and Henry began in the cellar. The police cleaned the coins with kerosene and vinegar, a lucky choice, as kerosene, a solvent, can safely remove grease and organic material from gold. Unfortunately, they also felt compelled to use knives to separate the coins that remained stuck together, probably the small one-dollar pieces. The policemen did Henry and Theodore no favor, scratching and gouging the tiny little gems and inflicting incalculable damage in the process. An inventory of the coins taken several months later revealed that fifteen percent of the one-dollar gold pieces had had their dates obliterated, while none of the higher denomination coins had unreadable dates. One can imagine the satisfaction of the policemen, the sense of accomplishment, in getting all the coins separated and safely stowed in the Central Station, all the while ignorant of the damage done to the coins. The police commissioner was apparently glad to be done with it and didn't want to be bothered any further. Charles D. Gaither, seemingly irritated by all the publicity, not to mention his distracted officers, refused to let numismatic experts look at the coins, stating that it "was all nonsense."

Even without seeing the coins, local collectors and dealers immediately understood the hoard would have some value. The thousands of one-dollar gold pieces in the hoard were already collectible beyond their intrinsic gold value, having not been minted since 1889. There was also a chance that some of the gold coins came from the branch mints, the main mint being in Philadelphia. The branch mints were founded in response to gold discoveries, first in the 1830s in the South, and then in the 1850s in the West. Coins from the branch mints were struck with mintmarks, "S" indicating San Francisco, "O" being New Orleans, and so on. The Philadelphia coins were struck without mintmarks. The branch mints were upstart backwater affairs, relying heavily on support from Philadelphia for operations. As a result, quality varied widely and many of the non-Philadelphia issues were limited to small quantities, meaning that by the 1930s many of the mintmarked specimens traded among collectors and dealers at substantial premiums.

Baltimore numismatists also anticipated that these coins would probably fall under the Gold Act exemption, which allowed the accumulation of gold that had "a recognized special value to collectors of rare and unusual coins." Dr. Charles E. McCormick, a Baltimore pharmacist and coin collector, said that "it would be a pity to melt up such coins," while local coin and stamp dealer Perry W. Fuller indicated that because of their collector value, he did not expect the federal government to intervene and force the coins to be "redeemed" in greenbacks. Fuller was wrong, because the feds were indeed watching. Fuller himself would be the first numismatist to get a good look at the coins, but for now the contents of the hoard, and the actions of the federal government, were still open to speculation. A cashier at the Baltimore branch of the Federal Reserve Bank suggested that the feds would wait until ownership of the gold was settled, and then force its exchange for currency.

As for the non-coin collecting public, suspicion of gold remained. Old gold buyers played upon public fear by advertising that their operations

Ruth Grob, Henry Grob, Bessie Jones, and Theodore Jones

were "licensed by the U.S. government," implying that possession or disposal of gold by any other means was illegal. Other ads claimed "we employ no solicitors," taking a shot at those who went door-to-door soliciting for old gold, a common practice at the time, and adding that the public should not "sell to strangers." Abraham Kimmel, a Brooklyn, New York resident, took full advantage of the situation by going door-to-door in Long Island, impersonating a U.S. Treasury agent and strongly suggesting that all gold items on the premises be turned over to him in order to "strengthen our currency." The gold canvasser carried faked credentials, stating that "all citizens are asked to co-operate to the fullest extent in this most important mission." Kimmel, paying minimum prices, was arrested after several days of harassing New York housewives and accusing those who declined to sell of being unpatriotic.

The *Saturday Evening Post,* sensing a popular cultural theme that might induce some additional circulation, commissioned the celebrated mystery writer, Mary Roberts Rinehart, to create a serial based on a hoard of gold hidden in a chest and tucked underneath a bed. In the first installment the unfortunate matron owner of the gold was "brutally and savagely done to death" with an axe. Perhaps she had "sold to strangers" or was otherwise reaping a deserved punishment for hoarding gold!

CHAPTER 7

A WEEKEND OF LABOR

Theodore and Henry had struck gold on the Friday before the Labor Day weekend of 1934. The first weekend brought numerous visitors, especially to Theodore's, many of them wanting to see the "treasure cellar." Robert King, the plumber who had recently worked on the pipes only steps away from the buried gold, came by to offer his congratulations. King was "the unluckiest man in Baltimore," as the *Baltimore News* put it, having dug up much of the cellar himself when preparing to lay new water pipes. The visitors did not necessarily get to see either Theodore or Henry. Both were reported to have taken trips over the weekend out of state. Exactly how these destitute children could afford to travel at this point in time went unexplained. Theodore, who probably went to Pittsburgh to see his sister and brothers, quite likely took along a few "souvenirs," and newspaper clippings, to prove to his incredulous siblings that lightning had indeed struck the family. Theodore also set the stage for a second thunderbolt, telling the press that he and Henry planned to have another go at the cellar. Neighbors continued their own digs, one newspaper noting that "lights were burning bright in almost every cellar."

Meanwhile, Levin was trying to figure out what to do with the dynamite in his hands. Beyond the law, there was an instant emotional connection with Henry and his mother, because, like Henry's deceased father, Levin himself had been stricken by the Spanish flu in the fall of 1918. Levin was hospitalized and not allowed to visit his first child for several weeks following her birth. "Harry O." conversed with Henry's mother and must have wondered to himself if his own wife might have walked in the same shoes. No doubt the empathy only increased his resolve to protect the families as best he could.

The studious attorney thus dug through the law books, working over the weekend to prepare a court filing for the boys, which was promptly entered the day after Labor Day. Levin's brief tipped his hand as to the legal route he planned to pursue, but also indicated that he grasped the concepts of the case immediately. Levin wrote that the coins had been "se-creted in the said cellar for a long time," and further that "said coins were not lying upon or on the ground." In stating these facts, Levin framed his case around what courts have come to consider two elements of the law of treasure trove: (1) that the treasure trove be buried or otherwise hid-den or concealed, and that (2) the treasure trove must have been buried for a long time, because it has "the thought of antiquity." Levin carefully questioned Henry and Theodore about the physical layout of the cellar, and in his petition alluded to the question of trespass. There was a door between the front and rear part of the cellar, and Levin realized that ques-tions might arise as to whether the boys had any right to be in the rear cellar. He headed this off by noting that the "petitioners were lawfully engaged in a joint enterprise," and that Theodore and his mother had lived in the building for some time. Finally, Levin made allowance for the federal gold recall, and asked that either the coins or "their equivalent in currency of the United States," be awarded to the boys.

Levin's brief hints at the tone of the initial conversations he had with Henry and Theodore. "Harry O." probably seemed like a physician, in-quiring about very specific details that didn't make much sense to the boys, blinded as they were by the yellow luster they had uncovered in the darkness. Levin himself needed to be sufficiently discriminating before engaging in what promised to be a lengthy legal battle. After meeting with

Henry Grob, Harry O. Levin, and Theodore Jones

the families, the attorney committed quickly and wasted no time launching a public relations campaign. "I am convinced they are the rightful owners," he announced on Tuesday, September 4. An editorial in the *Baltimore News* seemed to agree with Levin and expressed hope that "the finders may receive a goodly portion of it," especially in light of the fact that the first thing the boys wanted to do with the money was to help their mothers. Judge Albert S. J. Owens gave potential litigants ninety days to step forward, and now Levin would finally be able to put a face on the competition.

YO-HO-HO AND A BOTTLE OF RUM

"Lost and found articles are always interesting from the human standpoint. The greatest Teacher ever to live on this earth illustrated his teachings with the parables of the lost pearl, the lost sheep, the lost coin, and the lost boy. The discovery of the key to the location of lost or hidden treasure has been of fascinating interest to author and reader alike. When Robert Louis Stevenson wrote his immortal 'Treasure Island' he enveloped it with the most appealing and alluring quality of treasure trove. 'Fifteen men on a dead man's chest, Yo-ho-ho and a bottle of rum' brings to our minds Captain Bill and a certain 'seafaring man with one leg'. Buried gold has been the theme of writers and has given to their writings an entrancing interest, whether the reader be the growing boy or the sedate and settled old man. No one has started to read Poe's 'Gold Bug' and wanted to lay it down until he had reached the end."

Judge John Benjamin Guerry
Georgia Court of Appeals, 1935

While even a high-ranking judge could not ignore the compelling romance of a treasure trove, it could only be a pity, or perhaps some vague notion of eternal balance, that something diametrically dull would oppose it. Such is the law of treasure trove. Even the author of a standard study on treasure trove law admitted that, "No one . . . is likely to read the book through." A university law review added, "The true tales of treasure trove are by no means as exciting or as adventurous as one has been led to believe." Theodore and Henry hadn't the first clue as to what defined "treasure trove," but their attorney, Harry Levin, had no doubt done a good bit of research on the subject.

The phrase "treasure trove" is distinguished from several other types of missing property. "Abandoned property" applies to items from which an owner has deliberately walked away. Abandoned property can be legally claimed by anyone who finds it. The classic law school example is that of unattended horse manure on public highways, otherwise valuable fertilizer, which may be freely claimed by a finder. "Lost property" refers to something lost through carelessness or negligence. For example, if a stranger accidentally drops money on the floor of a hotel, a chambermaid can claim it. "Lost property" is differentiated from "mislaid property" by the intention of the person who lost it. Returning to the lucky chambermaid, suppose she finds money carefully tucked away in a desk drawer instead of lying about on the floor of a public corridor. In this case, the chambermaid is not so lucky, since the money goes to the hotel owner. Technically, the hotel owner must keep the money in case the person who hid it returns and can prove ownership. The idea behind the law is to preserve the chain of ownership if at all possible. In the case of "mislaid property," it is understood that whoever has carefully hidden valuables may well return for them. In the case of "lost property," this is less likely and so the finder is rewarded for the gift which fortune has bestowed upon them. Of course, the law is never perfect, and in the case of "mislaid" versus "lost" property, an incentive is created for finders to misrepresent the facts of the discovery, so that something that is technically "mislaid" appears to be merely "lost."

The remaining type of missing property is designated as "treasure trove." The English common law definition of "treasure trove" holds that it applies to gold or silver coins, plate, or bullion that is deliberately buried in the earth and not laying about upon the ground. In modern times, the definition has sometimes been extended to include currency as well. Both "mislaid property" and "treasure trove" apply to valuables that are deliberately hidden. However, "treasure trove" carries with it the additional thought of antiquity, the idea being that the owner is long since dead and unknown. If the owner is known, the find ceases to be "treasure trove" and reverts to the owner.

In cases where the identity of the owner can not be ascertained, different legal systems throughout history have made varying divisions of treasure trove between the finder, the landowner on whose land the find was made, and the state. In biblical times, for example, Jesus likens the Kingdom of Heaven to a treasure in a field, for which a man sells all that he has in order to purchase the field and so gain the treasure. Here, the implication is that treasure trove reverts to the landowner, which probably reflects local practice in this area of the Middle East at the time of Christ. An earlier Old Testament passage emphasized the responsibility of the finder of lost property to seek out the original owner, remaining silent on the disposition of treasure, should the original owner not be located. Classical Roman writings suggest that treasure trove was split evenly between the finder and landowner.

English common law awarded all treasure trove to the Crown, this practice dating back to at least the twelfth century. There was some justification for this, as treasure was sometimes secreted in the first place in order to avoid taxation. A further rationale for this practice was the idea that any property hidden by a deposed regime should be considered by right to belong to the subsequent monarch. The Crown, at its discretion, from time to time would make exceptions to its absolute claim to treasure. For example, treasure found on church property or cemeteries was sometimes shared with the church. The Crown also occasionally ceded its claim to treasure trove in specific parts of the country, no doubt in return for political considerations from local aristocrats. In modern times, the English Crown technically still claims treasure trove, but now "awards" finders the market value of the treasure, with museums being granted the first right to purchase anything of archaeological significance. The practice of awarding market value to the finder has been in effect since the latter part of the nineteenth century. Conversely, prosecutions for failure to disclose treasure trove have not occurred in England since the 1860s.

The framework for claiming legal ownership to Henry and Theodore's pot of gold was set, and Levin understood this immediately. There could only be three claims. Either someone could prove themselves an heir of the person who buried the gold, claim the gold as the landowner where it was found, or make a claim of treasure trove as the finder. If they could prove who buried the gold to begin with, ownership would be established and there would be no division of the spoils. On the other hand, if they discovered the gold or owned the land it was discovered on, there would be a question as to how the pot was divided, which in turn would rest on the precedents set in previous American treasure trove litigation. Levin searched carefully for related treasure cases, and found a number in his favor.

DON'T SAY ANYTHING ABOUT IT, AND THE LORD WILL BLESS YOU

Levin uncovered an Indiana case from 1922 that revolved around a workman who uncovered thirteen hundred dollars in gold coins in an earthen jar, buried to a depth of about six inches. Leo Todd, the finder, was excavating underneath a house for the purpose of constructing a cellar. The facts seemed to match Levin's case closely enough. Leo Todd could just as well have been Robert King, the unlucky plumber who had failed to strike gold while working in the 132 S. Eden Street cellar. The Indiana case reached the state appeals court, which invoked the law of treasure trove and ruled in the finder's favor. The conditions for applying treasure trove law had been met, namely that the discovered gold or silver had been deliberately hidden and was not lying about on the ground or in any other open place. Although there was evidence pointing to a certain previous inhabitant of the house who was known to handle gold frequently, this was not conclusive, and the money was awarded to Todd and not the landowner.

Levin also referred to a 1904 case from Oregon. It supported the case Levin was to set forth. Two brothers, aged eight and ten, uncovered seven thousand dollars in gold coins in a henhouse. One of them told the story in court: "I was in the back of the building, spading through the trash, and the point of my shovel struck something hard. I shoveled the trash away, and got the can on my spade, and was going to throw it in the sled. It was too heavy, so I dragged it out toward me a foot or so, and told my brother the can must be full of rocks. So I tried to take the lid off with my fingers. It was rusty and old, and I could not get it off, so I took the pick and chopped through the lid and when I pulled it out the lid came with it. In doing so I cut two of the sacks [inside the can] containing fives and twenties. So we looked through all the sacks, which were gold. My brother says, 'let's take it over home'. I says, 'No, let's take it up and show Dee Roberts [the henhouse owner]'. So we packed it up on the spade together. We packed it up the porch steps and Dee came out and says, 'What you got, boys?' We says 'a can of gold'. 'Where did you get it?' 'Out in the henhouse.' So Mary Roberts, Dee's wife said, 'Let's have it', so we gave it to them. They walked inside and closed the door in our face and we went back to work to finish up our job. About half and hour after, Dee called us out and says, 'Here's five cents boys. We put the money there some time ago, and were going to buy something with it. Don't say anything about it, and the Lord will bless you'. We asked how much was in the can. He said, 'Over seven thousand dollars.' " The Roberts claimed that they themselves had buried the gold, and were thus the legal owners, but the court dismissed this claim in view of the fact that the container around the gold was falling apart, and furthermore that the henhouse had not been cleaned out in years. While not immediately deciding in favor of the boys, the court ruled that the claim to the gold could not be made based on property ownership, but rather that the property owners had to establish actual ownership of the gold, a much more difficult task.

The "I meant to bury it there" argument seems to be an ongoing theme in treasure trove litigation. In another Oregon case from 1911, an employee found twenty-one ten-dollar gold pieces while cleaning out a warehouse. The warehouse owner insisted that his brother had "deposited and concealed" said coin in the warehouse, intending to retrieve it upon his return from travel. The brother was confronted before he had learned of the gold find and asked if he had buried any gold in the warehouse. He replied that he had not. The court ruled for the employee.

The general interpretation of treasure trove law in American legal practice was clear, and Levin seemingly had an open-and-shut case of "finder's keepers" on his hands. Levin, who was more thorough than confident, did his best to anticipate where any objections might arise. He knew that there would probably be claims to the gold from relatives of those who had supposedly buried it. He also knew that the gold was probably buried sometime around the Civil War, and that proving exactly who did the deed during those troubled times would be a long shot at best. The more compelling issue was whether the boys were trespassing by going into the back part of the cellar, and if so, what rights remained to them as trespassers. A general principal of law protects landowners against trespassers, and conversely prohibits trespassers from benefiting from any wrong they have done. It was this question that would weigh on Levin and the boys for a long time.

BALTIMORE IN THE CIVIL WAR

The year 1934 was not so many generations removed from the Civil War. Many Baltimore senior citizens in the 1930s had childhood memories of the "rebellion," as President Lincoln referred to it, not wanting to legitimize the Confederacy as a country in its own right. Although the city of Baltimore was largely physically untouched by the Civil War, the political loyalties of the citizenry were divided. Located just over the Mason-Dixon Line, there were both northern and southern sympathies within the city, even though the city itself was under the control of Union forces throughout the war. Both the Union and Confederate armies claimed Maryland enlistees, though those casting their lot with the southern forces sometimes had to find their way through Union blockades to do so.

The Confederates fired on Fort Sumter in South Carolina on April 12, 1861, and hostilities had begun. In Baltimore, control of the city was critical, as it possessed the only rail link from Washington, D.C. to the North. On April 19, northern forces from Pennsylvania and Massachusetts arrived at the train station in Baltimore, and a riot involving southern sympathizers, Baltimore police, and Union troops promptly erupted. Four soldiers and twelve citizens were killed. The Maryland legislature met on April 26 and adjourned without voting on the issue of secession. By the middle of May, the capitol of Annapolis and the city of Baltimore were firmly in Union hands.

With the city under military occupation, attention shifted to the political enemies of the North. On April 27, a day after the Maryland legislature effectively chose to side with the Union, President Lincoln suspended the writ of habeas corpus in certain areas and extended to the local military command the right to place under arrest and hold without trial any Confederate sympathizers. The first incarceration was made May 25 and was immediately challenged by Chief Justice Roger Brooke Taney, a Marylander. Taney maintained that habeas corpus could be suspended only with the consent of Congress. Lincoln ignored the judge's opinion and the military supported the President. With Congress out of session, Lincoln had now assumed absolute control of the federal government, far beyond his constitutional authority, justifying his actions by his inaugural oath to "preserve the Union" at all costs.

Soon the Confederate-leaning newspapers in Baltimore were suspended as their editors found themselves arrested. Members of the Maryland legislature, in addition to the mayor of Baltimore, were also arrested and held for varying amounts of time. Prominent residents of the city were further intimidated by having one of the guns from nearby Fort McHenry aimed at the fashionable Mount Vernon area of Baltimore.

Confederate forces approached Baltimore on several occasions during the war, though the city itself was never seriously threatened. Baltimore remained an important supply source for northern railroads and the shipbuilding industry, but also saw its share of war casualties and Confederate prisoners, thousands of whom were held at Fort McHenry. In April 1865, after Lincoln's assassination, his funeral train passed through Baltimore as it traveled from Washington, D.C., to Springfield, Illinois. The cortege included the Baltimore city council, among whose members was one Andrew J. Saulsbury. The day was rainy, and Saulsbury was probably glad to get back to his dry house, just a few blocks away from the parade route. Saulsbury, his family, and his servants lived at 132 S. Eden Street.

CHAPTER 8

ANDREW SAULSBURY

If a well-furnished home in nineteenth-century Baltimore lacked for twentieth-century conveniences, the next best thing one could have were full-time servants to help run the household. Andrew Saulsbury, a wealthy man, had two young black women who lived with him at 132 S. Eden, and a laundress who came in besides. Saulsbury's maids, Amanda Jackson and Roda Meacm, ages seventeen and twenty, may have been emancipated by Lincoln's 1863 proclamation, but the social order wasn't so quick to follow. Lincoln's own funeral train through Baltimore explained the hierarchy clearly enough. The whites were in front, followed by whites who aligned themselves with ethnic groups, then Jews, and finally blacks. Saulsbury was kind to his black help, at least on Christmas and special holidays. "He gave presents in gold to all," a daughter said. "The servants came in and were lined up and presented with their gold pieces."

Saulsbury hadn't come up with the idea of using gold coins as holiday gifts on his own. Indeed, the Christmas folklore of hanging stockings by the chimney is thought to have been originated by St. Nicholas himself, who deposited gold coins inside stockings drying overnight in the fireplace of a needy family. More contemporary to Saulsbury, Queen Victoria had in 1840 ordered that gold sovereigns be placed in Christmas puddings given to the royal staff. The tradition of handing the gold piece directly to the gift recipient was a bit safer, because there was always the danger that someone might swallow a coin by accident. This happened on at least one occasion, to a gentleman named Ernest Hatfield who accidentally ingested a Christmas coin baked in a pudding and required surgery many years later to remove it.

The United States mint got involved in the gift-giving business as well, increasing production of proof gold coins as Christmas time drew near. These coins, struck multiple times with highly polished planchets and dies, resulting in strongly mirrored surfaces and exceptional detail, could be specially ordered from the mint at slightly above face value. For the vast majority, like Andrew Saulsbury, who didn't resort to the celebratory presentations of Christmas puddings or U.S. mint proof specimens, a gold coin plucked out of ordinary circulation remained a distinctive way to make a monetary gift up until Roosevelt's gold recall in 1933.

Saulsbury gave his children gold gifts as well. Then, like now, cash was an easy gift to make, one that didn't require much thought. As Elizabeth Audoun, one of Saulsbury's daughters told it, "He did not bother about buying us presents, he gave us presents of gold, and he left the presents for the women folks to select for us." The gold coins, stored in a desk in the dining room, mesmerized the young Elizabeth. "When he opened the desk I always would go and stand beside him because the gold had a great fascination for a child, and I wanted to see it," she explained. There was another cache of coins that Saulsbury kept in his bedroom chest, containing not only gold but other coins of long-forgotten denominations, including two-cent bronzes and three-cent silvers. Large, old copper one-cent pieces were given to the children when the box was eventually cleaned out. "We had a perfect orgy spending them," said his daughter Martha.

Saulsbury's daughter, Elizabeth, had good reason to be fascinated by a drawer full of coins. Hard money had been scarce ever since the Civil War, when the Union authorized "legal tender" in 1862 to finance the campaign. One hundred and fifty million dollars of greenbacks were printed, and unlike previous currency issues, these were not redeemable in gold. Indeed, the United States government itself wouldn't accept greenbacks at face value in exchange for the glittering proof gold coins that the mint struck for collectors. Gresham's law, that bad money drives out good, held sway, and soon the Union greenbacks were trading among brokers at a discount, a hundred-dollar note fetching as little as forty one-dollar gold coins in 1864. Salmon Chase, the Treasury Secretary, attempted to stem the tide by selling U.S. treasury gold on the open market, to little effect. Gold, silver, and copper coins all disappeared from sight, as the public was wary of worthless Union paper and the varying prospects of reunification. In their stead arose a host of alternate forms of money, including private currency issued by individual merchants. As one New York reporter put it, "the saloon keeper, the cigar dealer, and the barber have turned banker." Hard money would not return into normal circulation until the 1870s.

MY FATHER'S HOUSE

The layout of Saulsbury's coin-filled home in the 1870s was much like it was in the 1930s. There was a front building and a back building, both three stories, connected by a one-story section that contained the kitchen and bathroom. The servants probably lived in back, with the family facing the park to the east on the front side of the brick house. From there the Saulsbury's looked out upon winding pathways, shady trees and a fountain in the center of Eastern City Spring, as the park was then known. Saulsbury never carried a mortgage on the property. "We were very comfortable," recollected a daughter. Inside the house one could find feather beds, carpets, paintings, clocks, a well-filled bookcase, easy chairs and the like, all in all the trappings of a "beautiful home," as one neighbor described it. Saulsbury's library in particular was valued more highly than any of the other household furnishings, and Andrew's family probably passed much pleasant time buried in books and overstuffed chairs, though it was still a lively affair, as there were eight children in the family by 1870. The children were "dressed well," according to a neighbor, no doubt keeping the servants constantly engaged in this task.

Among Saulsbury's paintings were two depicting the Confederate generals Robert E. Lee and Stonewall Jackson. Saulsbury's political convictions leaned toward the South, and his wife and children had been harassed by Union soldiers on at least one occasion. President Johnson offered a general amnesty to Confederate troops shortly after the conclusion of the war, on May 29, 1865, but this did not relieve the suspicion surrounding prominent citizens attached to the southern cause. To be sure, there was much remaining anti-Union sentiment in Baltimore, where citizens snapped up photographs of John Wilkes Booth at twenty-five cents a crack. On the other hand, it was not always wise to declare such allegiance openly, and occasionally someone was shot on sight for doing so. Saulsbury's friends were aware of his political stance. "He was an ardent southern sympathizer. That everyone knew," one daughter concluded.

The era of Reconstruction, the "second Civil War," consumed the country in the latter half of the 1860s and into the 1870s. It was in this environment that Saulsbury suddenly passed away young, at forty-six. He had been asthmatic and took sick several days prior to his death on November 28, 1873. The death was completely unexpected. "He was not seriously sick," thought one daughter. "I don't remember him being confined to the bed in that illness. He sat in a chair."

The funeral was conducted the following Sunday afternoon at 132 S. Eden. The minister, Reverend George W. Powell, delivered remarks based on the Gospel of John, the sixth verse of the fourteenth chapter. "In my Father's house are many mansions," he began. The same apostle later wrote of heaven, "and the streets of the city were paved in pure gold." The irony was lost on Reverend Powell's audience, unaware that they were mere steps away from earthly treasure in this terrestrial house of gold, where "moth and rust destroy and where thieves break in and steal," according to another of the Gospels. Saulsbury's widow may have been oblivious to the gold in the cellar, but she knew there was gold in his bedroom chest, and this she took to purchase a headstone for the grave. The gold "had remained at his head in life and she put it at his head in death, a lovely tombstone," recalled one of Saulsbury's daughters. A lengthy cortege re-plete with prominent Baltimoreans made its way to Green Mount Cemetery, where Saulsbury was laid to rest.

IT HAS BEEN GREATLY CHANGED

The Saulsbury descendants read about Theodore and Henry's hoard in the Baltimore newspapers and raced to stake their claim. Barely a week after the cellar of gold was discovered, Reuben Foster, a grandson of Andrew J. Saulsbury, obtained a court order from Judge Albert S. J. Owens appointing him administrator of his grandfather's estate, for the purposes of representing the estate in the hoard litigation. Foster had to do some legwork to determine that 132 S. Eden was indeed the former Saulsbury residence, as the street numbers had changed since Saulsbury's death in 1873. There were two daughters of Andrew J. Saulsbury still living, and Reuben and his aunts might have had a stroll down Eden Street to verify the identity of the onetime family home. The journey no doubt revived memories of an idyllic childhood ended by the death of a father, and one could not help but contrast the current state of the neighborhood with that of yesteryear. "It has been greatly changed," one of the daughters observed.

For Foster, who didn't need the money, the whole affair was a pleasant diversion. Foster's mother, a daughter of Andrew J. Saulsbury, had married well, into a wealthy family associated with the Chesapeake Steamship Company. His paternal grandfather had granted Reuben a substantial behest upon his reaching the age of twenty-one, including a home and ten thousand dollars. With these assets and income-producing ground rents, the young Foster was never compelled to work. Reuben took his training as an attorney, but never did practice law, choosing instead to stay well read and travel the world. When the gold hoard presented the need for legal engagement, Reuben contacted his good friend Charles F. Stein Jr., a local attorney, and convinced him to enter into what promised to be an entertaining battle.

The Saulsbury bunch weren't the only prospectors in Baltimore. Harry Chenven, who died at 132 S. Eden just a few short weeks prior, had family that also got wind of the hoard. It was the last chance for this hapless Russian immigrant to make good for his wife and only child. The wife, Goldie Benchman, who had reverted to using her maiden name, remained in Baltimore for a few years following Harry's hospitalization in 1915, operating a grocery store while supporting her mother and young son. By 1934, Goldie had moved to New York City and entered the garment industry, no longer characterized by the sweatshops of old, having been transformed by the power of organized labor, but it remained a wearying profession nonetheless. The son, Isaac, was now confronted with childhood memories of a crazy jeweler father, who had perhaps been hiding the family fortune all these years while he and his mother scrambled to make do. It was worth a trip to Baltimore to sort things out, and the Chenven's filed their claim with Judge Eugene O'Dunne in the Baltimore Circuit Court on October 3, 1934.

Others with shakier claims assumed their roles in the unfolding drama. Ernest G. Long, a metal worker living in Philadelphia, entered the litigation "as one of the descendants of James Lowry Donaldson." Donaldson was the family identified by Patrolman Edward Horner as having lived long ago at 132 S. Eden, his first best guess as to who might have buried the hoard. Horner got both the name and address wrong, confusing 132 S. Eden with the neighboring house to the north, but Long hadn't figured that out yet. Ernest was instead thinking about his Maryland ancestors who had found themselves on opposite sides of the Civil War, some casting their lot with the North and others with the South, and still others moving to South America, where the family had diplomatic interests. Long himself had been born in Uruguay, and so family members were familiar with exotic locales. His great-uncle, a military man, had written a book about Indian conflicts in the humid Florida swamps in the 1830s. Surely there was a pot of gold to be found in there somewhere.

Long's claim was at least a stab into the dark cellar. Other claims were more like the blind leading the blind. Mrs. Thomas H. Green of Detroit, a descendant of one Hannah White, also filed for the hoard. The best evidence she could produce was the fact that Hannah White, a seamstress, actually lived in the Eden Street neighborhood in the 1830s and 1840s. Similarly suspect claims came from Missouri, New York, and Illinois. In the end there were a total of ten parties to the suit, many less than the "scores of litigants" the *Baltimore Sun* had predicted on September 1, 1934. Potential litigants soon discovered that while it was one thing to file a claim, it was quite another to pay an attorney to travel to Baltimore and defend a weak argument. Within weeks the pool of litigants was whittled down to four parties. Harry O. Levin would fight for the boys, the Saulsburys and Chenvens would try to prove that their families buried the gold in the first place, while the elderly ladies Findlay and French would argue that they owned the gold by virtue of owning the property.

PROWLERS BEWARE

In between court filings, Henry and Theodore, now two youthful celebrities, found themselves inundated with mail from well-wishers, some of it originating as far away as Oklahoma. Not all of the mail was adequately addressed, and the Post Office arbitrarily delivered the letters of congratulations and advice to either Theodore's or Henry's residence. Theodore's mother said that the mail served to help the boys from "getting too fidgety" while waiting for the legal action to unfold.

A local retailer hatched the idea of using Theodore and Henry in a series of promotions. Morton Blum, reading Theodore's lament in the newspaper that he hadn't had a new suit in a long while, invited Theodore to the Hub department store and gave him the full treatment. The news-

Bessie Jones and Theodore Jones, with hand tools from the dig.
(Baltimore American, *September 2, 1934*)

papers covered the publicity stunt, and a full-length picture of Theodore, looking a bit uncomfortable in his stiff new clothes, appeared forthwith. "Uncle Mort," as Mr. Blum was known, put a bit of cash in Theodore's pockets as well, ten dollars up front plus three dollars a day, in payment for parading about the vicinity of the store at Charles and Fayette streets in downtown Baltimore. The store announced an "exclusive appearance" of Henry and Theodore, in conjunction with a Saturday sale on September 7, 1934. "Uncle Mort" interviewed the pair in the boys department of the store, a thinly veiled inducement to entice otherwise reluctant young boys, along with their mothers, to do some shopping for the new school year.

Public interest waned over the next few days, until September 11, when Theodore's mother appeared in the *Baltimore Evening Sun*, gun in hand, under the caption "Prowlers, Beware." Bessie Jones, the pistol-packing momma, reported a mysterious rattling of her doorknob several evenings prior, and declared that she was prepared to repel any prowlers. The .22 caliber weapon had been in the family's possession for some time, she said. It was, perhaps, a clue to Bessie's past, the best protection that one could get in those days against estranged husbands. There was not much other reason to keep a gun in a hungry household, until now, when Bessie found herself with new reasons to be concerned about her safety. "It's old, but it's still good. And it's fully loaded. If anyone comes sneaking around I'm going to do my best to be brave. I'll keep my finger on the trigger," Bessie said, adding that she would now be "sleeping with one eye open."

The gold, if not Bessie and Theodore, remained safe in a vault at the police headquarters. On December 4th, Judge Eugene O'Dunne ordered the gold turned over to the clerk of the city circuit court, adding a crucial note to the typed order with his own pen. "The clerk is directed not to deposit the funds in bank, but to retain them in kind in safe deposit box until the case is tried," he wrote. O'Dunne was taking special care that the coins not be prematurely turned into currency by the feds. Such niceties were lost on the families. "We are just sitting around and waiting for the court to decide who is to get the greenbacks in exchange for the gold," said Theodore's mother, Bessie, perhaps thinking that it was still more money than she had ever seen, regardless of what form it was in.

In the meantime, Henry had been getting into a bit of trouble with the police. On September 14, Henry and a friend, Walter Stankiwicz, got into an altercation with a recreation supervisor on the Broadway pier, several blocks south of Henry's residence on Caroline Street. A fight broke out after Daniel Lennon, the supervisor, attempted to prevent Henry and Walter from destroying some property. A patrolman was alerted by Lennon's calls for help, and Walter and Henry quickly found themselves in front of a magistrate who fined each five dollars. Walter paid the fine and was released the same day. Henry was without cash and was held overnight, then released the next day by the Baltimore Juvenile Court.

The warm summer weather that attracted Henry to the pier dissipated over the next few weeks, as the ninety-day limit for filing claims to the hoard approached. The owners of 132 S. Eden, Mary Findlay and Elizabeth French, waited until the very end to officially enter the competition. It was a bit of legal gamesmanship, but really not much of a surprise. Testimony was set for December 11, in Baltimore City Circuit Court, with Judge Eugene O'Dunne presiding.

PART 3

THE TRIAL BEGINS

Judge Eugene O'Dunne

CHAPTER 9

THEODORE'S TESTIMONY

"How old are you?" Judge Eugene O'Dunne asked Theodore, who had just been sworn in. "Sixteen," was his answer, and so the first word out of his mouth was a lie. He was fourteen at the time, but a grown-up fourteen, large for his age and more experienced than smaller boys who had spent more time in school than in the streets. Levin took up the questioning after the judge, establishing the physical layout of the cellar, and the circumstances by which Theodore and Henry found themselves digging holes in odd places. There was not a lot of new information. Theodore repeated, by and large, everything he had told the press in the aftermath of the Labor Day excitement. Embedded in his remarks was a deep sense of loyalty to Henry. Theodore may have lied on his own account, but he had not forgotten how Henry had accepted his "Pittsburgh manner" when others had not. At Levin's prompting, Theodore reminded everyone that the find was made jointly and that anything gained was to be split between the two fifty-fifty. "Ever since I have been in Baltimore, him and I have been pals, [and] we always went around together," Theodore testified.

The attorneys for the sisters Findlay and French questioned Theodore next, moving immediately to the issue of trespass in the rear cellar. Levin could not have been surprised, and perhaps had even prepared Theodore via a few practice sessions prior to the December 11 hearing. The attorneys, C. Arthur Eby and Emory H. Niles, had taken care to photograph most of the cellar, taking care to get an image of the door that hung between the front and rear parts of the cellar. The photographers had evidently gathered some attention in the building, and a most implausible rumor arose that the photography work had cost five hundred dollars, to which Judge O'Dunne dryly remarked, "That is at least above NRA prices," referring to the National Recovery Administration, a federal bureau created in 1933 and charged with creating fair business practices. Regardless of the price paid, Theodore identified the storage lockers in the front part of the cellar, of which one was allocated to each tenant at 132 S. Eden. He also fixed the spot of the hoard find, halfway along the east wall of the rear cellar. Theodore was careful to point out that the photographs didn't exactly match the state of the cellar at the time of the find. It was an important idea to impress upon Judge O'Dunne, because it undermined the evidence that Eby and Niles needed in order to make an argument about the partition separating the two parts of the cellar. Niles countered by asking Theodore whether he had asked the landlord, Benjamin Kalis, about going in the back of the cellar. Theodore had to admit that he had not.

The attorney for the Chenven estate took his turn, and was able to do little damage to Theodore. In the first place, Theodore really didn't know much about the old jeweler Harry Chenven, who had mostly kept to himself, and except for the matter of Chenven disposing of his chamber pot on the windows, Theodore couldn't offer much except that Chenven lived alone in one room and had a habit of coming home late at night. The Chenven attorney tried vainly to get Theodore to speculate as to the reputation of Chenven, whether he was miser, or whether he had perhaps left money in the house when he died. Levin successfully objected to the line of questioning. This was a hearing to establish facts, not to engage in speculation. The Chenven team was already grasping at straws, asking Theodore about any markings on the corroded copper pot that housed the fortune. Theodore said he hadn't noticed anything, which was already obvious to anyone who had examined the physical evidence. As Judge O'Dunne put it, "it is a bucket, dilapidated, disintegrated, covered with what appears to be verdigris inside and outside, of a completely green color." Another attorney pointed out that in some places the corrosion had eaten its way entirely through the green copper.

The court now heard from Henry, who Levin used to establish the idea of Henry and Theodore's habitual use of the cellar. Henry testified that he went over to Theodore's house every day, and that the two of them had spent much time in the front part of the cellar, just messing around as boys do. "For about three months straight we started going down there every day and playing," Henry reported, and further that they had been in the cellar just the day preceding the hoard find. The Findlay and French attorneys, as they had with Theodore, went directly to the issue of trespass, inquiring about the partition that hung between the front and back parts of the cellar. Henry allowed that there was a door there, but that it was never locked, and that he and Theodore had been back there several times for the purposes of chopping wood for Theodore's mother. Schonfield, the attorney for the Chenven family, then engaged Henry in a long discussion about the various windows in the cellar, and the tools that Henry and Theodore used for the great dig, all of which seems to have struck Judge O'Dunne as being rather pointless. "Do you have to go all over it again?" O'Dunne interrupted, and Schonfield quickly completed his exam of Henry. The Saulsbury attorneys finished Henry's testimony, establishing two points that they would use later. First, that there was a boot awkwardly wrapped around the pot, and second that there were many oyster shells in the earth surrounding the pot.

THE PALE OF SETTLEMENT

Schonfield, the Chenven attorney, had brought in witnesses from out of town, and requested that he present them next, to which Judge O'Dunne agreed. The Saulsbury and the Findlay-French teams were perhaps waiting for the other parties to play their cards first. Testifying were Harry Chenven's caretaker and friend from the old country, Harry Gamerman, as well as Chenven's sister and son. They were Russian Jews, among the large numbers of immigrants who crossed the Atlantic in growing numbers in the 1880s. Even before then, Jews were confined to the "Pale of Settlement," comprising much of western Russia, and including parts of modern day Lithuania and Poland. Five million Jews lived in the Pale, some forty percent of the world's Jewish population, and even within the Pale their movements were restricted, often requiring permits to live in larger cities.

March 1, 1881 saw the assassination of the Russian tsar Alexander II, murdered by a bomb in St. Petersburg. Alexander's death, blamed on Jewish revolutionaries, sparked an inferno of anti-Semitic activity. Mobs arose primarily in southwestern Russia, plundering Jewish homes and businesses, both in the countryside and in large cities, including Odessa and Kiev. The pogroms began at the spring Passover, and saw the Russian Orthodox perversely paint crosses on their homes to indicate that there were no Jews inside, evoking the image of blood painted over Jewish doorways in the time of Moses and the first Passover. The pattern was the same from city to city, the rioters given a day or two of leeway from the local authorities before the police made cursory efforts to dispel mobs, who simply broke up and regathered elsewhere. The few offenders taken into custody generally received light sentences.

Tsar Alexander III issued a weak statement affirming Jewish rights in May, which failed to prevent a new round of violence from breaking out in the summer of 1881. There were more in the spring of 1882, as riots in the city of Balta destroyed over a thousand Jewish homes and businesses. This spurred the first great wave of Russian Jewish emigration, much of it to America. A tiny contingent made the leap to Palestine, presaging the birth of the modern Israeli state in 1948. For those who stayed in Russia, the tsar issued the "Temporary Rules," which further restricted the geographic movement of Jews within the Pale. At the same time, the Russian government, forced to confront the atrocities in Balta, and growing international protest, used its influence to largely halt the physical persecution of Jews until 1903. In its stead arose a faceless bureaucracy determined to make Jewish life under the tsar as uncomfortable as possible.

The "Temporary Rules" were twisted by local authorities in the most arbitrary ways. Jews who left village homes for even a few days risked being barred from returning, under the explanation that Jews were no longer permitted to settle "anew" in rural areas. Jews who did not own their own village homes were prohibited from executing new leases, effectively expelling them from the rural areas. The restriction against settling "anew" was extended to prohibit almost all movement by rural Jews, to the point of disallowing Jews to inhabit property gained by inheritance. Those in large cities fared no better. Jews in Moscow and St. Petersburg, living there only by special permission to begin with, found authorities increasingly likely to cancel residence permits at a moment's notice. Many families were given only one or two days to leave the city, certainly not to live in a restricted rural area, but rather to fend for themselves in smaller cities. Two thousand Jews were so evicted from Kiev in 1886.

To these travel restrictions were added other restrictions. Jewish artisans were allowed to sell only their own material; also, they were subject to educational quotas. In addition, Jews were not permitted to practice law or to become officers in the military. In 1890 Jews were no longer allowed to vote in local elections. Later, Jews were formally expelled from Moscow, and the main synagogue closed the year thereafter. A chronicler depicted an image of the exodus from the city. "Eye-witnesses will never forget one bitterly cold night in January 1892. Crowds of Jews dressed in beggarly fashion, among then women, children, and old men, with remnants of their household belongings lying around them, filled the station of the Brest railroad. Threatened by police convoy and having failed to obtain a reprieve [some authorities had been bribed to extend the eviction period] they had made up their mind to leave, despite a temperature of thirty degrees below zero. In this way twenty thousand Jews who had lived in Moscow fifteen, twenty-five, and even forty years were forcibly removed to the Jewish Pale of Settlement." International outcry accomplished little, though fifty years prior to the Holocaust, Europe was not blind. "Shall civilized Europe, shall the Christianity of England behold this slow torture and bloodless massacre, and be silent?" asked one citizen in the *London Times*.

CHAPTER 10

THE SAULSBURY AND CHENVEN CLAIMS

By the early 1900s, economic persecution had made charity cases of nearly half the Jewish population in Russia. Worse, the Jews found themselves trapped between the fomenting socialism induced by the struggle of an agrarian empire competing with industrialized European neighbors, and an autocratic tsar who earnestly believed in the divine imprimatur upon his own office. On "Bloody Sunday," January 9, 1905, the government gunned down its own citizens, striking workers marching on the Winter Palace in St. Petersburg, a precursor to the Passover pogroms which would take place that spring. Throughout the rest of the year, riots broke out throughout the country, seemingly coordinated rather than locally organized. In four days in October, anti-Jewish violence in Odessa claimed three hundred Jewish lives, while forty thousand were materially ruined with homes and businesses ransacked. It was time to get out. Nearly half a million, ten percent of the Russian Jewish population, left for America between 1905 and 1910. Harry Chenven and his wife Goldie were among them, and it was Harry who carried the burden of what he had witnessed, perhaps one of the "many who lost their minds from the horrors," as one Jewish historian put it.

Years later, in Baltimore, after the gold hoard discovery, Harry Chenven's long-estranged widow decided not to enter the litigation. Whatever Harry had done to her, she put behind her. Harry's sister and son Zachary, on the other hand, chose to make the several hour trip from Brooklyn to Baltimore to reach whatever closure could be had in Harry's affairs. It was not the first time Zachary had traveled from New York to Baltimore, having visited his father from time to time over the years. Zachary had seen the ramshackle conditions at 132 S. Eden firsthand in 1931. Harry, the father, was evidently pleased whenever Zachary visited, and in May 1932 attempted to strike a bargain with his son in order that Isaac might come and live with him. If Zachary moved in, he promised, he would put the young man of nineteen years through medical school when he graduated from college. Zack was skeptical. "He had no visible means of support," he testified in court, adding that "he would not tell me" from where the alleged largess would come. Zachary instead returned to New York.

Schonfield, the Chenven attorney, had no further points to make. He could place Chenven "at the scene of the crime," demonstrate that Chenven was a jeweler who frequently handled old gold, and prove that Chenven was a man of an uneven nature with a history of mental illness. The idea of an unbalanced miser unnecessarily living in want was certainly the exception, but not without precedent. In nearby Philadelphia, a panhandler living in a dollar-a-week rooming house was found sprawled semi-conscious in a gutter, with seven thousand dollars in currency sewn in the lining of his coat. The man who had been begging for years had even applied for state relief. "Nobody needs it more than you," his landlady had said to him. The rich beggar died a day after being picked up by the police. Not surprisingly, the Philadelphia coroner's office was quickly besieged with calls from supposed friends who wished to lay claim to the currency. In Cincinnati, an elderly woman living without heat in the middle of the winter was found to have fifteen thousand dollars in gold stashed in cupboards and drawers, wrapped in old clothes. The woman was sent to a local hospital, where the social services director was appointed to be her guardian. A judge found the aged spinster to be of unsound mind. The gold was "redeemed" for its face value in currency and the proceeds were then handed over to the woman's guardian.

For Judge Eugene O'Dunne, the occasional exceptions were all noise. O'Dunne immediately ruled the Chenvens out of the case, not even waiting to prepare a written opinion on the matter. O'Dunne had several prob-

Close-up of the hoard location. The hoard container, or a likeness, is placed at the spot of the find. (Maryland State Archives)

lems with the Chenven presentation. The copper pot of gold appeared to have been buried much longer than the few years Chenven had lived at the property. Furthermore, the latest date on any of the coins was 1856. If Chenven, as an old gold buyer, had turned scrap gold into the U.S. mint to have it coined, it most certainly would have been dated in the twentieth century. The pot, Judge O'Dunne thought, had been buried long before Chenven even left Russia in 1908.

Zachary and his aunt, Betty Aaronson, went back to Brooklyn empty handed. Zachary worked his way through medical school, but the self-made man never lived the happiness that he seemingly had earned in the face of hardship His was a dark character, perhaps not unlike his father's. Still, the dutiful son took constant care of his mother, who lived in an apartment adjacent to her only son's medical practice. Dr. Zachary Chenven died in 1992, having seen his own son grow up in the fullness of America, unencumbered by the heaviness of immigrant experience, and becoming in turn a prominent physician himself.

THE GIFT THAT KEPT ON GIVING

With the Chenvens dismissed, the floor passed to the Saulsbury family to convince the court that their Civil War-era ancestor, Andrew J. Saulsbury, had secretly crept into his cellar at 132 S. Eden and buried a treasure. Saulsbury's grandson, Reuben Foster, and two aunts, Saulsbury's remaining children, all took the oath and gave testimony. That Saulsbury had been wealthy was unquestioned. A detailed inventory of his estate at the time of his death, in 1873, showed that he owned no less than thirty properties in the neighborhood surrounding Eden Street, not to mention a good bit of stock in a local building association, and seventeen thousand dollars in government bonds besides. The estate turned out to be the gift that kept on giving. The affairs of Saulsbury and his wife lingered in probate until 1898, as long-lost assets kept showing up. In all, the estate was valued at about a hundred thousand dollars—a few million in modern terms—and Saulsbury seems to have not kept the most meticulous records detailing the location of all his wealth.

Saulsbury had made his money in the soap and candle business, during his association with Armstrong and Company, a manufacturing concern within walking distance of his house on Eden Street. Saulsbury's first son was named James Armstrong Saulsbury, no doubt after James Armstrong, his business partner. There were three children in all by Andrew's first wife, who died young at the eve of the Civil War. He remarried shortly thereafter and had five more children, the last born in 1873, the same year in which Saulsbury suddenly died, at the age of forty-six. By the time of his death, Saulsbury had moved full time into real estate, consulting on the formation of building associations and dealing in local properties on his own account. He had also dabbled in politics, serving for several years on the second branch of the Baltimore City Council.

Andrew's time as a city councilman was in many ways pedestrian, dealing with the everyday issues of an expanding city, such as erecting street lamps, removing old water pumps, installing gas mains, and maintaining public roadways. If he had any preconceived agenda, it was to sack the Baltimore port warden, who had grossly exceeded his budget, and this Andrew successfully accomplished soon after joining the council, noting in his resolution that the city facilities there were in "dilapidated condition." A friend of Saulsbury's, James Webb, was the council president, and Saulsbury wasn't beyond allowing personal connections to influence his work on the council. In January 1868, he obtained permission for his former partner, James Armstrong, to expand his place of business. The following month, Saulsbury successfully petitioned for stepping stones to be installed on the street corner near his house on 132 S. Eden. Perhaps his wife had complained about the children's shoes getting dirty crossing the unpaved street. In any event, the stepping stones were quickly approved.

In matters of public policy, Saulsbury leaned towards the conservative side. He voted against German language instruction in the public schools, against the YMCA's using street lamps for the purposes of advertising, against creating paid city commissioners, and against minors playing in billiard parlors, the last resolution adding that anyone who reported such violations would receive half of the fines collected. He sold off school buildings and reduced public spending on education. Conversely, he supported most pro-business resolutions. Proposals to expand businesses, public marketplaces, and railroad interests generally received Saulsbury's vote.

CHAPTER 11

THE COPPER POT

The physical evidence was scant. A copper pot, thousands of coins dated before 1858, and the house in which they were buried. The Saulsbury heirs produced an "underground coppersmith," brought in to testify that the pot had indeed been in the ground since the 1860s, thus inferring that no subsequent owners of 132 S. Eden could have buried it. James D. Kavanagh, 57, the son of Irish immigrants, had been in the copper trade his entire professional life. His business had formerly been located at Pratt and Central Avenues, hardly a block away from 132 S. Eden. If anyone knew about the use of copper pots in the neighborhood, it was Kavanagh. The Saulsbury attorneys began the questioning, trying to establish that the pot had been buried for at least fifty years.

Q. Assuming this to be copper and assuming that it has been in the earth for some time, are you able, from your experience with copper and the copper utensils, to express an opinion by inspecting this vessel as to about or approximately how long it has been in the earth?
A. Well, I would say yes.
The Court: Listen, Mr. Kavanagh. Not knowing what the condition of the vessel was at the time was buried.
Q. Looking at that vessel as it is, could you say how long it has been in the earth?
A. Yes.
Q. Now, about how long would you say?
A. I would say to deteriorate in the condition it is in and the locality where it was, it would be there at least over fifty years.
Q. And for how long a maximum would you say it had been in the earth?
A. Well, now, that is very hard. It may be there a little more but it is just according to how it was exposed to the air.

Q. Suppose it was not exposed to the air but under the earth?

A. Then it would take longer for that to eat [through the copper].

Q. And about how long would you say?

A. I thought I put a right good time at that.

Q. You say fifty years, at least?

A. Yes, fifty.

Harry O. Levin now took up the cause for Theodore and Henry, the "infant petitioners," as referred to in the legal documents. Levin's job was to discredit the underground coppersmith in any way possible, and he dug his claws in quickly.

Q. In answering your question, Mr. Kavanagh, you simply did it by not touching it, nor did you examine it through any instrument of any kind, but just by looking at it, held about a foot away and you have expressed this opinion?

A. No, I seen that bucket before now.

Q. Where?

A. In the property room, about a week ago.

Q. At whose request?

A. By Mr. Strauss [attorney for the Saulsbury heirs].

Q. A week ago was the day after Christmas.

A. Oh, well, I know it wasn't then.

Q. When you say you saw it about a week ago you are wrong about that, aren't you?

A. As far as the date, I might be wrong on that.

Q. When did you see it, about?

A. I would have to do some thinking.

Q. Was it a month ago?

A. No, I don't think so, about three weeks I think.

Q. Is your opinion as to how long this thing has been in the ground as accurate as your statement that you saw it a week ago?

The Court: That is not a proper question.

Q. When you say this thing was buried at least fifty years ago, you are simply making a guess, aren't you?

A. No, I have handled copper that came out of the ground in my time and I have handled a great deal of it. I know a little bit about corrosion, and all of that, and from the appearance I have seen that bucket in at the time I seen it in the property room is a little different at the time I seen it now. Your coloring, your verdigris and your bluestone were more distinct on the inside of that bucket. Now, the longer that bucket is out and exposed to the air and everything, that changes the appearance of that article altogether.

Q. Do you know how long it had been exposed to the air before you saw it?

A. No, I would not be able to say that.

Q. So you did not see this immediately after it was taken out of the ground?

A. Oh, no.

Q. Your opinion is therefore based on having seen it after it had been exposed a number of times?

A. I am basing my opinion on when I saw it then.

Q. Your testimony is that it has been buried at least fifty years?

A. That is what.

Q. What maximum do you put on that?

A. That is about as long as I would put on it.

Q. Would you deny it had been buried eighty-six years?

A. No.

Q. It could have been buried eighty-six years, couldn't it?

A. It might have been buried one hundred and eighty-six years, if you want to put it that way. I am just giving you my opinion of it.

Q. You are now saying while you think it was buried fifty years, it could have been eighty-six years or one hundred and eighty-six years?

A. Not my opinion, I didn't put it.

Q. Whose opinion is it?

A. You made that assertion, "Couldn't it have been buried eighty-six years." I told you it could if you thought so.

Q. Could this thing have been buried eighty-six years.

A. I can't answer that question.

Q. Is it impossible for it to have been buried that long?

A. I would not answer that.

Q. Couldn't you answer that?

A. No, I gave you what I thought and you are not going to get me to force some other idea out of my hand that I won't say. If you know more about it than I do, you answer the question.

Q. Now, we can ask it all over again, Mr. Kavanagh.

A. You won't get a different answer.

Judge O'Dunne had heard enough of the testy exchange. "I think you are wasting a lot of time," he said to Levin. "I think he knows just as much about the age of this vessel as we can tell by looking at it." Kavanagh also testified that the kettle was not of a modern make, and that it was of a style not manufactured since he had started in the copper trade in 1899. He believed that the kettle was foreign in origin, possibly from Russia, Germany, or Japan. What Kavanagh couldn't testify to was the condition of the pot when it was buried. In the end his testimony carried little weight. It was obvious that the pot was old and deteriorated, but without knowing what it looked like when it was first buried, no one could say for sure how long it had been in the ground.

SOME FORM OF RELIEF

Theodore had told his story in court and returned with his mother to life at 132 S. Eden, still living on relief, but now imbued with hope and the reassurance of the powerful Levin that better times were coming. Bessie Jones didn't like taking relief, and thought to herself that if they ever got any money from the gold, she was going to give back some of what she had gotten from the relief workers.

In those pre-Great Society days, there was no ubiquitous federal welfare system, rather a patchwork of private and municipal organizations that met needs as best they could. The Baltimore Emergency Relief Commission was instituted in September 1933 and absorbed cases from the Family Welfare Association, the Bureau of Catholic Charities, and the Jewish Social Services Bureau. Their case load soared in 1934, going from twenty-three thousand relief cases in January up to thirty-eight thousand in May. By April, nineteen percent of the Baltimore population was on some form of relief, with blacks the hardest hit, at a rate three times higher than their proportion to the population suggested. The average household relief at the time was about thirty dollars a month, though little aid was given in actual cash. Most of the resources went directly to the basics of life: food, housing, clothing, and fuel. Those on the receiving end had to accept not only charity, but the disapproval of neighbors. "People on relief, whether deservedly or not, are rapidly acquiring the reputation of being chiselers," a Baltimore relief official said.

What one branch of the government gave, the other tried to take away. George A. Almoney, an operative with the Secret Service, had been pestering Judge O'Dunne to turn over the gold now in the custody of the court. Almoney appeared, "for the purpose of preserving the economic balance of the world," O'Dunne sarcastically observed. O'Dunne, perhaps to highlight what he viewed as excessive enthusiasm on the part of the Secret Service, examined Almoney and entered his comments into the record. "You are after the gold, aren't you?" O'Dunne began by asking, and Almoney answered in the affirmative. The Secret Service agent wished to exchange the gold for currency at the Federal Reserve Bank, "so it will cause no more trouble," as he put it. Still, Almoney wasn't sure it was really all gold. "We very rarely find a genuine gold dollar coin" he said, pointing out that much of the gold they examined turned out to be of counterfeit origin, made of brass. Almoney proposed that the pot be turned over forthwith to the Secret Service for testing. To this O'Dunne refused. "As possession itself is sometimes a strong factor in law, I thought it better to have the 3500 gold coins remain in the [court's] safe deposit box" O'Dunne wrote later. The two disagreeing branches of government could now litigate for the gold between themselves, or one side could back off. O'Dunne stood his ground, refusing to even divulge the location of the bank box. Almoney left the judge's presence, agreeing to investigate whether the coins in question had numismatic value beyond their gold content, in which case the Secret Service would allow that a trip to the smelters could be avoided, and that the coins could legally be held by the public. To this end he planned to consult with Perry W. Fuller, a local collectables dealer.

The whole interchange between Almoney and O'Dunne made for some interesting discussion in the internal memos of the Secret Service. Benjamin Bratton, the senior agent in Baltimore, wrote up a report for William H. Moran, the Chief of the Secret Service in nearby Washington, D.C.

There were several reporters present and it was not possible to keep the story from them," he wrote. "And one of them sneered at Operative Almoney and said, 'Oh! The Judge turned you down'. He then ran to [the] phone and from the item which appeared in the paper he represented he must have phoned in that the Secret Service had made a demand on Judge O'Dunne for the surrender of the gold coins and that the Judge had refused, etc. Another paper had a more reasonable account of the incident. It is thought necessary to mention this now, as later in the report it will be shown that the misleading article caused the U.S. Attorney here, Bernard J. Flynn, for whom I have the highest regard, to take the matter up with Operative Almoney and express dissatisfaction.

O'Dunne probably never had access to the Secret Service report, but no doubt would have chuckled over the discord among the overzealous observers that flowed from his courtroom. Bratton further opined that the Secret Service needed to wait until ownership was settled, but that, in any case, "after those high priced lawyers get theirs there will be small pickings for anyone else." A few days later Chief Moran told Almoney, by telephone, that the curator of the Smithsonian thought the hoard would be protected as numismatic gold, and shortly thereafter Bratton reported that collectors "have expressed the opinion that practically every one of the coins will be of premium value, if only because of the history of their finding."

Expecting that the federal agents would ultimately have to back off, Judge O'Dunne began pushing all parties involved to settle out of court. Harry O. Levin offered the Findlay-French team twenty-five percent of the take, which the Findlay-French attorneys declined, holding out for fifty percent. The refusal of the elderly ladies to settle didn't sit too well with the public. The Findlay-French attorneys summed it up later. "The case has received great publicity in the press, and, by reason of the journalistic atmosphere with which it has been surrounded, has appeared erroneously to be a struggle between two poor and deserving boys, who, by good fortune, found a treasure, and the heartless, or at least unfeeling and well-to-do heirs of a rich man [Saulsbury] on the one hand, and landlords [Findlay-French] on the other." Clearly, the public sympathy fell upon the children. Levin, ever the gambler, liked his chances and decided to let it all ride on O'Dunne's decision, spurning any attempt of the Findlay-French counsel to further negotiate.

Levin's abortive attempt to settle the case also completed the circle for the Schapiro heirs, the caretakers of 132 S. Eden Street who had abandoned the property in 1933, and chosen not to pay the ground rent of sixty dollars in September of that year. The true price of the ground rent payment was now understood. Their failure to pay had cost them their share of Levin's offer, surely worth thousands. Jennie Zimmerman, the Schapiro relative who had filed suit over the gold with everyone else, and who probably watched over the Schapiros in their final days, could do little more than brood about the seeming injustice of it all. She had lost any legal standing, and Levin's offer did not extend to her.

CHAPTER 12

JUDGE O'DUNNE AND THE SAULSBURY CLAIM

"Before attempting any discussion of the evidence, or of the law,
may I be permitted to say that no case, within my years of service on the
Bench, has been so full of romance or has been more ably presented,
both on evidence and on law, than has been this case."

Judge Eugene O'Dunne
Baltimore City Circuit Court, 1935

With no settlement forthcoming, Judge O'Dunne continued to accept testimony over the 1934 holiday season. The patient jurist attentively listened to the oral arguments from the attorneys, even keeping the court in session on Saturdays. He issued his opinion in February 1935, letting the suspense build by publishing it in two parts separated by a week. It was not unlike a contemporary radio serial, shamelessly delaying the conclusion of a story in order to entice the listener to return for another episode. For O'Dunne, the whole affair was a most pleasurable exercise of the law. He was in particular greatly entertained by counsel for the Saulsburys as they described the tenuous nature of the Civil War era, and the conditions that might cause one to hoard and hide all manner of valuables. "Under the magic spell of such eloquence, when we were transported to the years 1860–1864, I felt I could hear the beating of the drums, the marching of soldiers through the streets of Baltimore, and the echo of stacked arms on the Courthouse Square," O'Dunne wrote in the first part of his opinion, adding that one such presentation lasted five hours. The spellbinding accounts likely included tales of other Civil War–era caches, perhaps speculating as to the fate of the five thousand twenty-dollar gold pieces stolen from the New Orleans mint in January 1861 and never recovered.

The Saulsbury claim was front row center in the first part of O'Dunne's opinion, and in it he summarized the oral arguments that the Saulsbury's attorneys had put forth. The lawyers battled a high burden of proof, trying to demonstrate on the evidence alone that Andrew J. Saulsbury had indeed hoarded and hidden the gold. It was a circumstantial case that needed to be broken into small parts. First, they said, the coins were obviously buried after 1858, since that was last date on the coins. The coins must have been hidden by the owner of the house, or someone with ready access to the house, a person who could hide them while unnoticed and easily recover them at some point in the future. The hoarder would have to have been someone of substantial means who could afford to be separated from a great amount of wealth, and someone who was used to accumulating gold of small denomination, there being over twenty-eight hundred one-dollar gold pieces in the cache. Reuben Foster, the grandson, produced a one-dollar gold piece dated 1859 which was said to have been passed down through the family. And, the attorneys argued, the person who buried the gold most likely met a sudden death and was thus not able to tell anyone of its existence. Furthermore, the hoarder probably wasn't a previous owner of the house, since anyone moving out would have taken the hoard with them.

The Saulsbury attorneys ruled out any subsequent owners of 132 S. Eden, noting that the land records indicated frequent mortgages on the property. It would not make sense to mortgage a property worth two or three thousand dollars when one had probably five times that much buried in the cellar. Judge O'Dunne could hardly contest the title history. The property had traded hands frequently since the death of Saulsbury's widow in 1887, the succession of owners reflecting the tide of ethnic evolution in that part of they city. The Germans were first and the Russian Jews came next. The record was full of mortgages placed with local building societies, repeated borrowings ultimately put to a halt by the Findlay-French clan foreclosure on the property in 1933.

There were other arguments for the Saulsbury family. The copper pot itself had clearly been in the ground a long time. Of course there was no date or any other marking on it proving exactly where it came from or when. Still, the pot had been surrounded by oyster shells, and testimony from Saulsbury's children indicated that he frequently gave oyster parties to his gentlemen friends. The treasure container had been wrapped in a boot, and Saulsbury was known to have had odd boots made to order to accommodate a slight limp. Finally, there was the idea that the gold had most likely been buried in response to some economic crisis, perhaps at a time when banks had little credibility, during a time of national uncertainty, or when gold had reached an extraordinarily high value as related to paper currency. The entire presentation of the Saulsbury attorneys was made "with much dramatic effect," according to O'Dunne.

The facts seemed to match everything known of Andrew J. Saulsbury. He was a wealthy man, he hoarded small coin, he died suddenly, and his status as a Confederate sympathizer during the Civil War put his personal security at some risk. Judge O'Dunne listened, but he was more concerned with the question of precisely who had lived at 132 S. Eden, and when. Baltimore city directories had placed a Captain John J. Mattison at the address from 1853 to 1860. Saulsbury had purchased the property from Mattison in June 1865, but wasn't listed as living at 132 S. Eden until 1867. An exhaustive search of intervening city directories was made, searching them line by line, until it was found that another mariner, a certain Captain John E. Stevens, had lived at the address in 1864. O'Dunne was willing enough to accept that neither Mattison nor Stevens buried the gold, as both of the men continued to live in Baltimore in later years at different residences. Clearly they would not have left a seafarer's treasure behind in a former residence. The question was who else had lived there, and when?

Andrew J. Saulsbury was listed nearby at 138 S. Central in the 1865 and 1866 directories. His daughter Elizabeth, born in 1859, testified that she recalled the family moving from Central Street to Eden Street at the age of six, evidence which her attorneys then used to argue that Saulsbury had moved in immediately following his purchase of the property from Mattison in June 1865. Judge O'Dunne didn't give much credence to the daughter's testimony. She was an old woman by then. "I saw her on the witness stand," O'Dunne wrote, "and I say it would be almost pathetic to rely for unerring accuracy on her expressed recollection, which was memory blended with imagination and desire, mellowed with the gleam of seventy years of the flight of time." Compounding the gaps in the record of the residence was the absence of city directories between 1861 and 1863, doubtless due to the war. In the end, the Saulsburys could not demonstrate an unbroken chain of dwelling in the house, from Mattison to Stevens to Saulsbury. This troubled the judge.

Worse for the Saulsburys, the dates on the coins were difficult to explain. They ranged from 1834 to 1856, suggesting that the cache had been put away in the 1850s, not in the 1860s when Saulsbury and his family had moved into 132 S. Eden. A closer examination of the one-dollar gold pieces, which were minted beginning in 1849, revealed more clues. The gold dollars demonstrated that the hoard was underweight in coins of the year 1856, in relation to their original mintage (see figure 1). In other words, the coins weren't randomly gathered in the 1850s; collecting probably ceased sometime during 1856, before the 1856 dated gold dollars were completely in circulation. The 1856 date made no sense. The banking panic of 1857 was at least a year off, and the beginning of the Civil War four years beyond that. The distribution of the dates suggested that the hoard was pulled from circulation entirely in 1855 or 1856. Had the coins been collected over time, the dates might have been represented in closer proportion to their original mintages. There was no evidence for the argument the Saulsbury attorneys were forced to make. Andrew J. Saulsbury would have had to quickly assemble the coins sometime in 1856, and then have moved it from his Central Street home to Eden Street in 1865 or later. Did Saulsbury bury gold at 138 S. Central as well? It was hard enough to prove that he buried it at 132 S. Eden, let alone a previous residence.

O'Dunne allowed that the Saulsbury case was "plausible" while envisioning his own scenario. "It is equally plausible to assume that some of Captain Stevens' friends, unknown to him, and while Stevens was occupying the property, and while they were occupying it with him, may have buried treasure there, and been called to war and killed at the front and never come back and had opportunity to disclose the fact, or, it may have been pirate loot, which the holder was as much afraid to disclose as the Lindbergh kidnapping ransom loot. The mind of a Dumas, or Balzac, could spin fascinating plausibilities far outclassing those presented by the Saulsbury heirs….thieves, hoarders, pirates, or honest but scared men might have buried it and been unable to return. Of this there is no evidence, but it might have been," O'Dunne wrote in his opinion.

The judge was more inclined to believe that the coins had been buried during the war. However, the earliest that Saulsbury could have buried it would have been in June 1865, after the conflict was over and the White House occupied by a president whose political views were closer to his own. "It is difficult for us in these quiet times of peaceful depression to picture the excitement of the years immediately preceding the

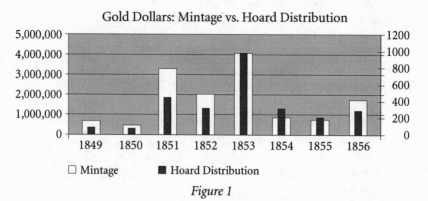

Gold Dollars: Mintage vs. Hoard Distribution

□ Mintage   ■ Hoard Distribution

Figure 1

Saulsbury's purchase in June 1865. In the four years preceding the Sauls-bury's acquisition of this property, much excitement swept over this city, state, and nation. For the two years immediately preceding his purchase, Baltimore was the stormy petrel of this drama, because of its border line position, and its key location as to control of the National Capital. . . . reason and imagination can best depict the state of mind of the inhabit-ants of Baltimore at this crisis of the war. There were innumerable high-handed and arbitrary acts of Federal militia, calculated to justly arouse citizens of Baltimore, unnecessary to now detail, but they inflamed public opinion," O'Dunne argued. He concluded by saying "I find in support of the Saulsbury claim nothing more than a plausible possibility falling far short of legal proof of ownership" The Saulsburys were thus ruled out of the contest, and the judge made everyone else wait a week to find out whether the poor boys or the Findlay-French ladies would win the first battle of this legal war.

CHAPTER 13

THE FINDLAY-FRENCH CLAIM

Although the Saulsbury case was one that rose or fell strictly on evidence, the Findlay-French case had to be built on the interpretation of written law. Complicating the case was the fact that Maryland, like most other states, had no statutory laws regarding treasure trove. The decision thus had to be drawn from legal tradition on both sides of the Atlantic, English common law being accepted as good a basis as any in such situations. The Findlay-French attorneys submitted a thirty-page brief to O'Dunne outlining the history of treasure trove law from the time of antiquity to the present. Emory Niles, a Rhodes scholar working for the Findlay-French ladies, engaged in some legal showmanship by sprinkling the document with numerous passages in Latin, no doubt extracted from ancient legal texts. Judge O'Dunne needed help with that part of it. "The Statute of Limitations has long since run on my ability to read Latin with any degree of legal intelligence," O'Dunne wrote, and so it was necessary that Niles take the brief back and perform the necessary translations. Not to be outdone, Levin entered a forty-page brief himself, citing many cases related to treasure trove and lost property. Levin brought in his younger cousin, an attorney named Sigmund Levin, to help with the research. O'Dunne was impressed with the Levin presentation. "My subsequent search has been able to add very little, if anything, to their work," he wrote.

The laws of antiquity that Niles detailed naturally supported his point of view. From the Roman era, the Justinian Code split treasure evenly between the finder and landowner, but only in situations where the finder was legally engaged on the owner's property. In cases of trespass, treasure passed in full to the landowner. English common law had originally agreed with Roman law, later changing as the power of the English Crown increased, allowing the Crown to seize treasure trove as it wished. Other European countries, including Spain and France, retained the Roman division of spoils. Louisiana, heavily influenced by the French, also enacted legislation specifying the sharing of treasure trove. Judge O'Dunne read through all the legal history, but he didn't have much use for the classical definitions of treasure trove. The requirement that trove be gold or silver was arbitrary. Why not other valuables as well? And why did something have to be buried in the earth? "If this ancient distinction is to [apply], any treasure which may be slightly buried in the earth, might, with a spring freshet, be washed to the surface, and thus lose its character as treasure trove; whereas, if later accidentally stepped upon by horse or man and pressed under the surface of the earth, it would revert to its earlier character of treasure trove. This might change from day to day, dependent upon the weather and the condition of the soil, and the amount of travel at such spot. Is there any sound reason in common sense for such distinction?" O'Dunne asked. Still, despite the arbitrary nature of what actually constituted treasure trove, O'Dunne was willing to accept that trove passed to the finder, based on other trove decisions in America, many of which Levin had cited in his brief.

The judge was more interested in the question of trespass, and what rights remained to Theodore and Henry as possible trespassers in the dark cellar. There had been much conflicting testimony regarding the state of the partition separating the front and rear cellar, and O'Dunne suspected at least one witness of outright deception. "There is considerable conflict in the testimony and much lying evidence as to whether this door was locked, or whether it was closed, or whether it was generally locked and generally closed, or otherwise," O'Dunne wrote in his opinion. Indeed, the testimony on this point seemed to reflect everyone's own interest in the case. Benjamin Kalis, the landlord employed by the Findlay-French clan, stated that prior to his renovations in late 1933, there had been a partition loosely standing at the opening to the rear cellar. He mounted the door with hinges and added a padlock, which he said was to prevent access to the back, where electric meters were newly installed, as there had been no electric service in the building up to that point. A key was left with a first-floor tenant to allow the utility company access to the meters, and another was kept in the office of the American Realty Company, which Kalis owned. Kalis initially claimed that the door was always kept locked, but under questioning from O'Dunne, Kalis squirmed around the issue.

Q. You did not go there from time to time to look at it, did you?
A. I did, your honor.
Q. How often?
A. Well, probably like on Eden street—

Q. Don't give me a lot of argument. How often did you go there to see if it was padlocked?

A. Not to see the padlock, but to inspect the property.

Q. How often?

A. At least once a week.

Q. And you always found it locked?

A. No, not all the time I went to the cellar, just to the property.

Q. That is what I want to know, did you or not [find the cellar locked]?

A. No, sir, I did not.

Q. You found it [the cellar] unlocked?

A. I could not say. The time I seen it, it was locked.

Q. Sometimes you found it locked, and sometimes you found it unlocked, is that right?

A. I say I did not go down specially to the cellar, I went to the property.

Q. I don't care what you went for. When you got there, did you or not find that the cellar door in the partition was locked or unlocked?

A. I did not pay attention.

Q. Then you don't know whether it was locked or unlocked?

A. I could not say.

Q. Now, we have all of that in [the record] to find out nothing.

What Kalis couldn't say, his carpenter, Charles Fleetwood, could. Fleetwood testified that the door was always kept locked and that he had used the office key to get in. On the other hand, he also had to admit that he had only been down there a few times. The Kalis plumber, Robert King, testified likewise.

But Harry Fleischer, a tenant in the second-floor front apartment at 132 S. Eden, had a different story to tell. It was Fleischer who had seen the bedraggled old widow Smulovitz chopping wood in the back of the cellar. Fleischer said that he had been in the rear part of the cellar many times, replacing electric fuses every few weeks, and that Kalis had even given him permission to store coal in the back. This directly contradicted Kalis, who had said he never gave anyone permission to enter the back of the cellar. Fleischer went further, charging that Kalis had actually installed the door and padlock after the hoard find, implying a bit of subterfuge on the part of the landlord, in order to claim later that the back of the cellar was fully secured. There was evidently some animosity between Fleischer and the landlord. It seems that Fleischer had previously complained about the bad smell and general uncleanliness of the cellar and asked Kalis to intervene. Nothing was done, according to Fleischer, until the boys made their startling find. The photographs of the cellar showed that the door to the rear part of the cellar appeared to be sturdier, and of much more recent origin, than the doors to each of the tenant's storage compartments in the front part of the cellar. Another tenant living in the first-floor rear apartment, Julia D'Alesandro, agreed with Fleischer, testifying that the door to the rear was habitually unlocked. Bessie Jones, Theodore's mother, no doubt understanding the import of the moment, agreed as well. "There wasn't no door hung there when we moved in and no hinges on it and no locks on it," she stated emphatically. "There had been an old door setting there, standing up against the building. There was no door hung there at all," Bessie explained to the court. Like Fleischer, she said that the door was hung and hinged after the gold was found.

The records Kalis kept didn't clarify the situation. There was a receipt from a local hardware store, for twenty-five cents, indicating that a padlock and key had been delivered to 132 S. Eden on December 16, 1933, during the building renovation. But there was no mention of what the lock was used for. And there was little in the Kalis work ledger detailing specific repairs to the door in the rear part of the cellar. Kalis had to explain that his ledger wasn't thorough. "We don't specify just exactly what a man is doing through the day, just so we give him credit for his time that he is putting in on like say 132 South Eden Street, and we give one or two items of what the man was doing," he admitted. There was another lock and key purchased in April 1934, and a labor charge of two dollars and seventy-six cents on April 19 for "putting up fence and repair cellar door." Kalis couldn't say for sure what the new lock was for, or exactly what "repair cellar door" meant. He was a busy man with hundreds of similar ledger entries and multiple tradesmen in his employ. One could not expect him to be intimately acquainted with the state of every door in every building he managed, and especially old doors in dark cellars. It was unpleasant for Kalis, obligated to the building owners for his management fees, while being drilled by sharp attorneys to explain the smallest details in his less-than-detailed ledgers.

JUDGE O'DUNNE ISSUES AN OPINION

There are, even in the most unfortunate of lives, greater or lesser moments of mercy and grace common to human experience. A kind word of studied empathy, a charity unshaken of dignity, a hearth of radiating warmth and companionship, these were all gifts the residents of 132 S. Eden could readily comprehend. Their blessings were few and appeared as if by chance, like the cross Theodore had uncovered on a dusty road, alone, waiting for a stranger to reunite him with his mother. But the moment at hand, the pot of gold at the end of rainbow, was not some stochastic chimera, like the automobiles Theodore imagined in the distance, wondering if they would stop and carry him home. The gold was real enough, and as happens in history, it was under the thumb of a maverick.

"When there was no war going on, he declared one," said the famed political commentator H. L. Mencken of Judge Eugene O'Dunne, adding that "when the natural supply of public enemies ran out, he manufactured them." O'Dunne seemingly reveled in the controversy that flowed out of his chambers. "Good copy could always be found in his courtroom," a law journal noted. O'Dunne had fashioned himself an independent Democrat early in his career, running for state's attorney three times and losing against the entrenched establishment. The Democratic power broker was the "King of the Underworld," O'Dunne concluded, describing his party leader. What O'Dunne failed to accomplish at the polls, he aimed to do from the bench instead, being appointed by the Maryland governor to the Supreme Bench of Baltimore in 1926. He fought segregation and corruption and had a reputation for stiff and unusual sentences, sending more than one man to the whipping post for wife-beating. He was unloved by his fellow judges, not afraid to criticize their work, and his own decisions were frequently reversed by the Maryland state appellate court. Forced off the bench at seventy by a mandatory retirement law, which he called a "constitutional imbecility," O'Dunne jumped immediately back into private practice, where "he remained active and belligerent until his last illness," according to one obituary. Above all, O'Dunne was his own man. "He feared only God," thought one colleague.

Politics aside, no one doubted O'Dunne's intelligence. Simon Sobeloff, later Solicitor General of the United States, backhandedly acknowledged O'Dunne's studious nature in a parody opinion written on the occasion of O'Dunne's retirement. The lengthy opinion ruling on a supposed automobile accident spoofed O'Dunne's tendency to invoke allusions of the classics and the antiquities, and his reputation for hard work. "A preliminary word may be in order with respect to the now almost universal custom of closing not only public libraries but, indeed all cultural institutions between midnight and 6:00 A.M. It is perhaps an indication of the decadence of the age that even scholars abandon their books during these night hours which, to one of my constitution, furnish such potent literary inspiration," Sobeloff wrote in jest. Sobeloff later had O'Dunne invoking Genesis, comparing the ark (the first known conveyance) and the modern automobile. Finally, O'Dunne is placed in London, writing opinions in longhand, temperature one hundred and six degrees, with ancient law tomes bound in human skin at hand. It was of course all a tribute. "Nobody but so devoted a disciple of Judge O'Dunne as Mr. Sobeloff could have so perfectly reproduced his judicial style," thought another colleague.

Levin liked his chances with O'Dunne. The two men were not so different, outsiders bent on justice, and more than willing to stand on their own against the established order. Levin was even more encouraged when O'Dunne began probing the Findlay-French attorney, during oral arguments, on the exact nature of trespass. O'Dunne posed a scenario to Emory Niles. Suppose the boys had been hunting rabbits in a public field and happened upon a pocketbook containing money and lying between the rails of the Baltimore & Ohio railroad tracks. Would the money belong to the railroad as a landowner, or to the children? Niles was of course forced to say that it belonged to the railroad. O'Dunne instead favored an "elastic" definition of trespass. If the boys were in the cellar for any other purpose except to access the Jones' storage locker in the front part of the cellar, was that not technically trespass? "By a parity of reasoning, they might be said to be trespassing during all of the five or six months that they daily played in the cellar generally, unless they confined themselves to their own coal bin, or wood shed locker there," he wrote. Or, if they were sitting on the steps leading downstairs, which were intended only for egress or ingress, would that not also be trespass? O'Dunne did not care for the legal hair splitting. "In a shack tenement of this character," he asked, "and as applied to these tenants, is that not drawing a line unwarranted by the practical aspects of life?" O'Dunne had considered the conflicting testimony on whether the rear cellar was locked or not, and in the end drew his own line, not willing to call the boys' act a trespass, while recognizing at the same time that the evidence wasn't obvious either way. O'Dunne now came to the climax, by edict ending the first important battle in this war of lucre. "I award the whole of the contents of the copper pot of some $11,427 face value, to the infant defendants as finders of treasure trove," he wrote on February 16, 1935.

The Jones and Grob families were expectedly jubilant, but cautious. The boys repeated the same platitudes to the press they had offered reporters when the coins were first found. The papers were only too happy to print it all again. "I'm going to get my mother a home out Canton way [a nearby Baltimore neighborhood], where her friends are," Henry said. "I always wanted to. I told her once that I was going to make her life easy." Theodore agreed. "That's the right idea. I'm going to follow Henry."

Both boys talked about reuniting their families in their imaginary new homes, each having siblings living elsewhere. Henry's mother, Ruth Grob, was equally excited. "I was sick lying on the couch when I heard about it," she said. "But when I heard that news—I got well pretty quick. I feel like I could cry." Ruth suggested that they were going to use the money to buy a small home and to put Henry through college. Bessie Jones felt likewise, but she was still waiting to actually see the cash. "I'm so happy I could jump right up and kiss Judge O'Dunne," she said. "He's a very nice man. I'm going on a shopping tour to get some clothes, too. But not until I get my hands on it. I'm not counting on it really until I get it. A bird in the hand's worth two in the bush." Theodore had some concerns as well. "There is just one thing that worries me," he said. "When the people from the relief headquarters, who had been paying us for two years, heard that we found the gold, [they] came down and made mother sign an agreement to pay back all of the money they had advanced to us. I don't know how much that will be, but its plenty." The two boys made an appearance on local radio the next day, no doubt answering all the same questions once more.

Whether or not Bessie Jones ever squared with the relief office is lost to history, but in Cleveland, a remarkably similar tale of interred gold and welfare ended in restitution being made to the Cleveland Associated Charities. Katherine Majewski, a Polish immigrant on welfare assistance for two years, had buried twenty-eight hundred dollars in gold coins in the basement of her landlord's home. James Mitchell, the landlord, subsequently revealed the hoard to local authorities, apparently an act of revenge related to a business dispute he had with Majewski. The Secret Service was called in, and Majewksi's welfare fraud was eventually uncovered. Majewksi's hoard was redeemed for currency and returned to her, but not until the city of Cleveland had been reimbursed for four hundred dollars. The U.S. Attorney elected not to prosecute, "in view of the fact that it would render Mrs. Majewski, who is 60 years of age, penniless and render her an object of charity for the balance of her life."

PART 4

THE AUCTION

*Henry and Theodore at the Perry Fuller
auction, 1935*

CHAPTER 14

PERRY FULLER, STAMP AND COIN DEALER

Yearning for the court victory that indeed came to fruition, Bessie Jones had been making what little money she could doing laundry by hand for most of 1934. A washing machine for his mother was one of the first things Theodore mentioned to a reporter just after the hoard find. Remarkably, an electric washing machine so appeared in their apartment between the time of the hoard find in September and O'Dunne's decision in February 1935. A new washing machine in those days was valued at fifty dollars, ostensibly a rather large sum of money in the Jones household. Theodore might have been especially industrious in the intervening months, or perhaps the money might have come from some other source. In any case, there was an electric percolator, a radio, and an iron besides. Not everyone on their block owned a radio, and Bessie and Theodore found themselves a new topic of conversation with those who did. The washing machine considerably eased Bessie's domestic drudgery, probably evoking envy among neighbors who went without. "I think it caused trouble in the family," recalled one elderly woman, reflecting on a time when she had the advantages of modern technology and her sisters did not. The boom in appliances, some thought, might drive the economy as had the automobile in the 1920s. The Jones electric bill, normally sixty cents a month, doubled to a dollar and twenty cents in November 1934. Bessie, possibly unaccustomed to residential electric service prior to moving into 132 S. Eden, became suspicious and went over to the landlord's office on 406 W. Saratoga, an hour by foot, insisting to see the bill in person. The bill was summarily presented and paid. Bessie returned home, a little more familiar with modern technology.

Henry's mother, Ruth, was engaged in her own enterprise, running "Ruth's Tavern" on the ground floor of her apartment building at 227 S. Caroline. The space had been used as a lunchroom several years prior, but with the lifting of Prohibition it was renovated into a more pressing concern, at least for the thirsty public. Ruth was licensed to dispense beer and light wines, and in fact had borrowed from Harry O. Levin the sixty dollars needed to acquire the license. But business was slow, and the few customers did not share too much enthusiasm for her son's good luck. "I found a penny on Hanover Street today, and I'm unemployed, but I'm going to give it all to the poor," said one to a reporter asking about found treasure, while another sarcastic patron added, "Jus' think of that. He's unemployed but he's gonna give it all to the poor."

Door-to-door salesmen were apparently enjoying good business at the Jones and Grob households, the published addresses of Henry and Theodore in the newspapers likely drawing their attention. Henry and Theodore were forced to devise a secret signal to announce their presence when visiting each other, so deluged were they with the 1930s version of telemarketers. Despite the fact that the gold was still locked up in a bank box controlled by Judge O'Dunne, word somehow got around that the boys and their mothers might be good sales leads.

Others were so not lucky in business. Perry W. Fuller, the Baltimore stamp and coin dealer who had been interviewed by the papers shortly after the hoard find, and who believed that the government would not seize the gold coins, found himself going bankrupt. Perry had grown up on an equine farm in North Carolina. He was thrown from a horse as a child, after a brother dared him to ride an unbroken animal, and as a result he was bedridden for many months. It was during this time he became fond of stamp collecting, and in later years he was known to be especially patient with young collectors. Theodore and Henry would have been surprisingly welcome in the upscale downtown gallery at 9 E. Hamilton Street where Fuller dealt in paintings, antiques, coins, stamps, and other curios. Fuller had come to the big city of Baltimore around 1910, to study medicine according to family lore, but could not stand the sight of blood and instead sought to make his professional mark elsewhere. He quickly became socially connected and married into the prominent Sherwood family, which was associated with the Old Bay Line shipping company. He became a full-time collectibles dealer around 1925, and by the 1930s was living in a house valued at twenty thousand dollars, enjoying the prestige of having a chauffeur and an art gallery in Baltimore's city center.

The façade of the gallery was inviting enough. The story underneath was less charming. The expansive manse where Fuller lived was not his own property but rather belonged to his mother-in-law, who lived at the same address. Fuller's business was likewise bankrolled by the Sherwoods, who had staked him to the tune of thirty thousand dollars. Fuller, with three children, now found himself in an uncomfortable position. Deeply

in debt to his wife's family, with no significant assets of his own, he somehow had to squeeze money out of a luxury business that depended on
discretionary spending at the height of the Depression. By 1935, Fuller
threw in the towel and initiated proceedings to dissolve the enterprise.
He left behind him a string of debts that were settled for six cents on the
dollar. Among his creditors was a Mrs. Robert E. Lee of Washington, no
doubt connected to the family of the Confederate general, who had likely
consigned Civil War material to Fuller. In particular, Fuller was recognized as an authority on Confederate postage. The Peabody Institute was
also listed, along with a host of businesses upon which Fuller relied for
daily needs such as printing, bookbinding, and advertising. Divorce followed, and Fuller had to scramble.

APPEAL

The American way of government, based upon "checks and balances," is
never as manifest as in the appellate process. Lower and higher courts toss
cases back and forth, a wave of exaltation or devastation riding on every decision. Emotion and media coverage inflame public opinion as every
controversial outcome faces the inevitable rehearing in some other venue.
Proceedings are seemingly doomed to be dragged on ad infinitum, leaving the underdog with always one more chance. Thus, it was no surprise
when both the Saulsbury and Findlay-French parties appealed Judge
O'Dunne's decision to the Maryland State Court of Appeals. Indeed, the
ink had hardly dried on O'Dunne's decision of February 16, 1935, before
both announced their plans to appeal the decision of the Baltimore City
Circuit Court judge, not even waiting until the next day. O'Dunne was
the least surprised. "I'm only a stoplight on the way to the court of appeals," he once said, knowing well that his batting average in the court of
appeals was not the highest.

Although O'Dunne's decision was now under appeal, all the parties
were amenable to proceeding with a public auction sale of the gold. The
last obstacle was getting past the Secret Service. But that problem had taken
care of itself. Federal agents in Baltimore ultimately had to admit that any
coins with numismatic value were legal to own as collectibles. The Secret
Service had failed to strong arm O'Dunne into sacrificing the treasure.
There was no getting around the Gold Act, which was quite explicit on
the matter. Collector coins were excepted from the recall, and surely anything as romantic as a Civil War-era gold coin buried in the ground for
seventy plus years qualified as a collector coin. On February 21, 1935, the
agents relented, months after expressing undue interest in a completely

Perry Fuller, center, with hoard coins

lawful situation. It was a good day for everyone else, especially the attorneys working on contingency. Judge O'Dunne thought the hoard would auction for around thirty thousand dollars.

It was a good day for Perry Fuller too, because he needed all the work he could get. The record is silent as to how Fuller was selected to auction the gold, but the choice was probably made by Charles A. McNabb and Harry O. Levin. McNabb, the deputy clerk of O'Dunne's court, was appointed by O'Dunne as guardian of the hoard, while Levin was appointed counsel to the guardian. It was a sweetheart deal for McNabb, who in time came to personally benefit from the cache. Levin probably conferred with the Findlay-French party as well, who happened to be personally acquainted with Fuller. H. Findlay French, the son and nephew of the two old ladies, was an avid stamp collector and client of Fuller's. They were all active in the Maryland Historical Society; indeed, Fuller and Mary Findlay had joined the society on the very same day. H. Findlay French wrote book reviews for the society's journal while Fuller used it as an advertising vehicle. The Saulsbury attorneys also knew Fuller, because one of them had represented one of Fuller's creditors!

Fuller had much to do. There was the matter of arranging the auction venue, and some thought was given to having the sale in New York. It was the financial capital of America and not surprisingly the numismatic capital as well. A Baltimore sale was more in keeping with the history of the hoard, and in the end Levin and Fuller made the sentimental choice and secured the ballroom of the Lord Baltimore Hotel in downtown Baltimore. Fuller advertised the sale in New York just to be safe, even though the auction won its fair share of free publicity in out-of-town newspapers. There was also an auction catalog to prepare, and even the crustiest coin dealer would have been most excited about being the first numismatic expert to inventory the coins that were now being held at the First National Bank on the corner of Redwood and Light streets.

Finally, Fuller had to prepare the coins as best he could for public sale. Cleaning coins is generally detrimental to their value, and the boys and Baltimore police had already exacted their share of damage. Fuller knew better, that there were proper methods to conserve gold coinage in ways that could improve both its appearance and value. Not being a chemist himself, he consulted with his dentist, who recommended a solution in which to boil the coins. Fuller treated the coins at the First National Bank and was pleased with the results. "They're not polished," he told the press. "That would have ruined them. They have simply been cleaned of corrosive substances. They are in unusually good condition." Fuller was now able to read the dates on most of the coins. Four hundred and twenty-one of the one-dollar gold pieces were indecipherable when he began. Fuller got the number down to thirty-nine. It was now time for the coin collectors to find out exactly what was in that bucket.

THE CATALOG

Fuller's sixteen-page catalog, issued sometime in April 1935, revealed the details. There were thirty-five hundred and eight coins in all, which Fuller divided into four hundred and thirty-eight lots. Most of the value was in the one-dollar and twenty-dollar pieces (see figure 2).

Denomination	Count	Total Face Value
$20.00	317	$6340.00
$10.00	81	$810.00
$5.00	255	$1275.00
$2.50	65	$162.50
$1.00	2789	$2789.00
Total	3508	$11381.50

Figure 2

The twenty-dollar coins, known as double eagles, had been minted for public use beginning in 1850. They were generally minted in large numbers at the Philadelphia and San Francisco mints, and these coins were not particularly scarce. The real prize was among the New Orleans double eagles, where the gold supply was limited to local sources. The hoard contained an example of the New Orleans double eagle from 1856, which had been minted to the extent of twenty-two hundred and fifty pieces, a trickle compared to the millions of double eagles pouring out of the Philadelphia and San Francisco coin factories. No special consideration was given the New Orleans coins at the time; indeed, collecting by mintmark was not popularized until the turn of the century. A nineteenth-century numismatist was generally satisfied with a single example of the 1856 date, regardless of where it originated. By 1935, the number of extant specimens of the 1856 New Orleans double eagles was probably thirty or less, and the coins were now recognized as far more desirable than their Philadelphia and San Francisco counterparts.

There were other scarce coins from New Orleans, including a ten-dollar piece dated 1849 and a five-dollar piece from 1847. The remainder of the hoard, by and large, was clearly not the work of a coin collector seeking rare specimens, but merely an assemblage of coins pulled out of everyday commerce. They were unremarkable by themselves, similar examples trading frequently among collectors and dealers with no one paying much attention. But while not rare, some of the coins were exceptionally preserved. Fuller's catalog described the coins only as "fine" or "very fine," a bit of timesaving on his part, as most numismatists used a much broader set of descriptions to specify condition. Among the lucky coins that had escaped the "restoration" performed upon them by the boys and Baltimore police officers were "matchless uncirculated gems," according to a New York coin dealer who later handled some of the coins on the aftermarket. Fuller himself hadn't been quite ready to use the "uncirculated" word. "Many appear never to have been in circulation," he admitted. "But because of the lack of definite knowledge regarding the origin of the treasure we have been conservative in the catalogue descriptions."

There were less rare coins from the Charlotte and Dahlonega branch mints as well, and all the coins were dated between 1834 and 1856. The year 1834 was significant. Before the government effectively abandoned the gold standard in 1933, there had been a continual struggle to keep both gold and silver coinage in circulation at the same time. One metal would rise in value in relation to the other as new sources were discovered and exploited, and the more valued metal would be hoarded and melted at a profit. The early nineteenth century saw much silver come out of South America and Mexico, and by the 1830s a five-dollar gold piece was worth five dollars and thirty cents in silver coins. Speculators scooped up every piece of gold coming out of the mint that could be had. The only way to alleviate the hoarding was to either decrease the amount of precious metal in the gold coins, or conversely increase the weight of the silver coinage. The government naturally chose the former option, debasing the gold to bring it into parity with the silver. As a result of the imbalance, the pre-1834 gold coinage was quite rare, and Fuller wasn't surprised when he didn't find any of the "old tenor" gold in the hoard. A lesser-sized Civil War-era hoard buried on a Texas farm was similarly lacking in pre-1834 gold issues. Unearthed in 1947, this find consisted of one hundred and sixty-six United States gold coins, all minted between 1834 and 1866. The premium on gold would turn into a premium on silver twenty years later, as California gold flooded the channels of commerce in the early 1850s.

In addition to taking shortcuts on the grading of the coins, Fuller also failed to record the mintmarks on the one-dollar pieces. Among the other denominations, fully twenty percent of the hoard coins were struck at branch mints. Yet among the nearly twenty-eight hundred one-dollar pieces, not a single mintmark was noted. Fuller probably considered it to be a laborious task and instead cataloged the one-dollar coins by date only. It was a disservice on the part of Fuller, who perhaps was pressed for time to prepare and distribute the catalog. Such coins typically ended up being purchased by sharp-eyed collectors and dealers who were able to examine the hoard coins personally prior to the sale. Out-of-town buyers, submitting bids by mail, had no such opportunity.

Henry and Theodore's discovery coin, the double eagle that Theodore could not initially identify, and which Henry had scraped with a knife, was not identified in Fuller's catalog. It was a curious omission, as Fuller took pains to describe certain other coins as scratched or nicked. There were a few dollars lost here; a piece specifically cataloged as the discovery coin most certainly would have fetched a bit more at auction. Fuller was not one to engage in excessive hype, and his sale catalog was devoid of overt marketing, simply stating the facts of the hoard discovery and proceeding to a terse inventory of the coins. In any case, if Henry and Theodore hadn't saved any "souvenirs," or perhaps the discovery coin itself, at least Harry Levin had some feel for the historical import of the situation and said that he would arrange for the boys to get a coin or two from the public sale.

CHAPTER 15

THE FINDLAY-FRENCH APPEAL

While Fuller carried out preparations for the auction, mailing out auction catalogs and getting the coins ready for public viewing, all the attorneys were preparing the appeal to the Maryland State Court of Appeals in Annapolis. The Findlay-French attorneys were apparently tired of their clients being thought of as two mean old women, and engaged in some damage control in their appellate brief. We "have always felt a definite moral obligation to reward the boys who found the coins, not only equitably, but generously," they wrote. And, they intended to pay the children a minimum of three thousand dollars from the auction proceeds, should the pot be awarded to the two ladies as the landowners. None of this was pertinent to the appeal. "In making these statements we realize that they are unusual to include in a brief in a court of law," the attorneys wrote. "If they are in any way improper, we crave the pardon of the Court. But we do not think they are," they added. The offer was "designed merely to clarify a situation that has been obscured by over-sentimentality and a distorted idea of the underlying condition of the persons whom we represent." The Findlay-French brief also revealed that the three-thousand-dollar offer was a condition of Levin agreeing to the public sale of the coins. Levin clearly had the upper hand, and knew it. The coins were going to be sold anyway, so why not take a minimum guarantee of three thousand dollars? The upside was one hundred percent of the pot if the Court of Appeals ruled his way, and now Levin knew that he and the boys would all get at least a thousand dollars each.

At the appellate level, all the attorneys were enjoined from rearguing the facts as established under Judge O'Dunne in the Baltimore Circuit Court. The only thing to be done was to argue for or against the conclusions drawn by O'Dunne and opposing attorneys, and no ink was spared in this endeavor. The lawyers, *en masse*, submitted briefs running over a hundred pages. It was their first opportunity to rebut the decisions that O'Dunne had authored in February, or in Levin's case, to remind everyone why the staunchly independent O'Dunne was correct in his thinking. The eight appellate judges read through the briefs and scheduled oral arguments for Tuesday, April 30, 1935, just two days before the public sale was to be held in Baltimore.

The Saulsbury attorneys made no offers similar to the Findlay-French legal team, instead reworking the case they had made before O'Dunne. O'Dunne's explanation that perhaps Captains Mattison or Stevens, residents of 132 S. Eden prior to Saulsbury, had seafaring associates who left the treasure behind did not square with the Saulsbury team. If this was a pirate's hoard, they asked, why were there no foreign coins present? And how could a low-paid sailor accumulate thousands of dollars in gold? Or, if he were a young soldier called off to war, why would he have not taken a friend or family member into confidence before heading into harm's way? It seemed to the Saulsbury attorneys that a great leap of faith was required to accept O'Dunne's theory. The judge's story required someone of great wealth to be living at the property in the Civil War era, who had continued and undisturbed access to the cellar, who hoarded gold coin, who told no one about the hoard and then died suddenly, and who *wasn't* Andrew J. Saulsbury. This line of reasoning, the attorneys thought, required a "succession and number of purely imaginary events."

The Findlay-French brief rested on an argument of the law, and in many places referred to previous Maryland Court of Appeals decisions that were obliquely related to the hoard case. They were, in effect, throwing the judges' words right back at them. In presenting their case, the Findlay-French attorneys first took issue with O'Dunne's "elastic" definition of trespass. O'Dunne was "merely throwing out a quasi justification of [his] decision, which was really based upon what the Court conceived to be equity and fairness to poor boys, rather than the clear and compelling legal principles upon which the appellants base their case," according to the attorneys. Further on the definition of trespass, they did not like O'Dunne's example of walking across a railroad track by chance and finding a pocketbook. "Our case is far stronger than that of a person who casually crosses a railroad track. To be analogous, the railroad case must be considered as one in which a person comes onto the right of way and actually digs up the road bed. No one would for a moment contend that such illegal conduct could result in the acquiring of rights by the person engaging in it," they argued.

The next issue raised was how and whether the English common law on treasure trove applied in Maryland. Certainly there were no statutory laws on the books either way. The Findlay-French attorneys wrote that the appeals court would effectively have to legislate the Maryland law through the decision they were about to make. "There is no Maryland statute regulating the subject. This Court in the instant case, will, therefore, be called upon to declare the Maryland law of treasure trove," they stated. Naturally the Findlay-French team had some strong ideas as to how treasure trove law should be written. They felt that treasure trove should be thought of as "mislaid" property, rather than being treated as its own special type of missing property. Recalling the case of the unlucky chambermaid, mislaid property was something deliberately concealed with the intention of returning for it. Mislaid property reverted to the landowner, of course.

The Findlay-French attorneys cited all the same cases that Levin had earlier found supporting the boys, but drew an important distinction. In all of these cases, they said, there had been no condition of trespass. How was it that one could acquire rights to property while trespassing on the land of another? If that were true, they argued, anyone could go on anyone else's land and begin digging. There was a single snag with this line of reasoning. The Court of Appeals in Georgia had ruled on a similar case just one month previous, on April 3, 1935. Two trespassers had uncovered fifteen thousand dollars in gold dust and bullion while digging underneath a large rock, even after being warned to stay off the property. It was an inexplicable decision, and the Findlay-French legal team could do little more than say that the Georgia court "stands alone in the absurdity of its conclusion." "It is manifest that the decision of the Georgia Court is in error," they remarked, and probably most observers agreed with that part of it.

The Findlay-French team thus attacked on two fronts, first saying that the common law of treasure trove should not apply, and secondly that the boys were trespassing anyway. At the same time, they fully realized they had already lost in the court of public opinion. "Hard cases make bad law," the Findlay-French team summarized. "This case would seem to be one of those in which commendable but unnecessary sympathy with the finders suggested, and has led to, a conclusion contrary to law and principle. The fact that the finders in this case were boys, and the fact that they had no unlawful intent when they trespassed, can make no difference in the legal consequences. These respondents are not grasping persons unwilling to recognize the claims of needy boys. They have already recognized these claims in part and have repeatedly committed themselves to add substantially to what they have already done."

CHAPTER 16

TRESPASSERS OR DISCOVERERS?

Levin naturally had no truck with the O'Dunne opinion, and took his opportunity to chime in with the "learned Chancellor" who, according to Levin, had "clearly and excellently stated" the case for the boys. With regard to the Saulsbury claim, Levin emphasized the legal standard that had to be met in order to award the pot to the heirs of that family. Levin reminded the Court of Appeals that Saulsbury's ownership had to be established "clearly and unmistakably." A plausible case was not sufficient to get the job done, even though Levin allowed that "several of the [Saulsbury] propositions are conceded."

Levin, like O'Dunne, pointed out problems with the Saulsbury timeline. The cache was obviously buried in 1856 or later, as that was the last date on the coins. Yet Saulsbury wasn't listed in the city directory at 132 S. Eden until 1867, and even if the testimony of his elderly daughter was to be believed, there was a still a nine-year gap between 1856 and 1865, when she testified that the family moved into the property. Levin speculated that the property may have even been vacant during some of this period, especially as one of Saulsbury's daughters mentioned that her father had had work done on the house prior to their moving in. All in all, Levin thought it more likely that the cache had been buried before Saulsbury got there. Certainly the war was over by then, indeed, Saulsbury didn't even purchase the property until June 1865. The era of Reconstruction was admittedly tumultuous, but surely it was far more likely for the gold to have been buried during wartime than in peacetime.

In order for Saulsbury to have buried the gold, Levin thought, he must have stopped hoarding in 1856, the latest date on the coins. Levin did not say it, but this suggested that Saulsbury started the collection at his Central Street residence, and then moved it to Eden Street along with the family. However, Levin felt that hoarders are always hoarders, and that it didn't make sense for Saulsbury to quit hoarding in 1856. There should have been coins dated between 1856 and Saulsbury's death in 1873. Mintages of one-dollar gold pieces remained substantial between 1856 and 1862, when the government introduced currency not redeemable in gold. Levin had to allow that Reuben Foster had produced in court a gold dollar dated 1859, said to have been handed down through the family from his grandfather, Andrew J. Saulsbury. There was also the testimony of Andrew's daughters that Saulsbury had kept much small coin close at hand in his residence. Levin countered by saying that an astute and prosperous businessman such as Saulsbury would not have been likely to put money in the ground, where it could not work for him.

As far as the two old Findlay-French ladies, Levin suggested that there was a philosophical progression of the law with regard to found property, with the strongest rights being accorded to the proven original owner, next to the finder, and finally to the landowner. And even at that, the landowner was treated only as an exception, specifically in cases where it was likely that the original owner would return. As an example, Levin cited the case of accidentally leaving a lottery ticket at the place of purchase. Beyond that, Levin wrote, this was an obvious case of treasure trove, and because Maryland had no laws governing trove, that American precedents should instead apply. Naturally he cited those in his favor, and pointed out that the Findlay-French team hadn't cited any treasure trove cases in their own favor.

But the real crux of the entire case was whether American treasure trove was to be treated as "lost" property or "mislaid" property. "Lost" property, according to the law books, defines a situation where an owner involuntarily or unintentionally parts with property and does not know where it is. Possession is retained by the finder. "Mislaid" describes property deliberately placed by a property owner who subsequently fails to reclaim it or forgets about it. This property goes to the landowner. Levin argued that American case law had effectively merged treasure trove into the law of "lost" property.

Levin's brief ended by discussing trespass, probably the one subject about which he was the most concerned. That there was conflicting testimony on this point he admitted, but his ace in the hole was the second-floor front tenant at 132 S. Eden, Harry Fleischer. Fleischer's tale of the aged widow Smulovitz, chopping wood with a candle in the dark rear cellar, seemed too poignant to be fabricated. More than that, it meant that the back of the cellar was not locked as a matter of habit. Even if it was, Levin cited the recent Georgia case awarding treasure trove to trespassers. With that highly controversial decision on everyone's minds, he left the case in the hands of the eight judges of the Maryland Court of Appeals.

"JUST LOOK AT THAT"

Fuller printed three thousand auction catalogs for the sale planned on Thursday, May 2, 1935. Requests for catalogs from nearly every state in the country came to Fuller's office at 9 East Hamilton Street, and Fuller predicted that the winning bids would total twenty-five thousand dollars. Auction lot viewing began on Monday of the same week, Fuller exhibiting the coins by appointment at the First National Bank under police guard. The coins were stored in paper envelopes with transparent faces, allowing the viewers a tactile interaction with the coins, a sensation lost in modern times with the explosion of hard plastic "slabs," which nowadays entomb nearly every coin of value.

The auction began at 2 P.M. Thursday, underneath the glass chandeliers in the ballroom of the Lord Baltimore Hotel. There were about one hundred in the audience, some dealers, some collectors, and some just spectators. Fuller hired an auctioneer, James H. Galton, to call the sale. Fuller sat next to Galton in the front of the room, calling out the highest mail bid for each lot before Galton broke into the banter that is the characteristic language of the auctioneer. Mail bids had been received for every lot in the auction, but few were successful, most of the participants preferring to see the coins in person in Baltimore and place bids for themselves at the auction.

The twenty-dollar gold pieces were listed at the beginning of the catalog. The first coin, a double eagle minted in Philadelphia in 1850, was sold to Rose Hendler, wife of the Baltimore ice cream king L. Manuel Hendler. The Hendlers were well-known Baltimore collectors, at one time gifting a Thomas Jefferson letter to the Maryland Historical Society, and Rose's presence at the auction was no surprise. She was a spirited bidder who won other lots besides. Rose paid thirty-six dollars for the first coin, and most of the other double eagles went for a couple dollars more or less. It was immediately clear to Fuller that the bidders were not paying for sentimental value. Most of the coins sold for their mere content of gold, a bit less than twice their face value. The 1856 double eagle from New Orleans was the one notable exception, selling at one hundred and five dollars, to a Samuel Glenn of Boydton, Virginia.

Fuller had sought additional publicity for the sale at the newly instituted Baltimore Coin Club, and had been approved for club membership on the same day as the auction sale. John Zug, a fellow member, took the bait and purchased at least seven double eagles in the sale, a date set from 1850 through 1856. Zug was evidently proud of the purchase and exhibited the coins a week later at the New York Numismatic Club, of which he was also a member. A friend of Zug's, Edward L. Weikert Jr., also attended.

The romance of Civil War-era gold no doubt struck a chord with Weikert. He himself, in 1893, had started his boyhood coin collection upon the chance finding of a one-dollar gold piece on the Gettysburg battlefield, near his birthplace. Weikert found more gold in the Lord Baltimore Hotel this day, bidding successfully on a number of five-dollar gold pieces.

The two boys came to the auction late by one account and left early by another. No one paid them much attention except a single reporter, and the auctioneer seems to have not pointed them out to the audience. This day, the coins were front row center, and the boys sat quietly in back of the room, in matching blue suits, both sets of clothing perhaps supplied by "Uncle" Morton Blum, who had outfitted Theodore at his downtown store the previous fall. Henry was particularly taken by the 1856 New Orleans twenty-dollar gold piece, and made a note of the winning bid in his copy of the catalog. A reporter has asked Henry, "How does it make you feel to have a man up there making your fortune for you?" Henry said nothing and pointed with his pencil to the one hundred and five dollar figure he had written in the catalog. "Well, just think, people are going to pay twenty thousand dollars for those coins you found in the cellar. Doesn't that thrill you?" On this day, Henry was tired of talking to reporters. "I know but just look at that," Henry said laconically, impressing his pencil upon the price written in his catalog. Theodore stared at the chandelier and played with his catalog, folding it in half before he even left the Lord Baltimore Hotel ballroom.

The four hundred and twenty-one lots were sold in a little over three hours. It was not an entertaining afternoon for the boys, or for most of the non-bidding spectators. The subtle interplay between bidders was only interesting to an observer who thoroughly understood the coins, the market, and the personalities involved. The anticipation had greatly exceeded the event. Still, there was a good deal of money being made for the children, or perhaps for the ladies who owned 132 S. Eden, or for the Saulsbury family who had lived in the house long ago. The auction realized almost twenty thousand dollars, far short of Fuller's estimate of twenty-five thousand and even further short of Judge O'Dunne's prediction of thirty thousand. The Baltimore bidders had proven themselves far more enamored of the gold itself than any stories attached to it. It was a reflection of the time, of the way that coins were collected in the Depression. A gold coin from a coin dealer was just as good as one that had been buried under mysterious circumstances. In any case, the nineteen thousand dollars were safe in the bank, and Theodore and Henry went home to wait and hear what the Maryland Court of Appeals had to say about who was going to get it.

LAWS ARE LIKE SAUSAGES

On July 2, 1935 the Maryland Court of Appeals issued the briefest of statements summing up nearly a year's worth of controversy between the boys and all others who would claim their golden pot. "The Court being equally divided in the opinion on the question arising in the above cases, it is ordered this second day of July 1935, that the decree be and it is hereby affirmed," wrote Carroll T. Bond, the chief judge of the court. Bond's statement meant that the court had split evenly down the middle, a 4–4 tie between eight judges on different sides of the issue, and further that O'Dunne's opinion would not be overturned. There was no written opinion, no airing of the internal debate, the court adopting the dictum often attributed to Otto von Bismarck. "Laws are like sausages," the German general thought. "It is better not to see them being made." The Findlay-French attorneys predictably and immediately filed a motion for reargument in the court of appeals.

Meanwhile, the auction proceeds remained under the control of Charles A. McNabb, the deputy clerk of the Baltimore Circuit Court. Assuming the court of appeals dismissed the motion for reargument, the cash was to be turned over to the children when they reached the age of twenty-one. In Henry's case, that meant waiting another five years, until May 12, 1940. Theodore, in theory, had to wait even a year longer than Henry, his twenty-first birthday coming on May 3, 1941. Theodore, of course, had been representing himself as two years older than he really was. As the boys waited, bureaucracy began chipping away at the hoard. Perry Fuller presented a bill for nearly eleven hundred dollars to cover the expenses of the auction sale. It was a reasonable amount for printing and distributing thousands of copies of the catalog, hiring guards at the bank, renting the hotel space, and preparing and collecting invoices. Reasonable or not, the money was disappearing. Fuller was only the first in line.

A careful observer of 132 S. Eden Street would have seen some interesting comings and goings in the summer of 1935. On several occasions, two brothers from another part of the city would park a Chevrolet sedan far down the street and walk up to the apartment of Theodore and his mother. Once, they left with someone from the apartment and drove over to the Henry Grob residence. There was a whole succession of new cars, perhaps the strongest expression of American independence, and often times Theodore was at the steering wheel. No one quite knew what to make of all of it, but they soon would.

PART 5

A MYSTERIOUS THEFT

1851 double eagle (twenty-dollar gold piece) from the Merrill purchase of Baltimore hoard gold in the summer of 1935. (Courtesy of Michael Merrill)

CHAPTER 17

A NEW TURN OF EVENTS

As if on cue, Labor Day 1935 brought incredible headlines to Baltimore having to do with mysteries of long-lost gold. The story would prove, in time, to be much more transparent than the 1934 version, though no less startling. The *Evening Sun* broke the story first, on Tuesday, September 3rd. Philip A. Rummel, stepfather of Theodore, was photographed in the family apartment at 132 S. Eden pointing to a mangled strong box, looking rather forlornly at a chest that was said to have contained several thousand dollars, before a theft occurred on the evening of September 2, Labor Day.

Rummel had married Theodore's mother that summer, July 22, 1935. Bessie felt compelled to use her real name on the marriage certificate, signing it with the name "Bessie Sines" and not "Bessie Jones," the alias she had been using in Baltimore. The clerk in the Baltimore courthouse either didn't recognize Bessie, or chose to stay silent on the matter. Bessie had been photographed in the papers on multiple occasions, and had been in the courthouse at least once before, to give testimony the previous December. In any event, nothing was made of the fact that Bessie Sines had quietly revealed her true identity, and so it was that Philip Rummel moved into 132 S. Eden with Bessie and Theodore in July.

Rummel, a World War I veteran, was born to German immigrants in Baltimore in 1893. He worked in the Baltimore City Sewerage as a laborer, a self-described "all-around man." Before that he had worked for the city in the street cleaning department, and before that on the highways, apparently in much the same capacity. In 1935, he was not always getting work, but generally managed to stay engaged with the city three or four days a week, working for the princely sum of forty-five cents an hour. It was, in today's terms, something close to the minimum wage. Philip's brother, George, was worse off, having been in bed for much of that year with back trouble. Compounding his financial woes was the fact that George had a wife and several children to support.

So, with Rummel earning perhaps seven or eight hundred dollars per year, and his brother in need, there was understandable surprise when he reported the theft of thirty-six hundred dollars from the 132 S. Eden apartment on the evening of September 2nd. The family had gone out that evening, about seven o'clock, to attend to the matter of a house they wanted to purchase in Overlea, a suburb on the northeast side of Baltimore. For the three hours they were gone, there must have been great anticipation about escaping the ramshackle conditions of Eden Street and moving into in their own house, finally liberated from landlords and disagreeable neighbors. They returned to Eden Street at about ten o'clock. Bessie and Theodore were well versed in misery, but until this moment, they had not experienced the kind of pain that could only accompany a fall from giddy exaltation. There was, they would later say, an unpleasant surprise waiting for them after they reached their second-floor apartment, perversely at the same moment they thought they were about to close the door on that chapter of their lives.

Philip and Bessie trudged over to the Eastern Police Station, the former site of glory where reporters had gathered to wolf down the boys' tales of precious gold one year earlier. Lieutenant Pfenning, who had counted part of the first find, took the statement the same evening of the theft. Philip and Bessie reported that a window on the fire escape had been forced open, and the apartment ransacked. Knives were scattered on the floor, locks on cupboards were broken, and most unfortunately, the lock on a trunk had been smashed. Inside the trunk was an empty pasteboard box that was said to have previously contained thirty-one hundred dollars in currency and five hundred dollars in gold coins.

I SORT OF FEEL LUCKY

Bessie, Theodore, and Philip Rummel needed to concoct a story quickly. There was the matter of explaining where the money came from, how that money found its way into the trunk, and of how best to engage the local police in trying to recover their loss. Rummel's first attempt was a non-starter. The money, he declared, was his life savings. A police officer assigned to the case, Lieutenant Ezekiel Williams, saw through the lie in an instant, realizing that great wealth stolen from a treasure house could not have been painstakingly accumulated by a part-time city laborer less than forty years old. Rummel, seemingly weak of character, later explained the situation in court.

Q. Did you tell them it was your life savings?

A. Yes, I told them because Theodore told me I should say that.

Q. When did he tell you?

A. At home, on that same day, the day of the burglary.

Q. Why did you tell a lie about it?

A. It was because Teddy told me to say it, it was the way Teddy told me to say it, and I went according to the boy. I knew I did not steal anything, and according to my stepson's statement, it would be all right. I thought it would not be a whole lot of paper reading, right when the crime was committed, when you tell a thing of that kind.

Rummel clearly hadn't absorbed the uproar of the previous Labor Day, when even the smallest details of the hoard were scrutinized by policeman, reporters, judges and attorneys. The next tale from the family, revealed to the police under questioning, inched towards the truth. The money, they said, had come from the sale of more gold coins, found during a "second" treasure find made in the 132 S. Eden cellar. Theodore summed it up to a reporter. "I went down to the cellar and dug on several occasions to see if there was any more gold, but did not find any. Once my stepfather accompanied me, but also returned empty-handed. Shortly after school closed last June [Henry] Grob said to me: 'I sort of feel lucky. What do you say we go down to the cellar and search again?' I got a pick and Henry got a shovel and we went down to the cellar. I dug and Henry sifted the earth with his shovel. We worked for a long time and did not find anything. We were about to give up when I said: 'Well, I'll give one more poke for luck.' I stuck the pick in the earth and the point struck something that sounded like metal. I said: 'We have struck something.' We dug and pulled out an old oyster can. We took the can upstairs and pulled the money apart. Then we divided it up. We decided not to say anything about our find. We only told my mother and stepfather."

Although Theodore's mother and stepfather got wind of the second find early on, Henry's mother Ruth didn't find out about it until some time later, at least according to a story Henry told Lieutenant Ezekiel Williams. The lieutenant later testified, "Henry Grob made a statement to me that they had divided the gold there [at 132 S. Eden Street]. He had his in a coffee can. He took it home and he ripped the mattress, pulled some of the wadding off the mattress, and made a space so he could put this can in. After he placed the can in the mattress, he sewed the mattress up, and he said one night, he and his brother [John Grob] were going to bed, after his brother got undressed, he said he made kind of a head-dive in the bed, and as he did, he head struck the can, and he immediately called to his mother. His mother came in, and then is when they found this coffee can of old gold coins, and [Henry] said he told his mother as to how he found it, and turned the money over to his mother."

In effect, Johnny Grob's supposed sore head had been caused by Theodore's one last swing of the pickaxe. It was all bad luck, thought Philip Rummel, who said the gold had turned into a curse for his new family. "Since the first gold was found in the cellar nothing but bad luck trailed the family, and now the curse is on me," Rummel said. "Attempts have been made to extort money from the family, and they have been threatened a number of times. Strange noises have often been heard about the house as if someone were trying to enter. It got so bad I went out and bought a gun. In order to protect things in the house I also nailed the window sashes down. Theodore has been threatened a number of times on the street. We have all lived in constant fear." Bessie added that an acquaintance of Theodore's threatened to "hit him over the head and take it away from him." Exactly what they were going to take away wasn't specified. Harry O. Levin, their attorney, was surprised to hear the family had any money at all, and noted that they had been relief clients all during his association with them. Nor had he yet been paid for any his efforts on behalf of the family, increasing his bewilderment at the latest news.

DOUBLE JEOPARDY

The opposing attorneys didn't believe a word of it. The idea that Theodore and Henry had struck pay dirt a second time only exacerbated the frustration they felt from losing the battle for the first pot of gold. "We think the fantastic tale of a second find is altogether unbelievable," said Emory H. Niles, one of the Findlay-French attorneys. The lawyers didn't have to sift through the earth themselves to know the truth. Many other people had had their own go at the cellar, and even Henry admitted that the cellar "looked like someone went through there with a plough." "They looked everywhere in there, but that one place," was how Henry rationalized it. The police didn't buy Henry's story either, reminding everyone that the whole cellar was dug up thoroughly after the first find. The Baltimore public, generally sympathetic to the boys, also had their doubts. "Opinion is about evenly divided as to whether or not the 'second find' was not dug up on August 31, 1934, with the first lot," wrote a Secret Service agent, reporting to Chief William H. Moran in Washington, D.C.

Eby and Niles, attorneys for the sisters Findlay and French, filed a petition to reopen the civil suit that they had lost in February. Civil suits, unlike criminal prosecution, in theory never reach ultimate closure. As long as an attorney can convince a judge that sufficient basis exists to reargue the case, the litigation can continue indefinitely. Judge Eugene O'Dunne considered the additional evidence, approved the petition on September 17, summoned witnesses, and set the hearing for September 20. He also ordered that no coins, or money derived from their sale, be disposed of in the meantime. The Findlay-French attorneys no doubt appreciated the order, but hedged their bets by engaging a private detective, one Ray Kennedy, to look into the matter further.

Harry O. Levin, the boys' own attorney, probably didn't believe the story either. He hadn't even heard about the newly found gold until September 3rd when a reporter told him about it. "I know nothing about it," Levin said. "The boys brought over part of the money to the police when they found it. A little later they brought a second batch. If this is a third lot, it is news to me." Levin thus had two clients who were not completely forthcoming with him, and he was embarrassed. There was also the none-too-small matter that the court had not yet awarded him his contingency fee from the auction sale proceeds. Levin was a full year into the litigation without a penny to show for it. There was nothing else to do except put on his game face and enter the courtroom.

Judge O'Dunne allowed a statement from Levin before the testimony was taken at the September 20 hearing:

> "I want to say neither my associate [Sigmund Levin] or myself know anything about any coins, other than those which were delivered by Theodore Jones and Henry Grob to the police. As an officer of this Court and particularly as counsel for the Guardian [Jones and Grob] appointed by the Court, I am in perfect accord with this, or any inquiry, having for its purpose the discovery of any coins other than those delivered to the police, and if there are or were others, withheld in the first place by these boys, or found since the original find, I intend, as counsel for the Guardian, to take such action as this Court directs, to recover them, or their value."

Levin went on to say that he expected that the first judgment for the boys (on which his contingency fee depended) would not be affected by any further action related to this second find.

O'Dunne cleared the courtroom and called the witnesses in one by one, so that the participants could not hear each other's testimony. The idea that Theodore and Henry hadn't had a good discussion beforehand about how they were going to testify was laughable, but one could not blame O'Dunne for at least trying to get at the truth. The proceedings were conducted without even stopping for lunch, so that no one could compare notes about the cross examinations. The witnesses were sequestered in the judge's chambers and called into the courtroom one by one. For the boys, this was judgment day, the one last opportunity they would get to come completely clean. But Theodore and Henry already knew what they were going to do.

THE KING OF COINCIDENCE

The second "pot" of gold, the boys said, had been found pretty much like the first "pot." Theodore pointed out some remarkable similarities. He had used the same axe, Henry had used the same corn knife, and once again Theodore was carrying the flashlight. The second container was buried about a foot down and was similarly green and corroded, just like the first pot. "We was digging around, and a piece flew up, the same as before," was how Theodore told it. The coins were all stuck together, and again most of them were one-dollar gold pieces. All in all, Theodore had crowned himself the king of coincidence on the witness stand. But he did not stretch credulity to insist that the pot was found in the exact same spot. No, he said, it was actually found a few feet south from the site of the first pot, in a corner of the rear cellar where two walls met.

Henry added his own set of coincidences. The "dig" was performed about the same time of day, four o'clock in the afternoon. The second pot was also copper, the same size as the first one, and with a similar cover. Emory Niles, attorney for the elderly ladies Findlay-French, listened to the recitation of similarities, and began to think ahead. During his cross examination of Henry he deftly proceeded from asking about the dig, to asking what happened to the money in the second pot, and then coming back to the dig, giving Henry every opportunity to slip up. Niles finally landed the question he had carefully passed over at the beginning. Henry was being played.

Q. Now, you remember that at the first trial we had some pictures of the cellar, and I am going to show you one, which shows where that first pot was found. Do you remember that?

A. Yes, sir.

Q. Now, will you take a pin and put it in this picture and show where the second gold was found?

A. The first [pot] was here (indicating) and the second was there (indicating).

Q. Where was the second one?
A. Directly a foot in front of it.
Q. I take it from this picture, this point you have marked, that you say the second find was west of the first find?
A. Yes, sir.
Q. Now, are you sure of that?
A. Yes, sir.
Q. Because I tell you now, that Theodore Jones said that was found south of the first find.
A. I can't tell you what Theodore said, I am telling you what is right.

Niles had made his point. Theodore claimed the pot was found in the corner, a distinct spot, while Henry placed it a couple yards away in the middle of the rear cellar space. The boys thus hadn't told a consistent story about where the second pot was found, nor could they even say exactly when it was found. Henry thought it was "about in May," perhaps fixing the date by the fact that he was no longer in school. Henry had chosen to celebrate his sixteenth birthday on May 12, 1935, by becoming a dropout. Theodore of course hadn't been in school for many years, and perhaps Henry thought it a pleasant thing to emulate his good friend. Theodore also thought the second find was in May, but like Henry couldn't fix the date any more than that. The next matter was the question of what was in the second pot, where the golden trail led. The boys claimed to have never counted the gold in the second pot, but rather split it piece for piece just like the first pot. This of course complicated the accounting, but Judge O'Dunne and the opposing attorneys got some help in that department.

CHAPTER 18

THE FAMILIES CELEBRATE

Wherever the gold came from, it was of little value to the families until it was converted into greenbacks and actually spent on something. Theodore and Henry could testify to a string of startling coincidences leading to the second find, but as there were no witnesses in the cellar, except perhaps the ghost of Andrew J. Saulsbury, it was really their word against no one else's. The gold on the other hand, and the greenbacks it turned into, was real enough and had its own story.

Ruth Grob testified that she had sold Henry's second find to an old gold buyer, "a Hebrew man" that happened to come to her door. "He came to my door, and I showed him a twenty-dollar gold piece, and asked him what he would give me for it, and he said twenty dollars, and he asked me did I have any more, and I told him, yes," Ruth said. "So I had it in my mattress, and I told him to wait until I came down, and he asked me how much it was, and I told him I did not know; I did not count it." Ruth thought the sale was towards the end of May 1935, but again, no one could put an exact date on the second find. She continued describing the transaction. "He gave me twenty dollars for the first piece, and he told me he would be back. He came back, and I had a little tavern there, and he took me in the back room, and he counted me thirty-four hundred dollars, and he said, 'You don't know me, and I don't know you, and you don't have to be scared.' " Henry didn't think much of his mother's deal. "She took a beating," he said. "It was worth five thousand dollars, I'm sure." Ruth was probably more interested in a quick and quiet transaction that put cash in her pocket. From there the cash went into multiple bank accounts, with deposits starting on June 10, 1935.

Ruth's decision to sell the gold at face value seemed strange at first glance. Surely she was aware that gold from the first find had sold for close to twice face value several weeks prior at the Lord Baltimore Hotel auction. But, like Theodore's mother, Bessie, she probably wanted to obtain cash quickly. She also knew that Levin was going to get a third of the first pot, and that the sale expenses were already deducted besides. In describing the moments after Henry's second find was found out, Ruth gave some idea of their thoughts. "Henry said, 'I will tell you, close the place and lock the door, and come back in the kitchen, I want to show you something,'" Ruth said. "I did, and he took me back and he pulled out a tin can of this money, and he said, 'Don't give it up like you did before, Mrs. Jones is going to keep hers, and you keep yours. Don't tell Mrs. Jones or Teddy that I told you that I had the money because they are afraid that you will give it up to the police like you did the last time. We did not get anything out of the first, you turned it in, and maybe we can get something for this.'" The families, at this point, were not at all confident that the proceeds from the first sale would ever actually materialize.

Ruth was doubtful they would receive their share of the first pot, and worried that the proceeds from the second pot would be seized. Two days prior to the trial, she had visited the Equitable Trust Company and withdrawn six hundred dollars in cash. The timing drew the suspicion of the court. "They told me my money was going to be stopped, and I was going to see someone if it could be stopped," she testified. "You heard this hearing was coming on, and you thought you had better get it out of the bank?" she was asked. "That is right, sir," came the reply. Ruth was also suspicious of Levin, and had brought in another attorney to represent Henry, a young man named Joel J. Hochman. Levin and Hochman had a telling exchange following the examination of Ruth Grob. "I do think that Mrs. Grob should be told to bring the money into Court to be held subject to what order there is as to the first case, second case, or whatever case it is," Levin said, making the subtle point that he had potential claims to the second pot. "Why are you interested in it?" Hochman shot back. Judge O'Dunne wasn't ready to impound anything. "Let us go on with this case now," he directed.

As for the money itself, Ruth Grob freely admitted to already having spent much of it. There was furniture, doctor bills, new clothes, back rent, and "poor people that helped me when I did not have anything." The family had moved out of their Caroline Street apartment in July 1935, to the more pleasant Canton neighborhood a couple miles east. They purchased a 1929 Ford coupe in July for ninety-five dollars, and only two weeks later they traded it in for a 1932 Ford V-8 priced at four hundred dollars. Ruth had a new place, new car, new furniture, and she topped it off by getting some gold dental work, a reminder to everyone she smiled at that this was someone who had arrived.

AN UPWARDLY MOBILE STEP

Bessie Jones had also been selling gold coins, and fixed the first sale of one thousand dollars face value to an old gold buyer working door to door. He was shabbily dressed, middle aged, and beyond that she knew nothing else about him. Unlike Ruth Grob, Bessie had a sense that the gold should bring more than face value, and she negotiated a price of twelve hundred and fifty dollars for the lot. With a large amount of cash in hand for the first time in their lives, the family went out and bought an old Ford for about two hundred dollars. The automobile was the ultimate symbol of the American middle class, an upwardly mobile step for Bessie and Theodore. The used car lot, a few blocks removed from 132 S. Eden at Baltimore and Dallas streets, was their virtual Eden, a grown-up's playground waiting for any with the means to enter. Their paradise following the June 20 purchase was short lived. The car developed mechanical problems, would not steer easily, and broke down at least once. The family, undeterred, traded in the gimpy jalopy for a new and unblemished 1935 Plymouth, at a cost of eight hundred dollars.

Plymouth was the brainchild of Walter Chrysler, whose eponymous automobile company lacked a low-priced line to compete with Ford and Chevrolet. Launched in 1928, two years after Ford ended its Model T production, Plymouth quickly found its niche and within four years had reached third place in cars produced by U.S. automakers. Redesigned in 1935, the Plymouth was a steel hulk, with a barrel of an engine protruding from the spacious interior. Theodore was taken with the magnificent machine, and it did not matter that he could not buy it himself. Rummel explained, "Theodore is too young to own it. Walter Scott [the dealer] said he would not sell to a child, Theodore was only a minor, and Mr. Scott said he thought it would be all right, if I bought it. Theodore said, 'You have it in your name,' and I said, 'Why do you want to put it on my name,' and he said, 'You take it in your name, you are all right, you are my father.'"

Bessie, Theodore, and his new stepfather, Philip Rummel, celebrated the grand purchase with a trip to Pittsburgh to see Theodore's siblings. "We hadn't seen my brother and sister for so long," Theodore said. The drive to the Steel City must have been glorious. There was of course the shiny automobile, good fortune to share with the rest of the family, and a large amount of cash and gold in the trunk. Theodore's hitchhiking days were over, riding the golden chariot towards a long-awaited reunion with his brother Eugene and sister Thelma. Rummel was steadier and cautious. Regarding the treasure in the trunk, he said, "I thought it was best to take it along, because everything was in the newspaper and I was afraid someone would go and steal it, so I went to Pittsburgh with Bessie." There were precautions taken once in Pittsburgh, too. Bessie stored her cache of gold and currency in her daughter's safe deposit box for the few days the family visited. Bessie, who had no bank account in Baltimore, apparently trusted the banks in Pittsburgh, and the relative anonymity of her married daughter didn't hurt either. But while Ruth Grob had let her money remain in a bank, Bessie and Philip were not ready to do the same. Later "they were sorry they did not leave it there," a police officer recalled.

In addition to the "shabbily dressed" stranger who appeared at her door in search of old gold, Bessie Jones sold gold coins over a period of several months to a pair of brothers, Yale and Eli Merrill. Yale, still a young man of twenty-nine, had recently started his own advertising and public relations firm following several years in the newspaper business, primarily as a sportswriter. The *Baltimore News* had thought highly enough of his work to send him to Amsterdam in 1928 to cover the Olympics. By 1934, Yale had his own firm, while his older brother, Eli, worked at a pawn shop in downtown Baltimore. Between the two of them they were looking for gold and for stories. It was, seemingly, a perfect match.

CHAPTER 19

THE MERRILL BROTHERS

Yale and Eli had been reading the papers like everyone else, and the idea occurred to Yale that he might purchase some of the gold and create a montage for promotional purposes, perhaps as a display in a department store. "[Eli] had mentioned the thing to me several times, and I was fascinated with it, and I made a trip to the library and read some of the literature," Yale explained later. The pair was well aware of the laws surrounding gold coins, that they had a legal right to handle gold coins with numismatic value. Between that and the fact that the courts had ruled in favor of Theodore and Henry, the two felt comfortable approaching the families in search of any gold they still might have.

So it was that the two brothers knocked on the door at 132 S. Eden one evening in June 1935. Bessie, Theodore, and Philip Rummel showed the two brothers a handful of gold coins, but declined to sell any of them. Yale left his office address with the family, then located at the American Building at Baltimore and Calvert Streets in downtown Baltimore. Bessie and Philip visited the office several days later, in part to ascertain whether or not Merrill was legitimate. Rummel explained it later. "When he came here, he wanted to buy this gold, and we thought probably he was a fake, and was trying to swindle us, and we would not sell it to him, unless we knew who he was. I thought it was all right when we found where his office was, and Bessie said, 'Do you think it is all right,' and I said, 'I think it is all right if the man can buy it, he is in business, we know who he is, he said not to worry about it, that there would not be anything said about it, it was only him and his partner.'" Satisfied with their investigation, Bessie and Philip invited the Merrills to come to 132 S. Eden that evening, and proposed selling five hundred dollars face value in gold coins for six hundred dollars in currency. The two brothers came as instructed but were put off until the next day when the price had risen to six hundred and twenty-five dollars. A deal was struck for six hundred and five dollars, Eli doing the negotiating, and the Merrills were now in the numismatic gold business.

The Merrills were apparently pleased with the deal, and a drawn-out series of visits between the brothers and the Rummel family ensued. "They were very peculiar people," Yale thought, "and there was a great deal of secrecy on their part." Yale and his brother were secretive too, taking care not to park in front of the building the eight or ten times they drove over to Eden Street. Philip Rummel was suspicious enough to write down the license plate number of their 1931 Chevrolet sedan. The brothers were not successful on most of their visits. The family was at the movies, another time out buying clothes, or away in Pittsburgh. "It was just a lot of foolish and funny things," thought Eli. Sometimes the brothers would arrive and be told the gold wasn't there, that it was somewhere else. Another deal was finally consummated, one thousand dollars face in gold in exchange for twelve hundred and fifty dollars in currency, and then a third trade of one thousand dollars face for eleven hundred and fifty dollars. The brothers explained that the last group contained fewer of the one-dollar pieces, which were slightly more desirable from a numismatic point of view.

Visit by visit, Yale and Eli Merrill became more frustrated and impatient while Bessie remained distrustful. Rummel recalled, "He [Yale] worried her—if you don't give it to him it will be—give it to him, sell it to him—it would not be any harm selling it to him, he would give her nice cash money, it would be in his hands and not worry about it—he always said, don't worry about it, why worry, give it to me and I will give you nice cash money, and I thought the fellow would give her counterfeit money and I took the money and rubbed it in my hand to see if the green would come off, but no green came off." The uneasy relationship came to an end after the third and final sale. "She said it is no more, and don't pester me any more," her husband recalled her saying to Yale Merrill.

In between sales, Rummel took the Merrills over to the Ruth Grob residence to see if a gold strike could be made there as well. The trip likely occurred at the insistence of the Merrills, because Rummel stayed in the car parked on the street. "Mrs. Grob is a person that gets a little excited," Rummel said, "She might be sick and I don't want to have any hard feelings with her, but maybe she can sell you some." The Merrills explained their business to Mrs. Grob, who was not at all pleased to see them. "She was very vehement in her denial that she had any coins; it seemed other people had been coming there, and trying to purchase the coins from her, and she became very excited, and we said, If you have not got any, it is perfectly all right," Yale Merrill recounted. Still, the Merrills had to be happy. In all they had purchased a total of twenty five hundred dollars face value in gold for three thousand and five dollars in currency, gold coins that easily could have fetched four thousand dollars at auction.

THE LAWYERS HAVE THEM ALREADY

Everyone tried to follow the money. Levin wanted to know where Ruth Grob's cash was, as he was entitled to his full share of the first pot, and wondering if the so-called second find was really a holdback from the first pot. Bessie and Theodore wanted the legal system they distrusted to find their stolen currency, suspecting the police themselves had stolen the cash from their apartment. The attorneys for the Findlay and French ladies wanted to know where the Merrill coins were. Represented by Simon Sobeloff, an attorney destined to become the solicitor general of the United States, the Merrills weren't going to do anything even slightly questionable, and in the interests of full disclosure Sobeloff himself

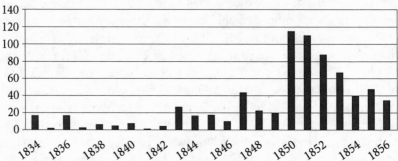

Figure 3

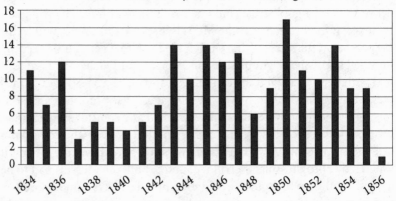

Figure 4

brought the Merrill coins into the courtroom for the September 20, 1935 trial. O'Dunne gazed upon the pile of coins, and the array of legal talent in his courtroom, and summed up the situation for posterity. "The worst has happened," O'Dunne remarked. "The lawyers have them already."

Eli Merrill produced an inventory of the gold coins he and his brother had purchased from Bessie Rummel. Neither had bothered to tally the one-dollar pieces by date, a tedious chore in their opinion. "We did not list the dates of the ones, it would have been quite a job," Yale explained. Nor did the two bother to note any mintmarks that might have appeared on the coins. The dates of the coins themselves still had a story to tell.

Part two of the hoard, at least the portion of it that landed in the Merrill's hands, was suspiciously overweight in coins of the 1830s and 1840s. While most of the part-one coins originated in the 1850s, the part-two coins showed a more even distribution between coins dated in the 1850s and those minted earlier. The implication was that somebody had picked out many of the earlier dated coins from the first pot, perhaps believing they were more valuable. There would have been no reason to make such a division by date when the coins were buried, as the secondary market for numismatic gold was virtually nonexistent in the Civil War era, though there were a few scattered collectors, mostly in New York and Philadelphia.

The number of one-dollar gold pieces in each batch was also significant. If one part of the hoard was truly older than the other, one would have expected to find fewer of the one-dollar pieces in the older hoard, as they were minted beginning only in 1849. Eighty percent of the coins in part one were one-dollar pieces, while the proportion in part two was eighty-four percent. Clearly the two pots—if indeed there were two pots—were buried in the 1850s at a time when one-dollar pieces were plentiful in circulation. The fact that the supposed second pot contained a significantly higher proportion of older coins among the higher denominations required some explanation.

AGREEABLE TO HUMAN NATURE

Besides the Merrills and the various old gold traders calling at the Philip Rummel and Ruth Grob households, a few coins had found their way into the home of George and Frances Rummel, Philip Rummel's brother and sister-in-law. George, a boilermaker, and his family lived several blocks from 132 S. Eden, at 311 S. Bond Street. Two brothers of German descent, George and Philip were not noted for their powers of personal communication. "He very seldom said anything," recalled Frances of her brother-in-law, Philip. Frances hadn't even been notified of the marriage of Philip and Bessie Jones. "I heard it unexpectedly and then I saw it in the paper," she said. The respective children were equally distant. To the children of George and Frances, their uncle Philip's stepson, Theodore, had no name but was simply "the boy who found the gold."

George had had a severe back accident on October 20, 1934, shortly after the first pot of gold was found. He was in bed for six months, and it was only natural that his brother, Philip, tried to do what he could for his brother's family. "Now and then my brother-in-law gave me a few [gold coins] when he came to the house," George's wife, Frances, said. This was news to the court. Until now, the discussion had centered on the disposition of the second pot. There had been no inkling that coins from the first find were anywhere except in the hands of the collectors and dealers who had purchased them in the May 1935 sale.

Under oath, Frances also detailed the sales of gold she had made for Bessie, gold held out of the first find and sold piecemeal so as to not attract attention. It was a small amount, perhaps one hundred and fifty dollars face value in gold coins. No one knew the exact total, though Frances estimated she had gotten one hundred and eighty-five dollars for all of it, which she had turned over to Bessie. She had sold gold coins on four or five occasions, to old gold buyers working the neighborhood door-to-door. Philip Rummel described one transaction, "My brother was in his bed with a broken back—this old man came around and said he was buying old gold and old money—the way he talked he was a licensed man—he was in business, and he always talked in Jewish. I don't know his name—he would go out and say like this—shhhh—say nothing." Rummel added that the discrete, Yiddish-speaking gold buyer had since passed away.

Judge Eugene O'Dunne wasn't surprised that there were at least a handful of pieces from the first part of the hoard that had escaped the attention of the court. "I can well understand human nature holding back a few of them. I think almost anybody would have been so tempted, and I think almost anybody would have held out a few, even as a souvenir or sample, but that is agreeable to human nature of certain varieties," he said, effectively excusing the behavior. The more pressing question was how O'Dunne was going to rule on the question of the second pot, whether it was legitimate or not, and what was going to happen to the precious metal inside.

CHAPTER 20

NO POT TO BE FOUND

Emory H. Niles, attorney for the Findlay-French ladies, was able to extract conflicting testimony on the composition and disposition of the supposed second pot. He also found it curious that no one could actually produce the container in court, even after all the discussion of the first pot's history in the December 1934 hearing. Theodore's explanation was non-responsive.

Q. Now, Theodore, where is the container you found this gold in?
A. I don't know where it is.
Q. What did you do with it?
A. I put it in the yard [the brick covered courtyard in between the front and back buildings at 132 S. Eden].
Q. What did this container look like?
A. It was—looked like it was galvanized [bathed in molten zinc].
Q. Did it look like the first one?
A. Yes, sir.
Q. Did this look as old as the first one?
A. Yes, sir.
Q. Was it about the same size?
A. Yes, sir.
Q. You saw the first one in Court here?
A. Yes, sir.
Q. And a lot of questions were asked you about it?
A. Yes, sir.
Q. Why didn't you keep the [second] container?
A. I just put it in the yard. I didn't think of keeping it.
Q. Weren't you afraid somebody would ask you questions about it?
A. I didn't know.
Q. Didn't you know it was important to keep it?
A. Yes, sir.

Remarkably, according to Theodore, the second pot pretty much resembled the first. It was yet another amazing coincidence in the story of the second find. Henry testified likewise, though he did not think the second pot was galvanized. The "galvanized" description seemed to originate with the Jones-Rummel clan. Both Bessie and Theodore used the word without being prompted for it.

As to the location of the pot, Bessie thought perhaps it was in the cellar. Judge O'Dunne and the attorneys were quite interested in seeing it, and so Bessie was dispatched after testifying and sent over to 132 S. Eden, accompanied by police officer Frederick J. German, in order to fetch the second pot. Meanwhile, the hearing continued. Bessie had thought she was done with 132 S. Eden for good, having moved out just a few days prior on September 9, 1935. The family had relocated to the Bond Street residence, no doubt tired of the personal threats upon them and the fact that their address had been published in the newspapers countless times. The robbery was merely the final straw, as the family had been looking for a new place to live anyway.

Bessie and the policeman arrived at the Eden Street property and found it completely locked up. It seems the landlord had decided once and for all to secure the cellar, the dark pit that had brought him and the property owners much grief. "Every door had a lock like it was nailed up," Bessie said. A first floor tenant let Bessie and the officer into the cellar, and gave them a candle to use, as the policeman had no flashlight. Not surprisingly, there was no pot to be found. Bessie did not give up. Several days later she reappeared in court, this time with the alleged second pot. She claimed to have found it in the front part of the cellar, which she had searched again along with her husband Philip Rummel. Judge O'Dunne still had the first pot in his safe and produced it for comparison. "It looks very much like the other that I have," he observed. Niles didn't buy it, knowing that it should have been easy to find something in the front cellar, where the ceiling height allowed one to walk freely. On the other hand he had no proof that Bessie and Philip had been scouring the antique stores looking for a duplicate.

INEBRIATED TO THE LEGAL LIMIT

Judge O'Dunne absorbed the arguments with all of his head but only part of his hand. He had had an accident at his summer home in Pennsylvania, the same Labor Day weekend the Jones-Rummel family reported the burglary at 132 S. Eden. Inspecting an electric pumping machine, O'Dunne lost the tips of three fingers on his right hand, two of them at the base of the fingernail. "There wasn't anything I could do but grasp my hand and send for a doctor," he said. "I had a cord tied tight around my wrist to prevent a free flow of blood, and waited about a half hour before the physician arrived." O'Dunne, ever the workhorse, was determined to do two things. First, get back to Baltimore, and second, not miss any court time in the upcoming September session. He explained his dilemma to the doctor. "I said to him, 'Now doctor, you know the pain I am suffering. I want you to prescribe a drink of whiskey which will tend to dull the pain but at the same time be consistent with the rules and regulations laid down by the Commissioner of Motor Vehicles.'" The doctor allowed him three-fourths of a glass of whiskey, and the stubborn Irishman, inebriated to the legal limit, sped back to Baltimore.

Having arrived at the courthouse back in Baltimore, O'Dunne could not sign his own name, and his October 2, 1935 ruling on the second find was given orally. Although he had reference to the stenographic record of the witness testimony, he probably did not take notes during the attorney's arguments. "Mr. Niles calls attention in his argument, to a great many instances of discrepancies between the testimony of witnesses. I could not pretend to remember all of the details to which he called attention," O'Dunne said. Niles of course pointed out that the boys hadn't agreed where the second find was, nor had they agreed on whether or not the pot was galvanized. There were other disagreements over the duration and number of times the family had been to Pittsburgh, and whether or not Rummel had been present when cash and gold were transferred between the Plymouth and the Pittsburgh bank box. There were other discrepancies Niles put forth, "quite a number of others which I do not recall," O'Dunne remarked. "From these, he [Niles] deduces as a conclusion that the whole story is a fabrication; that all the witnesses are lying; that there was but one find; that a perjured fraud has been put over on the Court," O'Dunne added.

The judge saw the contradictions in testimony as well as anyone else, but he was not sure they were so egregious as to conclusively imply deliberate lying. To those who read only the court records and felt otherwise, O'Dunne spoke directly in his ruling:

> "There are some . . . who say that a Court can much better determine
> the credibility of a witness from reading the printed record, than it
> can from seeing the witness on the stand, and in the flesh. I cannot
> agree . . . I have seen and heard all the witnesses. I have heard all of their
> contradictions and discrepancies. I have watched their demeanor.
> I have seen them frankly admit, like Rummel did, that he told the

policeman what in fact was an untruth, that this wasn't his life's savings, but that he had so stated to the policeman at the suggestion of the Jones boy, as a good explanation to be made [to] him when he was going to report the robbery. I suppose the boy had sense enough, after his previous experience, to know there was no use telling a police officer somebody robbed him of his gold coins—because the officer would have made them give that, like they did the first find. He [Rummel] came on the witness stand, plain, simple man (what was he, garbage cart driver or a simple city employee of the common laborer type?). He impressed me as being perfectly honest, and willing to admit without quibble or equivocation, that whatever he said in that respect was not so."

O'Dunne thought the different accounts actually lent credibility to the whole affair. "Instead of producing the impression that it is a concocted story of perjured testimony, it convinces me as to the truth of the present tale," he said in his opinion. "If they were going to concoct it they would have concocted it and put it together very much more copper-riveted than it come out now in places where it is somewhat disjointed." However fantastic and unlikely the saga of the second pot seemed to be, O'Dunne was not ready to call anyone a liar. He therefore made two findings of fact. "I find that there *was* a second find in these premises, 132 S. Eden Street, at or about the 27th of May [1935]," he said. And secondly, that "all of the contents, literally speaking, of the first pot, was not turned over to the police at the Eastern Station at that time [of the first find]." There were a few coins, he thought, which might have spilled out or been deliberately withheld.

Judge O'Dunne refused to impound any of the proceeds of the second pot. Indeed, he did not even settle the question of title to the second pot. The issue at hand was whether fraud had been committed with regards to the first pot, and O'Dunne was willing to overlook the odd coins that clearly had passed between Philip Rummel and his brother's family. O'Dunne had no problem with the Merrills' actions, either. "Remember, he is an advertising man," he said, speaking of Yale Merrill. "We all know what that is. He suddenly got excited over an idea that he could capitalize a collection of gold coins and use it as an advertising medium to boost himself and his business." As for buying the gold at below market value, the Merrill attorney, Sobeloff, argued that Yale and his brother had a perfect right to buy gold at a reasonable discount if they had opportunity to do so, and O'Dunne agreed, despite the suggestion of another attorney that the Merrills had "cheated the ignorant, low-witted Jones tribe." "Gold makes you open your eyes and stimulates the imagination, and sometimes dulls conscience, but I see nothing in it that affected his conscience," O'Dunne concluded.

Several days later O'Dunne maintained the injunction on all parties to not dispose of proceeds from the second find. That was as far as he was willing to go, and with that O'Dunne told everyone to take it to the Baltimore Court of Appeals, and recommended that any disagreement with his current ruling be combined with the already outstanding appeal for reargument of the first case.

PART 6

SECRETS AND THE
SECRET SERVICE

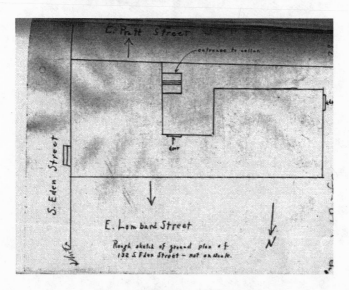

Plaintiff's exhibit, Maryland Court of Appeals April 1935, showing the layout of the 132 S. Eden Street property. (Maryland State Archives)

CHAPTER 21

AGENT BENJAMIN BRATTON

While the families had escaped O'Dunne's courtroom more or less unscathed, the U.S. Secret Service had not taken kindly to the secrecy of the families and the Merrill brothers in failing to disclose the so-called second find. For the local agents, who spent much of their time tediously chasing counterfeit currency backwards from bank tellers to depositors to merchants to customers, a gold hoarding case was a fresh opportunity to flex the muscle of the federal bureaucracy. Thus little time was wasted in interviewing those involved just a few days after the story of the second pot landed in the local papers. Baltimore Secret Service operative Benjamin Bratton took statements from Theodore, his mother, and stepfather on Friday, September 6, 1935. All three refused to sign the statements. "They are not signed because before these three people signed the statements they must have promises," Bratton wrote in his report to headquarters. Bratton thought the documents were legally valid anyway. "As it was agreed at the beginning that no promises would be made and the statements were made in the presence of Asst. U.S. Attorney F. Barton Harrington and the writer, and the stenographer has the notes it makes little difference. The statements can be used in Court if necessary, but not against Yale Merrill or his associates, as they were not present when the statements were made," Bratton added.

The Grob family was also elusive. Ruth was away in the tomato fields in Preston, Maryland as the Secret Service brought in Henry, at the time sixteen years old, and gave him a workout. "He was questioned at length by Asst. U.S. Attorney T. Barton Harrington and Detectives John Boniarski and Leo Vogelsang and self [agent Bratton] for about three hours without giving any information as to whom his mother sold the gold coins he turned over to her the day after the second lot was dug up in the cellar," Benjamin Bratton wrote in his report on the matter. Bratton was apparently impressed with Henry's performance after having talked to the Rummels the previous day. "The Rummels and the Jones boy are all morons, but Henry Grob is an intelligent boy and his mother is probably very smart; she is not spending freely, but is keeping at her work and saving the money," Bratton reported to Washington headquarters. Meanwhile, Bratton dispatched Agent George Almoney to Preston, Maryland, to interview Ruth Grob.

Almoney was the junior man in the office, the one who had to travel to Preston to get the statement. Ruth was either very forthcoming, or Almoney asked questions that pressed against the limits of his authority. In any event, her statement contained her marital history, the living situations of her children, personal financial information, and much detail regarding her sale of Henry's gold from the second pot. As for the secrecy of the second find, Ruth said "I did not turn the new find of gold over to Attorney Harry O. Levin, or notify the police about it because I never got anything out of the first lot found and I thought I would keep it."

Bratton met with the Merrill brothers as well, two men well acquainted with the laws concerning gold who were not going to be strong-armed by the Secret Service. This time it was Bratton who had to dance. "The Merrills both tried to pin me down to a definite statement that they could buy these premium coins and sell them without a license," Bratton wrote. "They have consulted their attorneys many times on this point and have been assured that they can do so. I told them that the Government must be satisfied that coins are bought and sold as premium [numismatically valuable] coins and that the strongest inference is apparent that recognized dealers in such coins are the only ones to benefit by the clause regarding premium coins. And at this time I could not regard them nor Ike Berman [Eli Merrill's employer] as recognized dealers or collectors, although Berman did buy some of the first lot at the auction. I refused to give them any other opinion." Bratton's statement strained his credibility, refusing to recognize the Merrill brothers as dealers or collectors even though he was interviewing them precisely because they had purchased collectible gold!

Bratton kept grasping at straws. "We [Bratton and Assistant U.S. Attorney Harrington] have gone over the Gold Reserve Act and find that it states a license is not required to buy or sell premium gold coins. There is hardly any doubt that every one of the coins has a premium value and the Merrills' claim they are making a collection or rare coins. As a matter of fact it is the opinion of this writer that they were speculating and have violated the spirit of the law, which is for the benefit of coin collectors and dealers in rare coins. I would like to know if there is any ground in the circumstances of this case for prosecuting the Merrills for buying the coins and the Rummel and Grob women for selling them. If after reviewing this report Chief can suggest where prosecution can be successful, I would appreciate very much some instructions," he wrote to Washington. The Washington office was silent on the question of prosecution, and Bratton had to let the matter drop. Of course, there is no record showing that the families, or the Merrill brothers, were ever told that the matter was closed.

CHAPTER 22

STRATEGY IN THE APPELLATE COURT

The Saulsbury attorneys, J. Paul Schmidt and Charles F. Stein, had had enough of the legal drama, not to mention the specter of the Secret Service, and advised the family to drop out of the marathon after the O'Dunne ruling. Stein was a good friend of Reuben Foster, the Saulsbury grandson, but friendship had its limits, and incurring additional court costs at the appellate level was simply throwing good money after bad. The Saulsbury clan agreed, leaving the boys, the Findlay-French ladies, and the Merrills to fight over the dwindling spoils, much of the second pot already having been spent or stolen. The Maryland Court of Appeals found its own economy and agreed to consolidate all the outstanding legal actions into a single case, which was heard in the January 1936 session of the court.

The standard for an appellate court to take action is high. As Simon Sobeloff, the attorney for the Merrills wrote in his brief, "there is a high public interest involved in preserving the finality of judgments…between litigants." Evidence that is newly introduced must therefore be of a decisive nature, and Sobeloff argued that any new evidence here did not meet that standard. For starters, O'Dunne had already made a finding of fact that there was indeed a second pot. And even if the boys had lied up and down about the second pot, Sobeloff argued that nothing substantially had changed from the first case, except for the amount of gold in the first pot. Surely the law would not hang on so trivial a thing as a few thousands dollars more or less in the golden pot. It was still buried treasure found by a tenant on a landlord's property.

Levin unsurprisingly concurred. "It must…be apparent that the applicant's original case would have been substantially benefited by…new evidence," he wrote in his brief to the Baltimore Court of Appeals. Whether the original pot contained a thousand or a million dollars should have had no bearing on who had the legal right to the prize, he thought. Levin was also displeased that the court of appeals had chosen to consolidate the two pots into one case. "Suppose the second find had been discovered by other persons?" he asked. Levin argued that the second pot was a separate event that required separate litigation. As for the first pot, Levin thought the current action brought by the Findlay-French attorneys was "a flimsy, undisguised attempt to procure in a devious and round-about fashion, a re-argument of the questions of title" that the court of appeals had already decided in July 1935. Levin and Sobeloff were mindful that the court had evenly split on the question of the first pot, and that any reargument at the appellate level could easily change the result.

Arthur Eby and Emory H. Niles, attorneys for the Findlay-French ladies, were indeed thinking the exact same thing. The earlier appellate decision had ended in a 4-4 tie, without the court issuing a written opinion that might have guided subsequent treasure cases. Eby and Niles, no doubt driven by a spirit of legal patriotism and a sincere desire to clarify and improve the practice of treasure trove law in Maryland, implored the Baltimore Court of Appeals to rehear the first appeal and to definitively settle the questions of trespass and treasure trove. "There has…been no opinion filed by this Court, and the legal questions involved in the appeals have not been determined…The failure of this Court to agree upon an opinion in this case indicates close questions of law or fact. We respectfully submit that, under these circumstances, a reargument of the case should be granted," they wrote in their brief.

C. Arthur Eby (left) and Emory H. Niles, attorneys for the
Findlay and French sisters.

Eby and Niles indicated they believed that there was no second find, that the story was altogether too fantastic to be true, and that witnesses had disagreed upon the circumstances of the second find when O'Dunne had segregated them in his court room and subjected each to examination by numerous attorneys. But the thrust of Eby's and Niles' argument was that the Court of Appeals had simply gotten it wrong the first time. The idea that trespassers could benefit from their intrusion in any way was terrible law, they thought. By now the university law reviews had gotten wind of the 1935 Maryland Court of Appeals decision and seemed to side with Eby and Niles. The Boston University and Georgetown law reviews both agreed that the Maryland Court of Appeals had made excessive allowance to trespass in their 1935 decision. Eby and Niles thus concluded their brief with a final request that the Court of Appeals re-argue the 1935 decision, and with that everyone now waited for the appellate judges to make their next move.

THE HOSPITALITY OF THE STATE

While the esteemed jurists pondered the vagaries of trespass and treasure trove law, Theodore found himself in a juvenile detention center. It was called the "Maryland Training School for Boys" in those days, perhaps a less politically correct sobriquet in a more severe era. Theodore's problems had started shortly after the purchase of the family's first automobile the previous summer. His first appearance in traffic court had been on July 13, 1935, on a charge of reckless driving. He was released on parole, and his stepfather, Philip Rummel, made reference to the situation in his court testimony of September 20. "The officer said it is according to the law, he should not drive it unless he has a license – that is the law, and if he didn't obey the law, he would be punished, and I told him he should not drive it, if he drives it, he will have to serve a term, and I am not going to fight for him and get myself into it," Rummel said, adding that Theodore had been recently driving anyway, but only with an operator as an escort.

Theodore's teenaged attraction to automotive excess was apparently unquenched, not unlike many of his peers who probably did the same thing but didn't get caught, and on January 30, 1936, he was once more in the Baltimore Traffic Court, appearing before Magistrate Donald Roman. Theodore was reported to have been driving recklessly at high speed, nearly hitting a milk wagon and a police officer to boot. He was driving with neither license nor registration, and he had attempted to evade arrest by turning his lights off. After listening to the arresting officer, the magistrate remarked that it was one of the most flagrant cases of reckless driving he had ever adjudicated. "Evidently you had been drinking," Roman said to Theodore. "You have had one chance here [referring to the earlier July 1935 charges]. You cannot have another. I am committing you to the Maryland Training School for Boys. The length of your stay there will be determined by your conduct."

Theodore's friends probably found the incident highly amusing, and no doubt he had numerous opportunities to recount his escapades in front of like-minded compatriots at the Maryland Training School for Boys in northern Baltimore. Theodore's mother, Bessie, told the court that she was going to get rid of the automobile, but it was too late. Theodore was left to enjoy the hospitality of the state of Maryland for four months, until May 1936 when Bessie found a clever attorney and a sympathetic judge. Henry M. Siegel, attorney for Bessie, argued that Theodore had been improperly sentenced, that the legal sentence for traffic violations was one hundred dollars, ninety days in jail, or both. Bessie apparently did not consult Harry O. Levin on the matter, though he continued to represent the family with respect to the gold litigation. In any event, Judge Albert S. J. Owens concurred with Siegel, and Theodore found himself a free man.

A POT OF LIES

The Baltimore Court of Appeals came to a decision on April 15, 1936, and Theodore had good news waiting for him upon his release from the "socializing course" at the Training School. It was not a complete victory, but the court had once again upheld O'Dunne's decision on the first pot. And if there were a few thousand dollars more in the pot than everyone had first thought, "its title would follow the decision" of the first appeal, the court ruled. The second pot, on the other hand, "would constitute a different right and liability, to be enforced in a separate action," wrote the court. The legalese meant that the contest for the second pot could start all over again. Eby and Niles, the Findlay-French legal team, now had to file papers arguing their rights to the second pot, contradicting all their earlier accusations that the "second pot" was nothing but fraud.

The appeals court felt that Eby and Niles hadn't made much of a dent in the September 1935 testimony, which detailed the tale of the second pot of gold. The team had put up no witnesses on their own behalf, no underground coppersmiths to debate the origin of the second vessel, no acquaintances of Theodore and Henry who might have testified that a substantial amount of gold was held out from day one. That the story was highly unlikely wasn't the point. The testimony under oath stood, unless perjury could be proved beyond a reasonable doubt. History could judge whether it was more likely to find a second treasure or to make up a tall tale. But that was not the proper legal framework with which to analyze the question. The appeals court needed to see either obvious judicial error on the part of O'Dunne, or substantive new evidence unknown at the time of the September 1935 trial. Neither condition was met in the court's opinion, written by Appellate Judge Walter J. Mitchell.

With the question of the first pot settled once and for all, Judge Eugene O'Dunne ordered the proceeds from the May 1935 auction sale dispersed. By prearrangement with the families, Levin was entitled to a one-third share, sixty-two hundred dollars and change, after the auction sale expenses had been deducted. Levin, by his own account, had spent "countless hours" on the case, researching minute and mundane details in dusty archives and writing endless briefs. There was also his partner and relative, Sigmund Levin, to be paid out of his own share. The rest of the money remained in the care of Charles A. McNabb, deputy clerk of the Baltimore City Circuit Court, acting as guardian for the two boys. Meanwhile, an injunction against disposing of any funds associated with the second find remained in effect. The Merrills had over three thousand dollars invested in their gold hoard, but it might have been lead for all they cared, not being able to sell a single gold coin without Judge O'Dunne's approval.

The courts allowed no sale, but had no problem with more and more litigation. True to form, the Findlay-French ladies accepted the invitation of the court of appeals to start it all over again with the second pot. On April 25, 1936, only a few days after the court of appeals decision, the Findlay-French legal team refiled in Baltimore City Circuit Court, suing anyone known to possess assets connected with the "second" pot, including the two families, their banks, and the Merrill brothers. Unlike the other old gold buyers, the Merrills had made the mistake of disclosing their identity to the families, and everyone knew the Merrill gold was safely in the hands of their attorney, Simon E. Sobeloff. The Findlay-French group was not dissuaded by the fact that much of the second pot had already been stolen or squandered. The gold under the control of Sobeloff was still a prize worth fighting for, and there were bank accounts that Ruth Grob held besides. Discarding their theory that the second find was no more than a pot of lies, the Findlay-French group now argued that there was indeed a second pot, and that if an act of trespass hadn't been committed the first time, then certainly it had occurred the second time.

A PERFECTLY LEGITIMATE DEAL

With no prospects of a "third find," the families now found it advantageous to delay proceedings as much as possible. The idea of simply outwaiting the Findlay-French ladies, now well into their seventies, probably crossed their minds. Ruth Grob, still using the attorney Joel Hochman instead of Levin, waited until June 30, 1936, apparently the last day allowed, to respond to the latest lawsuit. The Merrills, on the other hand, had more incentive to get things wrapped up, and the respective attorneys began negotiating.

On October 1, 1936, the Merrill brothers settled out of court with the Findlay-French sisters for five hundred dollars. Yale Merrill, ever the public relations man, knew all the right things to say in the brothers' defense. "We knew, of course, that the gold clause had been passed—we read the gold clause act, and according to our understanding of it, there was a clause in there that specifically gave the right to buy or sell coins of numismatic value. We also believed we had the right to purchase them because of the decision [of Judge O'Dunne awarding the first pot to the children]. We felt as if we were transacting a perfectly legitimate deal," Merrill recalled. But the Merrills could not escape the shadow of secrecy, the intimation of subterfuge that clouded their dealings with the Jones-Rummel family. There was no getting around the fact that they had all attempted to conceal the second pot. They had perhaps stolen from the public if from anyone. The news of the second find was owed to the populace of Baltimore, if nothing more than to deliver a diversion in times of depression, to allow everyone else to dream dreams of buried treasure and sudden prosperity.

The Merrills delivered their five hundred dollars to the Findlay-French ladies. The sisters' attorneys, like Levin, were hired on contingency and perhaps shared in the small settlement. The old women, although living in a neighborhood pleasant enough, apparently still needed the cash. The two "hardly had a pot to piss on," thought one grandson. To make ends meet, Elizabeth French worked as a house mother at the Gilman Country School, a private institution attended by many blue-blooded Baltimore children. Indeed, her own son had been in the first graduating class of 1903.

The Merrills were now free to dispose of the gold, and these coins were flipped quickly to other dealers, a son speculated. Philip Rummel had hinted at such a third party in his court testimony in September 1935. "He [Yale Merrill] said he had to get more somewhere, that a friend told him he had to get more, the fellow that started out in this wanted more, he wanted some in a lump," Rummel testified. The whole affair did not leave a bitter memory with the Merrills. There were two twenty-dollar gold pieces that were saved by Yale Merrill, who still believed in the romance of the Baltimore hoard even if the litigation had cost him a good deal of his profit, and tied up his investment much longer than he expected.

HARD TIME

While the Merrills had finally extricated themselves from the legal tangles, Theodore was in traffic court a third time. Bessie apparently did not follow through on her promise to get rid of the Plymouth, and Theodore continued to enjoy the family hotrod after his release from juvenile detention in May 1936. On October 7, 1936, Theodore was stopped for speeding on the Philadelphia Road in eastern Baltimore. To make matters worse, he was driving without a license, which had been denied him in connection with the reckless driving charge that landed him in reform school. Henry was with Theodore when the police had stopped them, but there was nothing the two friends could divine to soften the hand of the law. Theodore was held overnight, and he was in trouble.

The next day Magistrate George Eckhardt Jr. sentenced Theodore to three months in jail, likely having reviewed Theodore's traffic record and ensuring that the sentence was squarely within the law. There would be no technicalities this time. Theodore and Bessie now had an uncomfortable decision to make. Theodore had been giving his age as eighteen, in anticipation of getting his share of the first find, held by the Baltimore Circuit Court, upon his twenty-first birthday. He was in fact sixteen, and could have argued for sentencing as a juvenile. But he had already spent four months in the Maryland Training School for Boys, and perhaps felt that the devil he did not know was better than the one he did. There was also the matter that a stay in reform school was indefinite, the typical "socializing course" there lasting between nine and twelve months. Theodore took perhaps his final step towards adulthood, and elected to join the brotherhood of adult inmates in the Baltimore penal system.

Bessie could have been grateful for the prison term, knowing that adult justice might finally rein her boy onto the straight and narrow. Meanwhile, the battle over the second pot dragged on. The Findlay-French attorneys filed an amended bill of complaint, excluding the Merrills, on October 19, 1936. Levin, still working the gold case for Bessie and Theodore Jones, managed to stall the proceedings until the spring of 1937 by requesting a dismissal of the suit, which was denied in April 1937 by Judge Edwin T. Dickerson. Answers to the Findlay-French amended bill of complaint trickled in over the summer, first from the banks that held funds connected with the second find, and later from the attorney Joel Hochman, still working for Ruth Grob. Hochman was last in line again, putting off his response until August.

LIKE FATHER, LIKE SON

"It is not at all uncommon to find the hoards of a whole lifetime of hard work and self-denial squandered on the empty show of a ludicrous funeral parade and a display of flowers that ill comports with the humble life it is supposed to exalt."

Jacob Riis, *How the Other Half Lives*, 1890

In the midst of the wearisome litigation for control of the second pot, forces beyond the power of the law and social status made themselves manifest. After dropping out of school in May 1935, Henry Grob had seemingly settled into a blue-collar existence, and was working in the mayonnaise department of the Panzer packing plant for sixteen dollars a week. Henry and his mother Ruth remained in the Canton section of Baltimore, living in a small brick house with his sister and brother-in-law at 2816 Elliot Street, "a plain dwelling in a none-too-affluent neighborhood," thought one reporter. His neighbors thought of him as a "quiet, reliable, well-behaved youth."

In August 1937, Henry was suffering from a severe cold, but nevertheless went for a swim in the Boston Street harbor several blocks from the family home, disregarding the advice of a doctor. Henry developed pneumonia, the same disease that had felled the father he never knew, and he was admitted to the South Baltimore General Hospital. Antibiotics were not used as widely at that time, and in Henry's case these were either ineffective or perhaps not even administered. Henry probably arrived at the hospital in a terminal state. Judging by the minimal hospital bill, there was little that could be done. He passed away the evening of August 24, a week less than four years from the date of the hoard discovery.

Ruth spent a good portion of Henry's estate on the funeral. The Baltimore Circuit Court still held over five thousand dollars in his name, and even though she could not access the funds directly, her creditors seemed to accept that payments would be forthcoming. John Moran, the undertaker, was paid about five hundred dollars, while Oak Lawn Cemetery and Loeblein's Marble and Granite works inflated the total funeral expenses to nearly a thousand dollars. The court apparently felt the costs excessive, and authorized only partial payments pending final settlement of the estate.

The funeral was held in the Grob home on August 27. The pallbearers included Henry's friends Jesse Murphy, Henry Zimmerman, Harry Schreiber, Ray Gagney, James Marsh, and Lawrence Zalenski, who thought all the gold had brought nothing but bad luck to Henry. Theodore Jones was noticeably absent from the list. The close friendship of the two boys had not extended to the families. "Mrs. Jones and I do not get along very well," Ruth said. "Her daughter, Bernice, was stuck on my son, John, and I did not approve of her because she is married and has a little baby. I forbid them from going together. They do not like me for this."

In the family parlor, Henry was laid underneath a huge enlargement of a photograph of himself and Theodore made at the time of the first hoard find. "And that picture is just about all poor Henry ever got out of it," lamented his sister, Gertrude Eberhart. The service was conducted by Rev. C. J. Hines of the Emmanuel Evangelical Lutheran Church, and Henry was laid to rest near his father, in the Oak Lawn Cemetery on the east side of Baltimore. A Secret Service agent noticed the obituary in the newspapers, and thought enough of it to send a copy for the files in Washington, even though the Secret Service had long since ceased pursuing the case.

CHAPTER 23

THE COURT DECIDES

The final proceedings in the struggle for control of the second pot were conducted by Judge Samuel K. Dennis of the Baltimore Circuit Court. His opinion was issued shortly after Christmas Day 1937. "The burden is upon the plaintiffs…to show that there is a clear distinction between the two finds," the judge wrote at the outset of the opinion. Eby and Niles, arguing for the Findlay-French team, felt that the second find was clearly a trespass, even more so than the first find. "During the whole case…they [Theodore and Henry] had heard asserted many times the unwillingness of the owners of the land to permit them to dig in the back cellar," the two wrote. "Only on the theory that Jones and Grob had no comprehension whatsoever of the proceedings, could it be concluded that they did not know that whatever implied rights they may previously have had had been revoked," they thought.

Dennis pointed out that neither of the elderly ladies had ever personally expressed the "unwillingness" to which Eby and Niles had made reference. Indeed, not a single word from either of the sisters appeared in the transcripts, or even in the newspapers for that matter. They were the perfect clients for Eby and Niles, who "have protected their interests with dignity, intelligence and fairness," Dennis noted. But the fact remained that the terms of Bessie and Theodore's lease, if indeed a written lease even existed (none was ever produced in court), had not formally changed. The landlord Kalis had never put a "no trespassing" sign on the rear portion of the cellar, or ever asked anyone to sign a lease prohibiting access to the shallow space in the back.

Kalis had made a token attempt to control the back of the cellar after the first find, putting a lock on the entrance door, but the busy-ness of running a real estate enterprise did away with this scheme quickly. The tenants needed constant access to the back to replace fuses. Harry Fleisher, the tenant on the second-floor front told the story. "Right after the gold was found a lock was put on the door and I complained to Mr. Kalis

[that] I did not have the key to open [it] up and he gave the one key to the downstairs lady and he told her to put a lock on it, and I told him I have trouble with my meters and a week later the lock was taken off and it is again open," Fleisher recalled. It was too much trouble to control who could or could not get into the cellar of this low-rent building, and Kalis never imagined that a "second" pot might turn this trivial matter into the axis of another legal war.

Dennis could not find any significant differences between the two pots of gold. "In both cases we have the same landlords, the same tenant, the same agent, the same lease, the same boys, the same pseudo-cellar, the same barrier between the regular and pseudo cellars.... [and] the same right of entry," he thought. Dennis thought the second case might even be weaker than the first, because in the second case it was clear that Kalis had had an opportunity to clarify the question of the tenant's access of the rear cellar, but had never formally done so. In awarding the second pot to the boys, Dennis was equally cognizant of negligence by all parties, noting that much of the second pot had been lost by "folly, inexperience, extravagance and theft."

The Findlay-French attorneys could perhaps have had a third try at the Maryland Court of Appeals, though their chances would have been slim even if the appellate court agreed to hear the case, which was no sure thing. And why continue to litigate for a fortune that had been largely stolen anyway? H. Findlay French began making plans to divest his mother and aunt of their four-year headache. The legalities had come full circle. Judge Dennis, who had approved the ejectment proceedings at 132 S. Eden Street in November 1933, had now closed the door to the cellar for good.

FOUGHT BY ABLE, RESOURCEFUL PEOPLE

With the tedious litigation ground to a final halt, Ruth Grob was free to settle her son Henry's estate. There remained about six thousand dollars in the bank (see Appendix II), and several parties lined up to get their share. Charles A. McNabb, deputy clerk of the Baltimore City Circuit Court and trustee of the Grob estate held under control of the court, was awarded ten percent of the estate for administrative duties. It was a surprising amount, six hundred dollars for placing the appropriate legal notices in local newspapers, and for handling a few bills presented to the estate. There was no such bite taken out of Theodore's share. One could only surmise that Henry was penalized for being dead. And if the ten percent was not enough, McNabb billed for miscellaneous expenses beyond that, including thirty-five dollars for a trustee bond, which was paid not out of McNabb's share but directly by the estate.

Harry O. Levin made his own play. Levin appealed to the court for one thousand dollars, for rendered services related to "part two" of the hoard. It was a reasonable request. Levin probably had his own doubts as to the origin of the second pot, not unlike the opposing counsel. If in fact there was but one pot, then Levin had been considerably cheated by the families, since he was due one third of the total treasure. If there were legitimately two pots, then Levin was still owed for his counsel in fighting for the second kettle on behalf of Henry and Theodore. In January 1938, Judge Dickerson agreed, and five hundred dollars was deducted from each boy's share and awarded to Levin.

The city of Baltimore took their nibbles: an inheritance tax and a "trustee" tax that was paid out of McNabb's share. Henry's funeral expenses, which had not been completely paid the previous summer, were settled, and a payment was made to the attorney Joel Hochman, who Ruth had used for representation during "part two" of the hoard. Judge Dickerson probably considered Levin's work to have equally benefited both children and apparently had no problem with authorizing funds to Levin even if Ruth Grob had not explicitly relied upon him. There was no question that Levin had done the heavy lifting in the Maryland Court of Appeals; indeed, Hochman's name appeared on none of the briefs submitted to the appellate court.

The final tally left Ruth Grob with but thirty-six hundred dollars out of the auction sale proceeds, which had totaled nearly twenty thousand dollars. Judge Samuel K. Dennis summed up the situation in his December 1937 decision. "They were ... denied possession due to long, expensive legal processes, wherein they were fought by able, resourceful people; whereas they were penniless, inexperienced and ignorant," the judge wrote.

PART 7

SCATTERED TO THE WIND

*Henry H. Grob tombstone, Oak Lawn
Cemetery, Baltimore*

CHAPTER 24

TREASURE TROVE LAW

England had reformed its treasure trove laws in 1996. Treasure trove cases are still being argued in that country, with over twenty Roman coin hoards reported in one recent year alone. The English Crown technically still retains title to treasure trove, perhaps a nod to the regal traditions on the east side of the Atlantic. In practice, treasure finders receive awards equal to the market value of the find, but only if they have complied with the terms of the Treasure Act, which requires timely disclosure of the find to the appropriate authorities. Henry and Theodore would have failed that part of the test, at least for "part two" of the Baltimore hoard. The English government retains discretion to award landowners as well as finders, or conversely, in the case of trespass, to make no award at all to finders.

The case for reform was spurred by the explosion of amateur metal detecting in the 1970s. Certain finds of significant archaeological value were not governed by classical treasure trove law, which required that the objects be made primarily of gold or silver. For example, a find of fifteen hundred bronze coins dating to the fourth century was made in Buckinghamshire, just north of London, in 1986. Despite their considerable value, the coins did not fall within the medieval definition of treasure trove and were legally disbursed without ever being formally attributed and cataloged for posterity. The new laws govern objects made of all metals, including base metal coins which have no significant value as bullion but may be of inestimable value to scholars.

Old technicalities in the classical treasure trove law have also been done away with. English common law held that treasure was required to have been "deliberately hidden," something that could be difficult to prove conclusively. The new law applies to either lost or hidden objects, disregarding the motive for burying the objects in the first place. Found coins over three hundred years old, or other objects containing at least five per cent gold or silver, now fall under the definition of treasure trove. In addition, the containers of the hoards, often archaeologically significant in their own right, are now classified as treasure. By this law, Henry and Theodore's gold-filled copper pot, or pots, would have been preserved. Displayed in a Baltimore museum for many years, this pot has since gone missing.

Theodore and Henry would have had a fighting chance under the current English law. In the United States however, the situation might be different. The value of the hoard, more than ten million dollars today, would serve to attract much more competing legal talent than it did in the 1930s. Beyond the value of the treasure itself, the "celebrity attorney" phenomenon would no doubt also play a part. Moreover, the interpretation of treasure trove law in some states has changed since the middle of the twentieth century. The Supreme Court of Texas, in 1955, effectively ruled that "treasure trove" would not apply in that state. Their opinion cited the "present conditions in our nation" as not applicable to the common law doctrine of treasure trove, whose origins lay in the upheaval of kingdoms and conquerors and treasures concealed in the face of military devastation. The Texas court ruled that found property could be classified as either "lost" or "mislaid," but not as "treasure trove." "Lost" property is something lost through carelessness or chance, while property carefully hidden and later discovered is considered "mislaid." "Lost" property goes to the finder, but Henry and Theodore's pot of gold would more likely be categorized as "mislaid" property, and thus awarded to the landowners. The Texas court held out a glimmer of hope for treasure finders, adding that something "mislaid" for a certain amount of time could revert to "lost" status.

Tennessee followed suit in a 1985 case. There, trespassers using a metal detector located a cache of gold coins buried on the property of one Clyde E. Morgan. Although a lower court held for the finders, the Tennessee Court of Appeals reversed the ruling in favor of the landowners. In particular, the appeals court was disturbed by the allowance for trespass in the "finder's keepers" interpretation of treasure trove. The court stated in part, "We find the rule with respect to treasure-trove to be out of harmony with modern notions of fair play. The common-law rule of treasure-trove invites trespassers to roam at large over the property of others with their metal detecting devices and to dig wherever such devices tell them property might be found." In the decision, the court indicated that the rejection of "finder's keepers" applied not only to cases of trespass, but to all treasure trove.

Fortunately, for two modern-day children who might be as fortunate as Henry and Theodore, Texas and Tennessee are exceptions, and most other states continue to award treasure trove to finders, except in the case of trespass, which in this case would remain a question. Even there, various states are conflicted, and an Illinois case in 1992 suggested that trespassing finders may retain certain rights. About half the states have enacted statutes awarding treasure trove to finders provided that the finds are reported to local police and that a reasonable search, lasting from three to twelve months, is made for the original owner.

CHAPTER 25

THE COINS ARE DISPERSED

Few Baltimore hoard coins can be positively attributed today. Walter Breen, a prominent numismatic author, believed that many of the high-grade 1850s double eagles currently extant originated in the Baltimore hoard, but beyond this likelihood, attribution of specific examples is elusive. Several coins remain in the families of the principals. C. Arthur Eby, attorney for the Findlay-French ladies, had five children and gave each a gold dollar from the hoard. At least one of these survives. H. Findlay French, an experienced stamp collector, also acquired several Baltimore hoard coins. The Merrill brothers preserved two twenty-dollar gold pieces which remain in the family. Eli Merrill's employer, Ike Berman, is known to have made purchases from the auction sale in May 1935. The Saulsbury descendants retain a single one-dollar gold coin from 1859, used as evidence in the 1934 trial to establish that Saulsbury frequently handled gold. The coin was passed down in the family directly from Andrew J. Saulsbury. While technically not part of the Baltimore hoard of 1934, one can arguably connect the coin with Saulsbury's "original" hoard. Other families reported no knowledge of Baltimore gold still in their possession, including the Grob, Jones, and Perry Fuller descendants.

Several collectors and dealers are known to have purchased coins at the Perry Fuller sale, but few can be traced. The Baltimore hoard coins of Rose Hendler, Edward Weikert, Samuel Glenn, and John Zug have all been scattered to the numismatic winds. Two other Baltimore collectors, Charles McCormick and Louis Eliasberg, possibly were successful bidders at the Fuller sale as well. McCormick, one of the original organizers of the Baltimore Coin Club, had been quoted in the newspapers shortly after the hoard find, commenting on the legalities of holding gold coins. Eliasberg, a successful Baltimore financier who in time formed one of the greatest American coin collections ever assembled, perhaps attended the Fuller sale too, or might have been represented by John Zug, with whom he had a close relationship

Thomas Elder, a New York coin dealer, handled at least three hundred pieces of Baltimore gold on the secondary market. These coins appeared beginning in his auction sales of June 1935 and continued into 1938. The Elder coins probably came directly from the Merrill brothers. "Mr. Merrel [sic] told Mr. Rummel that he was going to New York. He said he would put the gold on sale," Theodore's mother said to a Secret Service agent during the investigation of the "second" find. Elder, by then a grizzled veteran in the coin business, found the Baltimore gold pieces to be among the finest he had seen, particularly the one-dollar gold pieces, "the most brilliant lot of dollars we have ever offered," he wrote. Elder's customers apparently agreed, bidding up most of the one-dollar gold pieces for upwards of two dollars and fifty cents, with some as high as four dollars. Fuller had gotten about two dollars each for many of the same coins, and Elder's ability to get higher bids than Fuller, in hindsight, was not much of a surprise. Elder had been in the auction business since 1903, and by 1940 had cranked out nearly three hundred catalogs. He was a nationally recognized numismatist with a client list to match, not to mention inside connections at the United States Mint in Philadelphia, while Perry Fuller was really a local player, and more of a stamp dealer at that.

A single coin from the Elder Baltimore group, an 1856 one-dollar gold piece, came into the hands of a well-known northeastern numismatist many years ago. The coin was accompanied by a note explaining that it was acquired from the Baltimore hoard via Tom Elder. Of course, such an attribution could be fabricated, but as the Baltimore hoard was not well known at the time, the provenance seems reliable. This is the only known coin from the Elder lot, many of which were "matchless uncirculated gems," Elder would reflect later.

LIFE GOES ON

Following the conclusion of the hoard litigation in 1939, Judge Eugene O'Dunne served another six years on the Baltimore Circuit Court bench, until forced into mandatory retirement at the age of seventy. The assumption of "senile deterioration" was a bit of "damned nonsense," according to H. L. Mencken, who felt that O'Dunne, judging the law, was far wiser than the legislators who made the laws in the first place. He was feted upon his retirement by a gathering of over four hundred colleagues, a bountiful testimony of admiration for this political maverick.

Simon E. Sobeloff, attorney for the Merrills, continued his meteoric rise in the legal hierarchy. The Baltimore hoard case had attracted exceptional talent, as Sobeloff's future career would attest. By 1952 he had risen to the level of chief judge of the Maryland Court of Appeals, and in 1954 he was appointed by President Eisenhower to the position of U.S. Solicitor General. In 1958 he became the chief judge of the U.S. Court of Appeals in the fourth district. He was thought to be a Supreme Court candidate, with one legal commentator suggesting that his principled stand against the communist witch hunts in the 1950s had cost him his shot at the acme of jurisprudence.

The Findlay-French ladies sold the 132 S. Eden property in 1939, following conclusion of the litigation. There was no longer hope of recovering any of the fortune, though the two ladies had come as close as possible, a single vote away on the Maryland Court of Appeals from sharing at least part of the windfall. H. Findlay French, the son, later discussed the case with Judge O'Dunne, who reportedly told him he might have ruled in favor of the ladies had he been assured that a substantial portion of the hoard would still end up with the children. The ladies passed away at advanced ages in the late 1940s. Their lives had spanned from before the Civil War, through the Depression, through the years of litigation over the gold, and into postwar America.

Misfortune continued to follow the Grob and Jones families. Philip Rummel, Theodore's stepfather, died the day after Christmas 1940, falling down drunk in front of a streetcar. The streetcar driver was taken to the Eastern District Police Station for questioning, the same station where Rummel had fabricated his story about the stolen currency in September 1935, telling a police officer that the theft represented his life savings. Shortly thereafter, Theodore lost his brother, Eugene, in Pittsburgh, who he had helped set up in the towing business with some of the hoard proceeds. Henry's sister, Emma, suffered from extreme obesity and, like Henry, died young. A relative recalled that her home needed to be partially deconstructed in order to remove the body. Henry's mother had now lost two of her four children, and she herself passed away the following year. Ruth was buried in Baltimore, adjacent to her children Henry and Emma in Oak Lawn Cemetery.

George Almoney, the Secret Service agent who interviewed Ruth Grob following the "second" find, died December 27, 1939. His doctors suspected he had been poisoned by individuals who he was investigating, and misdiagnosed what was merely a ruptured gall bladder. A noted amateur tenor, he died in a hospital bed singing Franz Schubert's "Ave Maria."

Harry Levin, the boys' attorney, continued to further his reputation as a liberal Republican. He represented the Baltimore *Afro-American* newspaper for many years, and was awarded a series of political appointments by the Republican Maryland Governor Harry W. Nice. In 1937 he was offered a judicial post on the Supreme Bench of Baltimore (later known as the Maryland State Circuit Court), but declined upon "mature consideration." A relative thought that the "mature consideration" was actually pressure exerted by senior members of the Baltimore Jewish community to refuse the appointment, on the grounds that there was ostensibly but one "Jewish seat" on the Supreme Bench. There was already a Jew sitting on the court, and it was felt that support for his re-election might fade if Levin accepted a second "Jewish seat." Levin died in 1966, not living to see his own son, Marshall Levin, gain the same judicial appointment in 1971.

A NEW IDENTITY

Theodore Jones became Theodore Krik Sines in 1938, using his legal name on his marriage certificate. His propensity to alter his age had not changed, and on this document he listed his age as twenty-two, when in fact he was just short of eighteen. The name Theodore Sines began appearing in Baltimore city directories after 1940. A son was born two years later, and Theodore began to make up for the bad luck that had befallen him and Henry. There was first a separation from the media, which Theodore's mother, Bessie, encouraged. The two had had enough publicity, and Theodore Sines never made any effort to remind the reporters who he really was. There were periodic retrospectives in area newspapers discussing the hoard, but none ever connected the Sines name with the magical tale of the pot of gold. The stories petered out over time. Henry was dead, and no one could find Theodore.

In April 1937, Theodore began collecting interest payments on the first part of the hoard. The court still held about five thousand dollars of Theodore's money in a savings account, but allowed the interest to Theodore. Like clockwork, Theodore and his mother filed papers with the court every six months asking for the bank interest which was paid twice annually, typically fifty or sixty dollars. The last interest payment was collected in April 1939, and Theodore's final payday came in May 1939, on his nineteenth birthday, when his share of the funds from the 1935 Fuller auction sale was finally disbursed to him personally. Theodore was never a wealthy man, but by all accounts the money was put to constructive use.

His working life, which lasted about forty years, was spent at Bethlehem Steel as a shipyard mechanic, earning the respect of his colleagues as a skilled machinist. He was a leader, not surprising for one who was forced to grow up early in life, and on at least one occasion entered the management ranks, but quickly tired of it and rejoined the men in the yard getting their hands dirty. There was a brief stint in the army at the close of World War II, served stateside in Texas. Theodore had joined the army in July 1945, and was honorably discharged in December of the same year. His son remembered him as a good provider for his family, keeping the children well clothed and well fed. Theodore did not talk much and kept to himself, perhaps haunted by the misery of his childhood and compelled to take care of those who came after him. At the same time he was a hard man, strict with the children who always called him "sir," protective, and not one to give compliments. He stayed at home, preferring to let the women take the children on outings, perhaps to a beach on the Chesapeake Bay, or some other diversion outside the city. But Theodore mellowed later in life, as many do, drawing closer to his church and to his children.

A lifelong smoker, Theodore Sines was diagnosed with cancer in 1977 and passed away shortly thereafter at the age of fifty-seven. It was a common malady among steel- and shipyard workers, many of whom suffered from lung cancer and other asbestos-related illnesses. Fifteen years later Judge Marshall Levin, the son of Harry O. Levin, ruled against asbestos manufactures in what was believed at the time to be the largest asbestos trial in history. The reform was much too late for Theodore. His funeral was well attended, which might have surprised him, a son thought. Theodore was more loved than he realized.

132 S. EDEN STREET TODAY

The property at 132 S. Eden Street is today the boiler room of the American Alloy Foundry, which consumes most of the entire block west of 100 S. Eden Street, intersecting Pratt on the south side and Lombard on the north. The 132 S. Eden property itself was razed around 1980 and is today covered by a concrete slab at the ground level. Not all the houses in this block had cellars—the water table is low in the area (the adjacent block to the east is aptly named "Spring" Street) and it was not unusual to hit water at a depth of several feet. Some of the cellars were more accurately called crawl spaces, dug only to depths of several feet. Such was the case at 132 S. Eden, where the rear cellar was dug more shallowly, perhaps due to problems with water at the time of excavation.

A lone original row house stands at 108 S. Eden, at the opposite end of the street, north of which is an empty lot unhonored by even a "Do Not Park" sign. A narrow alley on the west side of the foundry runs between Pratt and Lombard, the same alley that Bessie and Theodore looked out on from their apartment in the rear building at 132 S. Eden. The east side of the street remains a park, City Spring Square, as it was at the time of the hoard find. Indeed, this is the second oldest park in the Baltimore, acquired by the city in 1818.

The American Alloy Foundry was established by Charles Gunther in 1942 and is today operated by his grandson, Robert Eagan. Originally situated between row houses on either side, the foundry site had in previous years been occupied by a bottling company, an ice cream company garage, and a grocery store. A faded advertisement surviving on the north side of the building urges passers by to enjoy "Whistle," possibly a product of the Joseph Goldman Bottling Works, which occupied the site into the 1920s.

American Alloy is a small business offering custom metal casting at reasonable prices with quick turnaround. They have cast parts for antique cars, antique trains, slot machines, and a plethora of other applications.

Clients have included Disney World (where a bronze orangutan may be found at the "Tree of Life" in the Animal Kingdom), the National Park Service, and the Smithsonian. Recently, the foundry cast parts for the "Bells of Remembrance," a set of memorial bells that have been erected at the September 11, 2001 crash sites. Another project is the construction of an engine block for a replica of the Wright brother's first airplane, commemorating one hundred years of aviation.

Throughout the years the foundry has employed local workers, a practice which doubtless helped the company survive in the aftermath of the riots following the assassination of Martin Luther King on April 4, 1968. Robert Eagan, the current owner, noted that among area business, some were left untouched while others were completely ransacked. The American Alloy Foundry was among those that escaped devastation. In the wake of the riots, National Guard troops bivouacked in the City Spring Square on the east side of Eden Street.

The foundry was also threatened by the specter of public housing in the area, most notably the Lafayette Courts project to the northeast. The government made overtures to seize the foundry property by eminent domain, but later apparently decided it would be more advantageous to leave employment opportunities in the area. The Lafayette Courts development was razed in the mid-1990s, at a time when large cities across the country could not escape the failures of high-rise public housing. Today it has been replaced with the Pleasant View Gardens project, which was designed to evoke the classic Baltimore row house architecture.

The American Alloy Foundry, which today fills the 132 S. Eden lot, in addition to much of the 100 S. Eden block in Baltimore.

Robert Eagan, 52, has worked exclusively in the foundry since childhood. Without an obvious successor, Eagan operates by hand amid sixty years of accumulated casting tools and equipment, as a skilled craftsman capable of quickly and accurately delivering custom parts to his customers. It is a niche market, and one he obviously enjoys. While much of the casting business has moved offshore, Eagan stands as a lone artisan who has embraced his craft and clearly revels in making his customers happy. The man and his company are "old school," the "last of the Mohicans," as Eagan puts it.

Much of the interior of American Alloy Foundry is still original, and certain portions of the building echo, as close as one can get, what life must have been like in the back building of 132 S. Eden, where Theodore Sines and his mother resided in 1934. The strongest impression is the coldness of the rooms, which in 1934 could have only been alleviated by going outside and retrieving fuel from the cellar for the furnace, presuming that one had the resources to pay for the wood or coal.

The property at 132 S. Eden is again reverting to its "house of gold" status as gentrification in Baltimore pushes east from the downtown area towards Little Italy and Fell's Point. The block of 100 S. Eden has an estimated value of two million dollars, certainly an attractive return on the four thousand dollars that Charles Gunther paid for the site in 1942. The odds of a similarly minded foundry craftsman such as Eagan finding his way to overseeing the business are small, particularly in light of the capital now required to purchase the property. It seems quite possible that the 132 S. Eden site will in future years be resurrected to the residential splendor that Andrew J. Saulsbury enjoyed in the 1860s, when he entered the cellar in the rear of the house and buried a fortune in the earth.

Eagan has no illusions that any gold remains underneath his property. Indeed, much of the property was scavenged when it was demolished, particularly for the old bricks that were popular for creating classic looks in residential interiors. Eagan noted that entire brick walls were knocked down and disappeared quickly, and is certain that anything more interesting would have been found at the time and quietly carried away. City code required that the cellar at 132 S. Eden be refilled, and today a search of the property would be highly problematic, as any secrets the remaining foundation of this house has to reveal are buried under a concrete slab and guarded by the prohibitive cost of excavation.

APPENDICES

APPENDIX I

A SELECT CAST
OF CHARACTERS

Chenven, Harry. 1881(?)–1934. A one-time jeweler, he was a resident of 132 S. Eden, from about 1927 until the time of his death. His son Isaac participated as a Chenven heir in the litigation for the hoard.

Dickerson, Edwin T. Born c. 1879 in Maryland. Baltimore City Circuit Court judge who oversaw the final phases of the hoard litigation. Dickerson is listed as an attorney residing in Baltimore at 3004 Garrison Boulevard in the 1930 census, living with two sisters and a nephew.

Eberhart, Paul. Born 1910 in Berks County, Pa., died December, 1977 in Ephrata, Pa. He married Henry Grob's sister, Gertrude, and was living in the same apartment building as Henry at the time of the hoard find.

Eby, C. Arthur. Born c. 1883. Baltimore attorney who represented the sisters Findlay and French in the hoard litigation.

Findlay, Mary Pillar Boyd. 1861–1948. Co-owner, with her sister Elizabeth French, of 132 S. Eden Street at the time of the hoard discovery. She never married. The Findlay sisters are listed in the 1930 census as living together with two black servants at 1510 Bolton in Baltimore.

Fleetwood, Charles E. 1888(?)–1965. Carpenter who worked for Benjamin Kalis on the 132 S. Eden Street property.

Foster, Reuben. 1897–1979. Grandson of Andrew J. Saulsbury, he was appointed the administrator of Saulsbury's estate for the purposes of litigating the hoard.

French, Elizabeth Hollingsworth Findlay. 1856–1949. Co-owner, with her sister Mary B. Findlay, of 132 S. Eden Street at the time of the hoard discovery. She was married to George R. French and widowed before 1905. They had one son, Henry Findlay French.

French, Henry Findlay. 1886–1980. The son of Elizabeth French, he made statements to the press shortly after the hoard find. A World War I veteran, French was an attorney and the director of the Industrial Bureau of the Association of Commerce.

Fuller, Perry W. 1889–1979. Fuller was the auctioneer of the hoard in 1935. He is listed in the 1930 census in Baltimore with a wife and three children. His first wife was Anita Sherwood.

Gamerman, Harry. Born c. 1864, in Russia, emigrated to the United States in 1907. A fellow jeweler and close friend of Harry Chenvin.

German, Fred. Baltimore patrolman, involved in the investigation of "part two" of the hoard.

Grob, Gertrude. Born c. 1914, most likely in Baltimore. Sister of Henry Grob. She married Paul Eberhart.

Grob, Henry H. Born May 12, 1919 in Baltimore, died August 24, 1937 in Baltimore. Co-discoverer of the Baltimore gold hoard.

Grob, John. 1889–1918. Father of Henry Grob.

Grob, John H. Born c. 1917. Brother of Henry Grob.

Grob, Ruth. Born Ruth Crist c. 1893 in Baltimore, married October 21, 1912, in Baltimore, to John Grob. Mother of Henry Grob. She is listed as being married to Leo Stockman in the 1920 census, then listed as Ruth Fisher in the 1930 census, living with her sons Henry and John at 227 S. Caroline St. in Fell's Point.

Hendler, Rose. Born c. 1888 in Maryland. She was a successful bidder at the 1935 hoard auction. She was married to L. Manuel Hendler, the President of Hendler Creamery Company, a prominent local ice cream concern that was eventually bought out by Borden. Both her and her husband's parents were born in Russia.

Hochman, Joel J. Born c. 1900, in Maryland, to Russian immigrants whose native language was Yiddish. Hochman was a Baltimore attorney hired by Ruth Grob for portions of the hoard litigation. In the 1930 census, Hochman is listed as an attorney living with his parents at 1648 Ruxton Avenue.

Jones, Theodore Krik. Born May 3, 1920, in Ohio, died August 28, 1977, in Baltimore. Co-discoverer of the hoard with Henry Grob. He was married to Marie H. Kroupa on March 3, 1938.

Kalis, Benjamin. 1894–1992. Real estate agent employed by Mary Findlay and Elizabeth French to manage the 132 S. Eden property. Kalis was born in Russia and came to Baltimore around 1900. He oversaw the conversion of the 132 S. Eden house into separate apartments during the winter of 1933–1934.

Keogh, William. Baltimore police sergeant, involved in the investigation of "part two" of the hoard.

Lample, Gustav. 1892–1962. Police sergeant who counted the coins on August 31, 1934.

CAST OF CHARACTERS

Levin, Harry O. 1888–1966. Attorney for Henry Grob and Theodore Jones.

Levin, Sigmund. 1907(?)–1985. He is listed as a co-attorney with Harry O. Levin on some court documents. Known as "Siggy," he was a cousin of Levin's.

McCormick, Dr. Charles E. 1889(?)–1974. Baltimore pharmacist and charter member of the Baltimore Coin Club. He was quoted as a "local collector" in the press shortly after the hoard was discovered. It is probable he attended the hoard auction sale in 1935.

McNabb, Charles A. Born c. 1880 in Maryland (the 1920 and 1930 census data is inconsistent). Deputy clerk in 1920, chief clerk of the Baltimore court in 1930. He is listed as a married homeowner, with no children living at home in both the 1920 and 1930 census.

Menchine, W. Albert. Attorney used by Ruth Grob in parts of the hoard litigation, apparently a partner of Joel J. Hochman. Harry O. Levin's state senatorial opponent in 1924 was William G. Menchine, likely a relative.

Merrill, Eli. 1903–1988. Along with his brother Yale, he made purchases of hoard gold from the Rummel family and was later sued by the Findlay and French sisters. The Merrill parents were Russian immigrants, arriving in America in 1893. The 1930 census lists Eli as a salesman in a loan office (probably a pawn broking concern). Another brother, Morris, was also in the pawn broking business.

Merrill, Yale. 1906–1993. Along with his brother Eli, he made purchases of hoard gold from the Rummel family and was later sued by the Findlay and French sisters. He is listed as a sports editor in the 1930 census and later worked in public relations.

Niles, Emory H. Attorney for the Findlay-French party in the hoard litigation.

Owens, Albert S. J. Baltimore judge who handled the initial hoard claim in September, 1934 and set a waiting period of ninety days for additional claimants to present themselves.

Pfenning, Daniel. 1911–1979 (likely). Police lieutenant who counted the coins on the evening of August 31, 1934.

Rummel, Phillip A., Jr. 1898–1940. His parents were both born in Germany. The stepfather of Theodore Jones, Rummel was a World War I veteran. He married Bessie Jones on July 22, 1935.

Schapiro, Ida. 1855(?)–1931. Owner of 132 S. Eden in the 1920s. Findlay and French foreclosed on 132 S. Eden, held by the Schapiro estate, in December 1933, after the Schapiro estate failed to make the 1933 ground rent payment.

Stankiwicz, Walter. 1916–1995 (likely). Stankiwicz was arrested, along with Henry Grob, for getting into a fight near the Broadway pier on September 15, 1934. The Stankiwicz family lived at 209 S. Eden as of 1930 (1930 census, Baltimore district 32).

Stockman, Leo. 1894–1939. Stockman lived with Ruth Grob for a short time around 1920. Listed as a film operator in Baltimore city directories from 1918 to 1922, also listed in the 1920 census with "wife" Ruth, and her children listed as stepchildren. WWI veteran.

Weikert, Edward L., Jr. 1890–1971. A man of many occupations and fraternal organizations, he was most notably elected to the state House of Representatives in Pennsylvania in 1926. Weikert attended and was a successful bidder at the 1935 auction.

Williams, Ezekiel. Baltimore police lieutenant involved in the investigation of "part two" of the hoard.

SETTLEMENT OF THE
HENRY H. GROB ESTATE

Following the death of Henry Grob, his mother filed with the Circuit Court to assume her son's estate as the surviving heir. The estate consisted of Henry's share of the 1935 Fuller auction sale, plus interest. Following is the auditor's report to the court, submitted March 30, 1938.

Assets:

Principal of trust estate (in Savings Bank of Baltimore)	$5798.00
Interest paid 10/1936	$48.21
Interest paid 4/1937	$73.06
Interest paid 10/1937	$73.94
Interest paid 4/1938	$62.50
Total Estate	$6055.71

Disbursements:

Trustee commission, less 1% for tax on same, Per 3/15/38 court order	$545.01

[Charles A. McNabb, the deputy clerk of the circuit court, was named trustee of the estate and authorized to pay estate expenses and administer any related legal issues. For this service, Judge Edwin Dickerson allowed a 10% share of the estate to McNabb. This seems to have been somewhat of a sweetheart deal as McNabb's only responsibilities consisted of paying several bills as mentioned below.]

1% trustee tax to Register of Wills, Baltimore City	$60.56

[The Baltimore municipality got in on the action as well, claiming a 10% share of any trustee payments.]

Trustee Expenses:

Attorney	$10.00
Clerk	$22.50
Auditor & Notices	$32.00

[McNabb was required to pay court costs related to the estate disposition. Naturally these were paid for out of the estate and not out of McNabb's share. Harry O. Levin acted as McNabb's attorney.]

Daily Record order notice to creditors $7.00

[A notice was taken in the legal newspaper informing any creditors to present themselves to the court.]

Fidelity & Deposit, Trustee's bond $35.00

[McNabb was required to file a bond for the amount of the estate, to protect the estate in the event that he disappeared with the proceeds, over which he had control. Once again, this was paid for out of the estate and not out of McNabb's portion.]

John A. Moran, funeral bill	$300.00
Oak Lawn Cemetery lot	$181.00
Loeblein's Marble and Granite Mfgs.	$100.00
South Baltimore General Hospital	$19.00

[On September 30, 1937 Ruth Grob asked the court to pay for Henry's funeral expenses, using the estate balance to cover the bills. Her initial request was for actual costs, which Judge Dickerson apparently considered excessive, allowing only $600 at the time. The cemetery lots were sold in groups of four, which may have contributed to Dickerson's decision.]

Harry O. Levin counsel fee $500.00

[Levin asked the court for $1,000 for his services in actions related to "part two" of the hoard. This amount was approved by Judge Dickerson on January 3, 1938. Half ($500) was taken from the Grob estate, and $500 was taken from the Jones portion still held by the court until Jones' 21st birthday.]

Register of Wills, Baltimore City, Inheritance Tax $42.44

[Once again, the city got some of the hoard proceeds, with a 1% inheritance tax paid on the remaining amount.]

SETTLEMENT OF THE HENRY H. GROB ESTATE

John. A. Moran $156.50
Oak Lawn Cemetery $93.00
Joel J. Hochman, attorney $150.00

[These amounts were paid per an order by Ruth Grob on March 30, 1938. This represented the amounts remaining to be paid to the funeral home and cemetery. Hochman represented Ruth Grob beginning in September 1935, when news of the second find became public.]

  To Ruth Grob directly (paid January 3, 1938) $200.00

[On the same day that Levin received $1,000 from the court for services rendered, Ruth Grob appealed to the court for personal funds. The petition read in part, "That your petitioner is destitute and has no funds whatsoever and inasmuch she will be entitled, as the sole heir of law of said Henry H. Grob deceased, to the entire sum, it is right and proper that the court allows her to withdraw the sum of $200 which she requires for immediate necessities." The court approved the request. Following all disbursements, the remaining total of $3,601.70 was given to Ruth Grob on April 11, 1938.]

FULLER INVENTORY OF PART ONE OF THE HOARD

The Fuller inventory is derived from the contents of the Perry Fuller catalog issued for the May 1935 auction sale. This inventory is similar to that published by Walter Breen in the January 1952 issue of *The Numismatist*, with minor corrections.

Twenty-Dollar Gold Pieces (Double Eagles)

Date	Philadelphia	New Orleans	San Francisco	Total
1850	92	5		97
1851	79	10		89
1852	47	2		49
1853	27			27
1854	12			12
1855	6		12	18
1856	1	1	23	25
Total	264	18	35	317

Ten-Dollar Gold Pieces (Eagles)

Date	Philadelphia	New Orleans	San Francisco	Total
1839	2			2
1840	1			1
1841	1			1
1842	2	1		3
1844	1			1
1845	1	1		2
1846	1			1
1847	13	7		20
1848	5	2		7
1849	10	1		11

(continued)

Date	Philadelphia	New Orleans	San Francisco	Total
1850	6	2		8
1851	1	3		4
1852	1			1
1853	4	3		7
1854	1		1	2
1855	7			7
1856	3			3
Total	58	22	1	81

Five-Dollar Gold Pieces (Half Eagles)

Date	Philadelphia	New Orleans	Charlotte	Dahlonega	Total
1834	15				15
1835	2				2
1836	12				12
1837	3				3
1838	6		1		7
1839	1				1
1840	8				8
1841	1				1
1842				1	1
1843	12	5	2	1	20
1844	6	6	2		14
1845	10	3			13
1846	4		4	1	9
1847	20	1	1	1	23
1848	8		5	1	14
1849	6		1	1	8
1850	5			2	7
1851	13				13
1852	20		5	2	27
1853	12		3	3	18
1844	11	1		6	18
1855	15		3	1	19
1856	3				3
Total	193	16	27	20	256

Two-and-a-Half-Dollar Gold Pieces (Quarter Eagles)

Date	Philadelphia	New Orleans	Charlotte	Dahlonega	Total
1834	2				2
1836	5				5
1839				1	1
1843	1	4	1		6
1845	2				2
1847		1			1
1848				1	1
1850	3				3
1851	5				5
1852	11				11
1853	14				14
1854	7				7
1855	3				3
1856	4				4
Total	57	5	1	2	65

One-dollar Gold Pieces

1849	95
1850	78
1851	452
1852	322
1853	976
1854	316
1855	215
1856	296
Total	2750

The mintmarks on the one-dollar gold pieces, if any, were unnoted. In addition, the auction contained a single lot of thirty-nine one-dollar gold pieces which could not be identified as to date. In addition to the coins listed in the catalog, Fuller likely held out fifty one-dollar gold pieces which were paid for at two dollars each.

MERRILL INVENTORY OF PART TWO
OF THE HOARD

The Merrill inventory includes the coins purchased from the Jones-Rummel family in the summer of 1935. This inventory was produced in court after the news of the second find became public. The number of coins for each date is given by denomination in the following table.

Date	$20	$10	$5	$2.50
1834			10	1
1835			4	3
1836			10	2
1837			2	1
1838			5	
1839		1	4	
1840		1	3	
1841		3	2	
1842		4	3	
1843		3	7	4
1844		1	9	
1845		1	12	1
1846			12	
1847		4	6	3
1848			6	
1849		3	5	1
1850	2	8	5	2
1851	4	2	5	
1852	4	2	4	
1853	3	2	9	
1854	2		7	
1855		2	7	
1856			1	
Total	15	37	138	18

The mintmarks on the coins were not recorded. In addition to the coins listed above, the Merrills purchased 1,092 one-dollar coins which were not inventoried as to date. The total face value listed is thus $2,497, three dollars short of the $2,500 face value known to have been purchased. This leaves the possibility that a single three-dollar gold piece was found in part two of the hoard and not listed specifically in the Merrill inventory, being an odd piece. This obsolete denomination was minted between 1854 and 1889, generally in small quantities.

NOTES

BCCC2 indicates the stenographic record of the Baltimore City Circuit Court #2, testimony taken in 1934 and 1935 and transcribed by the court reporter. *HLA* indicates the Harry Levin Family Archive, a scrapbook of news clippings assembled in the 1920s and 1930s by Harry O. Levin.

Part 1 (pp. 3–24)

Chapter 1. The House at 132 South Eden Street (pp. 3–9)

I

census taker who visited the residence, U. S. Bureau of the Census 1930, Baltimore City, district #37, 23.

An English word falls upon the ear, Jacob Riis, *How the Other Half Lives: Studies Among the Tenements of New York* (New York: Charles Scribner's Sons, 1890), 87–100.

an earlier census, U. S. Bureau of the Census 1920, Baltimore City, district #63, 9.

a Baltimore work relief administrator, Richard Lowitt and Maurine Beasley eds., *One-Third of a Nation: Lorena Hickok: Reports on the Great Depression* (Urbana: University of Illinois Press, 1981), 344.

Harry Fleischer was under oath, BCCC #2, docket A-579, 1934, 252–63.

II

for the first time on November 15th, BCCC #2, docket A-579, 1934, 121.

eight industrious years, U. S. Bureau of the Census 1920, Baltimore City, district #97, 3.

active in the labor movement, Interview with Michael Kalis (grandson), 4/23/2003.

six hundred dollars, BCCC #2, docket A-579, 1934, 331.

reported finding no one else, BCCC #2, docket A-579, 1934, 121.

team of ten workers, BCCC #2, docket A-579, 1934, 127.

bums, panhandlers, and smoke hounds, *Baltimore Evening Sun,* 4/12/1939.

Stove pipes extended, Sanborn Fire Insurance Maps (Baltimore), Sanborn Map Company, 1914.

naturally divided the property, BCCC #2, docket A-579, 1934, 122.

frozen at least twice, Maryland Court of Appeals, Records and Briefs, April 1935, cases 35–36, French exhibit B.

According to Fleetwood, BCCC #2, docket A-579, 1934, 145.

King agreed, BCCC #2, docket A-579, 1934, 148.

Two boys watched, Interview with Cora Cohen (daughter of Benjamin Kalis), 5/3/2003.

look over things at least once a week, BCCC #2, docket A-579, 1934, 130.

III

Real estate developers in Baltimore, Mary Ellen Hayward and Charles Belfoure, *The Baltimore Row House* (New York: Princeton Architectural Press, 2001), 109–10.

[Oscar and Ida Schapiro] had purchased the property, Baltimore City Superior Court Land Records, SCL #3352, folio 142, 4/29/1919. Land transactions in Baltimore are indexed by block number; the 100 South block of Eden Street is block 1391.

Ida died a widow in 1931, City of Baltimore Health Department, Death Certificate #E68739. Her husband had died in 1926, Death Certificate #E05827.

due in September 1933, Baltimore City Superior Court Judicial Record, SCL #14, folio 174, 11/8/1933.

a concept employed in various cities, *Baltimore City Paper* Online, 3/29/2000, http://www.citypaper.com/2000–03-29/charmed.html.

in a run down condition, humblest sort of means, Judge Samuel K. Dennis, opinion in case 21483A, Baltimore City Circuit Court #2, 12/28/1937.

thirty-eight dollars a month, U. S. Bureau of the Census 1930, Baltimore City, district #37, 23. The 1930 census indicated whether the residents owned or rented, and what the rent was set at in the latter case. Whether the rent was always paid or not is not noted.

ground rent had been in the family, Maryland Court of Appeals, Records and Briefs, April 1935, cases 35–36, 96. The ground rent was first acquired by Mary Boyd, an aunt of Elizabeth French and Mary B. Findlay, in 1851.

application for membership in the Maryland Historical Society, Maryland Historical Society, Baltimore MD, 2/11/1930.

the two sisters paid nearly one hundred a month, U. S. Bureau of the Census 1930, Baltimore City, district #599, 6. The Findlay and French rent at 1510 Bolton Street was set at ninety dollars a month, while others on the same street paid one hundred dollars or more.

born into a naval tradition, J. Thomas Scharf, *History of Delaware 1609–1888* (Philadelphia: L. J. Richards, 1888), 194.

took his own turn in the military, Gilman School Bulletin, Winter 1981, Baltimore, MD.

spent most of his professional career, *Baltimore Sun,* 9/14/1980.

keeping a vigilant lookout for any movement of negroes, *Baltimore Sun,* 1/21/1921, 18. Note that restrictive covenants preventing sales to nonwhites were not struck down by the Supreme Court until 1948, *Shelley v. Kraemer,* 334 U.S. 1. The author is grateful to John Kleeberg for this citation.

file an ejectment proceeding, Baltimore City Superior Court Judicial Record, SCL #14, folio 174, 11/8/1933.

Chapter 2. Bessie Sines and Theodore Jones (pp.10–16)

IV

Some time around 1932, *Baltimore Sun,* 2/17/1935, 15.

Worked in a glass factory, who was divorced, U. S. Bureau of the Census 1930, City of Pittsburgh, district 2-414, 8.

If my Dad opened his mouth, Interview with Edward Sines, 3/14/2003.

from time to time used other dates. Theodore's marriage certificate, filed in 1938, indicates a birth year of 1916. He may not have been old enough to marry without parental consent. In 1941, he gave his birth year as 1918 when completing his application for a Social Security card. The 1930 census, along with his death certificate, agrees with the 1920 date. His gravestone agrees with the 1920 date. The May 1918 date given on the Social Security application is virtually impossible, since he had a sister born November 17, 1918 (State of Ohio Certificate of Birth for Bernice Louise Sines, #108621).

Theodore once told a reporter, *Baltimore Sun,* 2/17/1935, 15. Theodore's parents were likely divorced sometime before 1928, when his father remarried a Clara Lally in Ohio (Pickaway County marriage license application, 5/9/1928).

made the trip at least once, picked up a cross, *Baltimore Post,* 9/1/1934, 3.

shortly after New Year's Day, BCCC #2, docket A-579, 1934, 337.

fresh wallpaper, Maryland Court of Appeals, Records and Briefs, April 1935, cases 35–36, French exhibit B. The entire house was papered in December 1933, at a cost of forty-six dollars.

As Bessie put it, BCCC #2, docket A-579, 1934, 77.

Bessie took in laundry, *Washington Post,* 9/2/1934, M1.

Kalis even put the electric bill under his company name, BCCC #2, docket A-579, 1934, 345.

V

Harry Chenven, although the Baltimore City Circuit Court #2 records spell the name "Chenvin," we use the spelling "Chenven" which has been adopted by Harry Chenven's descendants.

one room, third floor, BCCC #2, docket A-579, 1934, 35.

An old description of the property, Baltimore City Register of Wills (Inventory of Andrew J. Saulsbury), 2/18/1874, JHB 99, folio 375. Here, the back building is described as two stories with an attic. Subsequent renovations may have modified the attic to make it more livable as a separate rented space.

easy of entry, *Baltimore Evening Sun,* 9/11/1934, 15.

Chenven kept a padlock, BCCC #2, docket A-579, 1934, 37.

moved into the ramshackle building in 1927, BCCC #2, docket A-579, 1934, 97.

apparently lacking even a simple toilet, French Exhibit B, Maryland State Court of Appeals, April 1935, docket #35. A ledger of repairs to the property shows that second- and third-floor toilets were repaired on August 21, 1934, shortly after Chenven's death.

He used to keep a vessel, BCCC #2, docket A-579, 1934, 84.

My mother hollered up at him, forced to explain the soiled windows, BCCC #2, docket A-579, 1934, 45.

Harry Gamerman, Testimony of Harry Gamerman, BCCC #2, docket A-579, 1934, 94–109.

247 S. Broadway, Baltimore city directories, 1916–1918.

The Chenven family disagreed, Interview with Dr. Norman Chenven (grandson of Harry Chenven), 7/5/2003.

suspected Gamerman of passing counterfeit money, National Archives, Record Group 87. Daily report of Benjamin Bratton, Secret Service operative, 2/9/1935.

Chenven's sister in New York, Testimony of Betty Aaronson, BCCC #2, docket A-579, 1934, 109–11.

neighbors later thought the house had been vacant, *Baltimore Sun,* 9/1/1934, 9.

died of a stroke, City of Baltimore Health Department, Death Certificate #F04136.

VI

An Italian-American girl wrote to the President, *New York Times,* 3/19/1933, 1.

A Syracuse woman read this account, *New York Times,* 3/24/1933, 12.

an event heralded by full page newspaper ads, for example, Atlas Beer (*Chicago Daily Tribune,* 4/2/1933, 9), Schlitz (*Chicago Daily Tribune* 4/7/1933, 12), Budweiser (*Chicago Daily Tribune* 4/11/1933, 20), and others.

Winking an eye at his profession, *Chicago Daily Tribune* , 4/7/1933, 1.

the price of various quantities of beer, *Chicago Daily Tribune,* 4/7/1933, 2. A twelve-ounce stein was now sold for fifteen cents, compared to the twenty-five cents previously charged in saloons and speakeasies.

A federal chemist, *Chicago Daily Tribune,* 4/10/1933, 1.

French vintners, *Chicago Daily Tribune,* 4/15/1933, 10.

We were supposed to turn in our gold, recollection of Ruth Neuenschwander, c. 2002.

Peter Kaminsky, of Queens, *New York Times,* 1/9/1934, 9.

Russian immigrant who worked as a machinist, United States Census 1930, New York City, enumeration district #1176, 23B.

White House china, *The Numismatist,* November 1971, 1609.

Louis Eliasberg, a Baltimore financier, Q. David Bowers, *Louis E. Eliasberg, Sr.: King of Coins* (Wolfeboro, NH: Bowers and Merena Galleries, 1996), 70.

Chapter 3. Henry Grob (pp. 17–21)

VII

Pittsburgh manner, Baltimore *Evening Sun,* 2/16/1935, 14.

initiated me by beating me up, *Baltimore News and Post,* 2/16/1935, 2.

We always went around together, Testimony of Theodore Jones, BCCC #2, docket A-579, 1934, 26.

I used to go there every day, Testimony of Henry Grob, BCCC #2, docket A-579, 1934, 54.

the larger of the two boys, Testimony of Theodore Jones, BCCC #2, docket A-579, 1934, 13. Photographs of the two together (for example, in *Popular Science Monthly,* December 1934, 29), depict their relative size.

looking much older than his age of fourteen, photographs in the *Baltimore American,* 9/2/1934, L3.

Henry's father was a blue eyed blond, World War I draft registration card for John Rudolph Grob, 6/5/1917. The birth date on the card, suggesting an age of eighteen, is a typographical error. John Grob's identity is established by the address on the card (the same as on Henry's birth certificate), the fact that he claims a wife and three children as a draft exemption (Henry had three older siblings), and the fact that the card itself gives an age of 28, disagreeing with the stated birth date.

Henry, born May 12th, 1919, City of Baltimore Health Department, Birth Certificate #B73595, 5/12/1919.

never knew his father, City of Baltimore Health Department, Death Certificate [John Grob], #D22018, 10/13/1918. The cause of death is given as "bronchial pneumonia," one of the manifestations of the Spanish flu.

been beaten all over with a club, Alfred W. Crosby, *America's Forgotten Pandemic, The Influenza of 1918* (Cambridge, UK: Cambridge University Press, 1989), 39.

A children's rhyme, Ibid., 53.

was probably a friend of the family, World War I draft registrations for Leo

Stockman and John Rudolph Grob, 6/5/1917. Stockman ended up serving overseas from June 1918 to May 1919 (*Maryland in the World War, 1917–1919; Military and Naval Service Records*, Vol. I–II (Baltimore: Twentieth Century Press, 1933).

Stockman was a womanizer of the worst sort, Baltimore City Divorce decrees, #B20604 (4/3/1920) and #B37017 (September, 1932). Stockman lived with at least four women, two represented by these divorces, also with Ruth Grob, and also with an Anna Stockman, his spouse at the time of his death. The divorce decrees present additional evidence of his infidelities.

loved and left any number of women in his short life, City of Baltimore Health Department, Death Certificate #F59798, 7/16/1939. Stockman died at the age of 44.

abandoned and left with a young child, Baltimore City Divorce decree, #B20604 (4/3/1920).

Stockman was remarried by 1925, Baltimore City Divorce decree, #B37017 (September, 1932).

Ruth described it later, statement of Ruth Grob to Secret Service Agent George Almoney, taken 9/9/1935. U.S. National Archives, Record Group 87, closed investigations file C-11369.

taverns being illegal in this period, United States Census 1930, Baltimore City, district #30, 23. At this time Ruth was living with her two sons, Henry, age 10, and John, age 13, while the two daughters (Emma and Gertrude) are unlisted at the same address.

picked vegetables in the fields, *Baltimore News and Post*, 2/16/1935, 2.

working there for ten dollars a week, BCCC #2, 9/20/1935, 201.

a Baltimore relief social worker, Richard Lowitt and Maurine Beasley eds., *One Third of a Nation: Lorena Hickok Reports on the Great Depression* (Urbana: University of Illinois Press, 1981), 359.

VIII

second grade education, Interview with Edward Sines, 3/14/2003.

spell the name of his good friend Henry Grob, Testimony of Theodore Jones, BCCC #2, docket A-579, 1934, 12.

once driving a milk wagon, *Baltimore Sun*, 2/17/1935, 15.

planned to call the Rinky-Dinky-Doos, *Baltimore Evening Sun*, 9/1/1934, 3.

been playing in the front portion almost daily, Testimony of Henry Grob, BCCC #2, docket A-579, 1934, 55.

get some relief from the ninety degree days, *Baltimore Sun*, 9/2/1934, 3. There were thirty days over ninety degrees in 1934, twice the normal number for the summer.

had been repaired between August 7th and 27th, Testimony of Benjamin Kalis, BCCC #2, docket A-579, 1934, 127.

entered the back part of the basement several times before, Testimony of Theodore Jones, BCCC #2, docket A-579, 1934, 12.

each boy would contribute a nickel in dues, Judicial Opinion of Judge Eugene O'Dunne, Maryland Daily Record, 2/16/1935, 3.

it might be for playing cards, Testimony of Henry Grob, BCCC #2, docket A-579, 1934, 54.

It was Henry's idea, Testimony of Theodore Jones, BCCC #2, docket A-579, 1934, 13.

an axe, a corn knife, and a flashlight, Testimony of Henry Grob, BCCC #2, dockets A-579, 1934, 56, 72.

ten feet wide and twenty feet long, Testimony of Theodore Jones, BCCC #2, docket A-579, 1934, 8. The width of ten feet was Theodore's estimate. The property width itself was twenty feet, however, the back building did not extend across the whole width. The length is the author's estimate from contemporary fire insurance maps.

wearing the cross he had found, Baltimore News, 9/1/1934, 3.

chose a spot next to the brick wall, Testimony of Theodore Jones, BCCC #2, docket A-579, 1934, 48–50, and Henry Grob, 57. The exact spot is not clear from the testimony, but from the accompanying photographic exhibits the spot is clearly at the middle part of the east wall in the rear cellar.

Chapter 4. Treasure in the Cellar (pp. 22–24)

IX

he hit something sounded like of tinny, Testimony of Henry Grob, BCCC #2, docket A-579, 1934, 59. The discovery account in the Baltimore Newspapers reads somewhat differently from the court transcript. The Baltimore Sun (9/1/34, 20) reported that the first coin was identified quickly by Henry, at which point Theodore said, "I was digging in that hole — hands, elbows, knees and everything." Coins then came up with every dig until about half the hoard had been unearthed, at which point the copper pot was extracted. Both sources agreed that Theodore could not identify the discovery coin, a twenty-dollar gold piece. Theodore may not have been able to decipher or understand the inscription on the coin, which read "TWENTY D."

The newspapers reported its weight, Baltimore News and Post, 9/1/1934, 3.

one might use to pack tomatoes, Henry Grob, BCCC #2, docket A-579, 1934, 61.

Someone later noticed the imprint of a gold coin, Harry Levin, BCCC #2, docket A-579, 1934, 91.

is highly resistant to corrosion, see "Coin World," 9/26/2005, 60, regarding the effects of burying coins of various compositions in soil.

The two used the hammer, Testimony of Theodore Jones, BCCC #2, docket A-579, 1934, 20.

sat on the dirt floor and dreamed dreams, Baltimore Sun, 9/1/1934, 20.

Henry and my dad weren't dumb, Interview with Edward Sines, 3/14/2003.

Part 2 (pp. 25–52)

Chapter 5. Laying Claim (pp. 27–31)

X

He had small feet, Testimony of Henry Grob, BCCC #2, docket A-579, 1934, 63.

I always said I'd be a millionaire, *Baltimore Evening Sun,* 9/1/1934, 3.

Henry and Theodore's first thought, *Baltimore Sun,* 9/1/1934, 20.

Take it out of here, Testimony of Henry Grob, BCCC #2, docket A-579, 1934, 64.

Paul, a soldier at Fort Hoyle, *Baltimore Sun,* 9/2/1934, 3.

paraded around the pile of gold, *Baltimore Sun,* 9/1/1934, 20.

a United States district attorney was quoted, *Baltimore Sun,* 9/2/1934, 3.

He done his best to turn it over to the police, Testimony of Henry Grob, BCCC #2, docket A-579, 1934, 64.

Robert Perry, of Bradford, Ohio, *Dayton Journal,* 9/16/1937, cited in Secret Service gold investigation files, U.S. National Archives, record group 87, entry 29.

Henry and Paul collected Theodore, *Baltimore News* 9/1/1934, 3. Accounts of the comings and goings of Henry, Theodore, and the police on the evening of August 31 are conflicting. The stenographic record of the 1934 litigation indicates that Henry and his brother-in-law Paul went to the police first (64), then went over to Theodore's with the police. The newspapers (for example, *Baltimore Sun,* 9/1/1934, 20) indicate that both boys went to the police first. Regardless of the order, Henry and Theodore were without question acting together.

Theodore had been trying to clean up the gold, Testimony of Theodore Jones, BCCC #2, docket A-579, 1934, 24.

stuck together in bunches, Testimony of Bessie Jones, BCCC #2, docket A-579, 1934, 80.

We've got about $7000 in gold pieces here, *Baltimore News,* 9/1/1934, 3.

a face value of $7882, *Baltimore News,* 9/1/1934, 3. This batch of gold consisted of 218 twenty-dollar gold pieces, 81 tens, 255 fives, 64 two-and-a-halfs, and 1277 ones.

after the legal tangles were ironed out, *Baltimore News,* 9/1/1934, 3.

turned over an additional $3542 worth, *Baltimore News,* 9/1/1934, 3. This consisted of 99 twenty-dollar gold pieces and 1562 one-dollar pieces. The *Baltimore Evening Sun* (9/1/1934, 13) reported that this batch was turned over at Theodore's, while the *Baltimore News* (3) and *Baltimore Sun* (9/1/1934, 20) indicate that the second batch was turned over at the police station. The stenographic record of the 1934 litigation, 24 and 81, agrees with the transfer location of 132 S. Eden.

The boys were rather forthcoming, *Baltimore News,* 9/1/1934, 3.

first statements to the media, *Baltimore News*, 9/1/1934, 3.
new clothes for holidays, Interview with Edward Sines, 3/14/2003.
I was wearing this yesterday, *Baltimore News*, 9/1/1934, 3.

XI

child of Russian Jewish immigrant parents, U. S. Bureau of the Census 1930, Baltimore City, district #209, 4B. The birthplace of Levin's parents is given as "Russia" in the 1930 census; however, Levin's descendants believe the family may have come from what is now Lithuania.
well known defender of the disenfranchised, *Baltimore Sun* obituary, 1/5/1966.
successful attorney, the 1930 census indicates that Levin owned his own home, valued at $15,000 at the time, and was married with two children (U. S. Bureau of the Census 1930, Baltimore, district #209, 4B).
probably on the morning of September 1st, Levin was named as the boys' attorney in the *Baltimore News*, 9/1/34, 3. Henry's mother, on September 1, signed a petition prepared by Harry Levin (BCCC #2, case file 20009A).
the agreement to split the hoard proceeds, *Baltimore Sun* 4/23/1936, 26. The terms of the agreement were not publicly revealed for some time.
may have referred the two families to Levin, *Baltimore News*, 9/1/1934, 1.
Afro-American newspaper in Baltimore quoted Menchine, *Afro-American*, 10/12/1923, 1, also in HLA 6.
The Post was quite open about that part, *Baltimore Post* 10/11/1926, also in HLA 28.
I should be Irish?, *Baltimore Sun*, 10/14/1926, also in HLA 39.
use of the N-word, *Afro-American*, 10/23/1926, 20, also HLA 26. This appeared in an Altfeld advertisement in which Altfeld accused Levin of using this inflammatory slur.
The big corporate interests are firmly entrenched, HLA 19.

Chapter 6. The Baltimore Gold Rush (pp. 32–36)

XII

special guard at 132 S. Eden, *Baltimore Evening Sun*, 9/1/1934, 13.
a look at Harry Chenvin's empty apartment, Testimony of Theodore Jones, BCCC #2, docket A-579, 1934, 37.
seemingly plausible theory, *Baltimore News*, 9/1/1934, 3.
Donaldson was involved in the Brazilian coffee trade, *Baltimore Evening Sun*, 9/1/1934, 1.
The family he had in mind was actually named Wilson, 130 S. Eden was occupied by a John S. Miles in 1870, whose daughters and sons-in-law lived in the house over the next thirty years. One son-in-law, Captain John G. Wilson, imported coffee from Brazil. Wilson likely died before 1900, not being listed in the census that year, while his wife and an elderly sister re-

mained. U.S. Census 1870, Baltimore City third ward, 11, U.S. Census 1880, Baltimore City enumeration district #34, 15, U.S Census 1900, Baltimore City enumeration district #58, 3. Also testimony of Martha Saulsbury Short, BCCC #2, docket A-579, 1934, 239, establishing the residence of Wilson.

dealt with numerous visitors, *Baltimore News,* 9/1/1934, 1.

Her name was Jennie Zimmerman, BCCC #2, case 20345.5. Among the litigants filing was Jennie Zimmerman, on behalf of the heirs of Israel and Ida Schapiro (the spelling of the last name is given variously as "Schapiro" or "Shapiro" by different sources).

conducted their own cellar excavations, *Baltimore News,* 9/1/1934, 3.

scores of claimants are expected, *Baltimore Sun,* 9/1/1934, 9.

Theodore had already lied, *Baltimore News* 9/1/1934, 1. Theodore's age is given as sixteen here, also in the *Baltimore Sun* (9/1/1934, 20) and finally in the *Baltimore Evening Sun* (9/1/1934, 13).

asked him if he had a girlfriend, *Baltimore News,* 9/1/1934, 3.

being supported by the Family Welfare, *Baltimore Sun,* 9/1/1934, 13.

Reporters encouraged local residents, *Baltimore News,* 9/1/1934, 3.

XIII

refused to let numismatic experts look, *Baltimore Sun,* 9/2/1934, 3.

An inventory of the coins taken several months later, opinion of Judge Eugene O'Dunne, published in *The Daily Record,* Baltimore 2/16/1935, 3. At this point, 421 of 2840 one-dollar gold pieces are identified as dateless. Although the eventual auction cataloger of the hoard was able to distinguish dates on most of these coins, the fact that a casual observer could not do the same in February 1935, suggests that these one-dollar gold pieces were damaged. Perry W. Fuller, the auction cataloger, identified only 39 as dateless in his May 1935 auction catalog. Fuller cleaned the coins before the auction, which likely improved the legibility of the inscriptions.

branch mints were upstart backwater affairs, Richard Doty, " 'An onerous & delicate task': Franklin Peale's Mission South," Coinage of the Americas Conference at the American Numismatic Society, New York, November 1989, 67–82.

it would be a pity to melt up such coins, *Baltimore Sun,* 9/2/1934, 3.

A cashier at the Baltimore branch of the Federal Reserve Bank, *Washington Post,* 9/2/1934, 2.

licensed by the U.S. Government, *Chicago Daily News,* 4/5/1933, 5, advertisement for the U.S. Smelting Works. Also *Chicago Daily News,* 9/4/1934, 11.

a common practice at the time, Interview with Gilbert Sandler, 7/13/2004. Sandler, a Baltimore historian, indicated that door-to-door commerce was much more popular during this period than the present day, with junk men going from house to house collecting glass and scrap metal, including old gold items such as eyeglass frames.

Abraham Kimmel, a Brooklyn resident, *Brooklyn Eagle*, 8/6/1942,16, cited in Secret Service gold investigations, U.S. National Archives, Record Group 87, entry 29.

the celebrated mystery writer, Mary Roberts Rinehart, *Saturday Evening Post*, 4/8/1933. The serial was combined and eventually sold as a single volume under the title, "The Album."

Chapter 7. A Weekend of Labor (pp. 37–44)

XIV

Robert King, the plumber who recently fixed the pipes, *Baltimore News* 9/3/1934, 3. King's name was unknown by the reporter, but his identity is fixed by King's later court testimony in BCCC #2, docket A-579, 1934, 147–49.

Both were reported to have taken trips, *Baltimore Sun*, 9/2/1934, 3 and *Baltimore News*, 9/3/1934, 3. The *Sun* reported that Grob went out of town with brother-in-law Paul Eberhart, while the *News* reported that Jones went to visit relatives (probably his siblings) in Pennsylvania.

planned to have another go at the cellar, *Baltimore News*, 9/3/1934, 3

lights were burning bright in almost every cellar, *Baltimore American*, 9/2/1934, 3.

Levin was hospitalized and not allowed to see his first child, interview with Harriet Berkis (daughter of Harry Levin), 1/10/2005. Harriet was born December 9, 1918.

Levin's brief tipped his hand, BCCC #2, case file 20009A.

I am convinced they are the rightful owners, *New York Times*, 9/4/1934, 21.

An editorial in the Baltimore News, *Baltimore News*, 9/3/1934, 18.

gave potential litigants ninety days, *Baltimore Evening Sun*, 9/11/1934, 15, also *Baltimore News* 9/10/1934, 16.

XV

Judge John Benjamin Guerry, Georgia Court of Appeals, 1935, 179 S.E. 634.

a standard study on treasure trove law, Sir George Hill, *Treasure Trove in Law and Practice* (London: Oxford University Press, 1936), vi.

A university law review, *Boston University Law Review*, June 1935, 656–60.

no doubt done a good bit of research on the subject, Levin's son, Marshall Levin, also an attorney, later had the opportunity to demonstrate the family's knowledge of treasure law while a Harvard Law School student under Edward "Bull" Warren, one of the most feared professors in the history of that esteemed institution. Levin, the son, was to become no less a remarkable figure than his father. During World War II he enciphered and deciphered communications between Churchill, Stalin, and Roosevelt. Later in life he lectured at Harvard Law School, emphasizing that "terror does not reign" in his classroom. Warren was sufficiently impressed by the case to make reference to it in his *Cases on Property* (2nd edition, 1938). Interview with Robert Levin (grandson of Harry, son of Marshall), 7/6/2004. Also see "The Greatest Interruption," "Harvard Law Bulletin," Fall 2001.

The classic law school example is that of unattended horse manure, Haslam v. Lockwood, 37 Conn. 500 (1871). The author is grateful to John Kleeberg for this citation.

In modern times, the definition has sometimes been extended, American courts have held since 1861 that paper currency is treasure trove as well. See Huthmacher v. Harris's Administrators, 80 Am. Dec. 502, 503–4 (Pa. 1861). The author is grateful to John Kleeberg for this citation.

if a stranger accidentally drops cash on the floor of a hotel, Hamaker v. Blanchard, 90 Pa. 377. In this case the cash was proved to be not the property of a guest and was awarded to the chambermaid who litigated for it.

the chambermaid is not so lucky, *Jackson v. Steinberg,* 186 Or. 129.

Jesus likens the Kingdom of Heaven to a treasure in a field, Matthew 13:44.

An earlier Old Testament passage, Deuteronomy 22:1–3.

Contemporary Roman practice, Hill, 13.

English common law...awarded all treasure trove to the Crown, Hill, 187.

prosecutions for failure to disclose treasure trove, Hill, 226.

Levin searched carefully for cases which supported his cause, these cases were cited in a Levin brief, BCCC #2, case 21483.5.

XVI

A 1922 case in Indiana, N.E. 922.

sudden riches and duplicity are no strangers, 44 Or. 108, 74 Pac. 913.

I meant to bury it there, 58 Or. 218, 114 Pac. 100.

XVII

the cortege included the Baltimore city council, Scott Sumpter Sheads and Daniel Carroll Toomey, *Baltimore in the Civil War,* (Linthicum, MD: Toomey Press, 1991), 81.

among whose members was one Andrew J. Saulsbury, testimony of Elizabeth Saulsbury Audoun (a granddaughter), BCCC #2, docket A-579, 1934, 181. Audoun placed Saulsbury on the city council in 1865, though another source indicates he served only from 1868–1870, see J. Thomas Scharf, *History of Baltimore City and County,* (Philadelphia, PA: Louis H. Everts, 1881), 193.

lived at 132 S. Eden Street, The exact date Saulsbury and his family moved into 132 S. Eden is unknown. Elizabeth Saulsbury identified the year as 1865, BCCC #2, docket A-579, 1934, 178. The family previously resided one block west, at 138 S. Central Street, per the 1865 Baltimore city directory, and also according to the Elizabeth Saulsbury testimony (174).

Chapter 8. Andrew Saulsbury (pp. 45–52)

XVIII

two young black women, U. S. Bureau of the Census 1870, Baltimore City, third ward, 11, also testimony of Elizabeth Saulsbury Audoun, BCCC #2, docket A-579, 1934, 181.

may have been emancipated by Lincoln's 1863 proclamation, Maryland had a large population of free blacks before the Civil War, numbering eighty-four thousand in 1860. Daniel R. Randall, Cooperation in Maryland and the South, *Johns Hopkins University Studies in Historical and Political Science, Sixth Series, Nos. 11–12,* 1888, 512.

Lincoln's funeral train through Baltimore, Scott Sumpter Sheads and Daniel Carroll Toomey, *Baltimore in the Civil War,* (Linthicum, MD: Toomey Press, 1991), 81.

He gave presents in gold to all, testimony of Margaret Saulsbury Short, BCCC #2, docket A-579, 1934, 236.

Queen Victoria in 1840, accidentally ingested a Christmas coin, Alan Percival Major, Coins and Christmas Pudding, *The Numismatist,* December 1983, 2496–97. Also see *The Telegraph,* 10/18/2005, on the demise of coins in Christmas puddings in modern day Britain.

United States mint got involved in the gift giving, Walter Breen, *Walter Breen's Encyclopedia of United States and Colonial Proof Coins, 1722–1977,* (Albertson, NY:FCI Press, 1977). Production of one-dollar gold piece proofs, particularly in the late 1880s, increased toward the end of each year. Also see Roger Burdette, *Unneeded in Commerce,* "Coin World," 4/17/2006, 96–97, citing Mint correspondence indicating large orders of one-dollar gold pieces near the holiday season.

He did not bother about buying us presents, Testimony of Elizabeth Saulsbury Audoun, BCCC #2, docket A-579, 1934, 185.

gold had a great fascination for a child, Testimony of Elizabeth Saulsbury Audoun, BCCC #2, docket A-579, 1934, 182.

like two cent bronzes and three cent silvers, perfect orgy spending them, Testimony of Martha Saulsbury Short, BCCC #2, docket A-579, 1934, 226. Martha noted that her mother had to take the two- and three-cent coins to a bank for redemption. These coins had been abolished in 1873; see Neil Carothers, *Fractional Money,* (New York: John Wiley & Sons, 1930), 236–38.

wouldn't accept greenbacks at face value, correspondence between William Boerum Wetmore and Samuel and Henry Chapman, 7/3/1904, collection of the American Numismatic Society. Wetmore notes in a letter to the coin dealers Chapman that an 1864 proof set was purchased by his father from the U.S. mint, in the same year, for $101.25 in currency. The proof set had a face value of about forty dollars, mostly in gold. Elsewhere, a Philadelphia coin dealer sold 1868 silver proof sets, consisting of about two dollars face in silver, during their year of issue for $4.50 in greenbacks ("Mason Coin and Stamp Collector's Magazine," March 1868, 112).

selling U.S. treasury gold on the open market, Albert Bushnell Hart, *Salmon Portland Chase,* (Boston, MA: Houghton Mifflin Company, 1899), 284–86.

the saloon keeper, the cigar dealer, and the barber have turned banker, Carothers, 166.

XIX

much like it was in the 1930s, Baltimore City Register of Wills (Inventories), 1874, JHB99, 375, gives a description of the property following Saulsbury's death in 1873.

winding pathways, shady trees and a fountain, see contemporary city maps at the Enoch Pratt Free Library (for example Md. Map 869B1.A3, 1869, part 11), also Scharf's *History of Baltimore City and County,* 280.

never carried a mortgage on the property, Testimony of J. Paul Schmidt, BCCC #2, docket A-579, 1934, 158.

We were very comfortable, Testimony of Elizabeth Saulsbury Audoun, BCCC #2, docket A-579, 1934, 181.

Inside the house one could find, Baltimore City Register of Wills (Inventories), 1874, JHB99, 366. Saulsbury's library was valued at forty-one-dollars, feather beds at fourteen and twelve dollars, and so on.

a 'beautiful home', as one neighbor described it, Testimony of Mae Hudgins Neudecker, BCCC #2, docket A-579, 1934, 219.

seven children in the family by 1870, U. S. Bureau of the Census 1870, Baltimore City, third ward, 11.

The children were 'dressed well', Testimony of Mae Hudgins Neudecker, BCCC #2, docket A-579, 1934, 219.

had been harassed by Union soldiers on at least one occasion, BCCC2, docket A-579, 1934, 231. This was the testimony of one of Saulsbury's daughters, which was cutoff before she could give full details. She had not actually seen it herself and the testimony would have been inadmissible as hearsay.

Two depicting the Confederate generals, Maryland Court of Appeals, Records and Briefs, April 1935, cases 35–36, Saulsbury brief, 20. The paintings may have been the work of James Kimball Harley, a society painter who had done a portrait of Andrew J. Saulsbury himself (BCCC2, docket A-579, 1934, 238). The present day location of the Saulsbury portrait is unknown.

occasionally someone was shot on sight, Robert I. Cottom Jr. and Mary Ellen Hayward, *Maryland in the Civil War: A House Divided* (Baltimore, MD: The Maryland Historical Society, 1994), 112.

He was an ardent Southern sympathizer, Testimony of Elizabeth Saulsbury Audoun, BCCC2, docket A-579, 1934, 196.

Saulsbury passed away young, the collected obituaries of Saulsbury are given in BCCC2, docket A-579, 1934, 169–72.

He had been asthmatic, Testimony of Elizabeth Saulsbury Audoun, BCCC2, docket A-579, 1934, 205.

The minister, a Reverend George W. Powell, BCCC2, docket A-579, 1934, 171–72.

the streets of the city were paved in pure gold, Revelations 21:21.

moth and rust destroy, Matthew 6:19.

she put it at his head in death, Testimony of Martha Saulsbury Short, BCCC2, docket A-579, 1934, 238.

XX

obtained a court order, *Baltimore Evening Sun,* 9/8/1934, 16.

It has been greatly changed, Testimony of Martha Saulsbury Short, BCCC #2, docket A-579, 1934, 233.

a wealthy family associated with the Chesapeake Steamship Company, Interview with Sally Foster (daughter of Reuben Foster), 3/11/2004.

who had reverted to using her maiden name, U. S. Bureau of the Census 1920, Baltimore City, district 282, 8A. Goldie is here listed as divorced.

moved to New York City and entered the garment industry, Interview with Dr. Norman Chenven (son of Isaac Zachary Chenven, grandson of Harry Chenven), 7/5/2003.

worth a trip to Baltimore to sort things out, *Baltimore Evening Sun,* 10/3/1934, 34.

Ernest G. Long, a metal worker, born in Uruguay, U. S. Bureau of the Census 1900, New Jersey, Burlington County, Riverside Township, district # 32, 22.

still others moving to South America, Correspondence, email from Craig D. Lowry, 8/2/2004 and 2/1/2005. Ernest Long's great-great-uncle, Robert K. Lowry, was the first American consul to South America.

had written a book, James Lowry Donaldson, *Sergeant Atkins, A Tale of Adventure Founded on Fact,* (Philadelphia: J.B. Lippincott & Co., 1871).

Hannah White, a seamstress, a Mrs. Hannah White is listed in Baltimore city directories between 1829 and 1842, as living on Pitt Street, between Eden and Caroline (one block east of Eden).

Mrs. Thomas H. Green of Detroit, BCCC #2, case 20345.5 gives a list of nine parties to the suit. A tenth is mentioned in the case testimony, BCCC #2, docket A-579, 1934, 363–64.

XXI

found themselves inundated with mail, *Baltimore Evening Sun,* 9/6/1934, 38. An example of one of these letters remains in the possession of the Sines family.

reading Theodore's lament in the newspaper, his stiff new clothes, *Baltimore American,* 9/2/1934, L3.

put a bit of cash in Theodore's pockets, *Baltimore Sun,* 9/2/1934, 3.

Prowlers, Beware, *Baltimore Evening Sun,* 9/11/1934, 34. Bessie Jones later suggested the gun was more recently purchased as a result of hearing noises in the apartment, *Baltimore Evening Sun* , 9/3/1935, 40.

pistol packing momma, the author acknowledges Dr. Joel Orosz for suggesting this appellation.

adding a crucial note to the typed order, BCCC #2, file 20345.5, court order 12/4/1934.

Such niceties were lost, *Baltimore News,* 9/3/1934, 3.

an altercation with a recreation supervisor, *Baltimore Sun,* 9/15/1934, 20.

Part 3 (pp. 53–80)

Chapter 9. Theodore's Testimony (pp. 55–58)

XXII

Sixteen, Testimony of Theodore Jones, BCCC #2, docket A-579, 1934, 5.

A deep sense of loyalty to Henry, Testimony of Theodore Jones, BCCC #2, docket A-579, 1934, 26.

A most implausible rumor, Testimony of Bessie Jones, BCCC #2, docket A-579, 1934, 335. The Findlay-French attorneys produced receipts for the photography work totaling thirty-five dollars (347).

It is a bucket, dilapidated, disintegrated, Judge Eugene O'Dunne, BCCC #2, docket A-579, 1934, 90.

We started going down there every day, Testimony of Henry Grob, BCCC #2, docket A-579, 1934, 55.

XXIII

paint crosses on their homes, S. M. Dubnow, *History of the Jews in Russia and Poland, Volume II,* (Philadelphia: The Jewish Publication Society of America, 1946), 253.

A chronicler described the exodus from the city, Ibid., 406.

Europe was not blind, *London Times,* 11/5/1890.

Chapter 10. The Saulsbury and Chenven Claims (pp. 59–62)

XXIV

nearly half the Jewish population, S. M. Dubnow, *History of the Jews in Russia and Poland,* Volume III, (Philadelphia: The Jewish Publication Society of America, 1920), 24.

riots in Odessa claimed three hundred Jewish lives, Ibid., 127.

Nearly half million, Ibid., 148.

Harry Chenven and his wife Goldie, Harry's immigration date is from, BCCC

NOTES TO PAGES 59–62

#2, docket A-579, 99. Goldie's immigration date is from the 1920 U.S. Census, Baltimore City, enumeration district 282, 8A.

many who lost their minds from the horrors, Dubnow, Volume III, 129.

no visible means of support, BCCC #2, docket A-579, 1934, 115.

a panhandler living in a dollar a week rooming house, *Philadelphia Inquirer,* 4/2/1936 and 4/3/1936, cited in the Secret Service gold investigation files, U.S. National Archives, record group 87, entry 29. Much of the currency was in gold certificates, which had been withdrawn from circulation in tandem with gold coinage.

an elderly woman living without heat, *Cincinnati Post,* 2/27/1940, cited in the Secret Service gold investigation files, U.S. National Archives, record group 87, entry 29. The hoard, containing some French coins, was thought to have originated with the woman's parents, her father being of French ancestry.

several problems with the Chenven presentation, BCCC #2, docket A-579, 1934, 117–18, also *The Daily Record,* Baltimore, 2/11/1935, 3.

his was a dark character, Interview with Dr. Norman Chenven, 7/5/2003.

XXV

a detailed inventory of his estate, Baltimore City Register of Wills (Inventories), 1874, JHB 99, 365–78.

lingered in probate, Baltimore City Register of Wills (Accounts of Sale), 1898, TWM 77, 346–67.

move full time into real estate, BCCC #2, docket A-579, 1934, 179–80. Saulsbury left Armstrong and opened his own real estate office in 1871.

Andrew's time as a city councilman, *Journal of Proceedings of the Second Branch of the City Council of Baltimore at the Sessions 1867–1868,* (Baltimore: John Cox, Printer, 1868), also *Journal of Proceedings of the Second Branch of the City Council of Baltimore at the Sessions 1868–1869,* (Baltimore: E. G. Armiger, Printer, 1869).

A friend of Saulsbury's, James Webb, Webb was a pallbearer at Saulsbury's funeral in 1873 and also acted as an administrator of Saulsbury's estate, BCCC #2, docket A-579, 1934, 160, 172. James Webb is listed as being a soap and candle manufacturer in the 1864 Baltimore city directory, on Ensor Street, and may have had a prior business relationship with Saulsbury and his partner James Armstrong.

a former partner, James Armstrong, the 1864 Baltimore city directory lists "Armstrong, James & Co." as a soap and candle manufacturer on Concord Street near Pratt. Elizabeth Saulsbury Audoun stated that her father was associated with this firm, BCCC #2, docket A-579, 1934, 179. On the personal side, James Armstrong and Thomas Armstrong were both pallbearers at Saulsbury's funeral, BCCC #2, docket A-579, 1934, 172.

Chapter 11. The Copper Pot (pp. 63–68)

XXVI

son of Irish immigrants, U. S. Bureau of the Census 1930, Baltimore, district #213, 1.

Saulsbury attorneys started the questioning, BCCC #2, docket A-579, 1934, 264–69.

Harry Levin now took up the cause, BCCC #2, docket A-579, 1934, 269–76.

XXVII

still living on relief, *Baltimore Evening Sun,* 9/3/1935, 8.

Bessie Jones didn't like taking relief, *Baltimore Evening Sun,* 2/16/1935, 1 and 14.

Baltimore Emergency Relief Commission, Baltimore Emergency Relief Commission First Annual Statistical Report 9/1/1933–8/31/1934, Howard C. Beck, Administrator.

acquiring the reputation of being chiselers, Richard Lowitt and Maurine Beasley, eds., *One Third of a Nation: Lorena Hickok Reports on the Great Depression,* (Urbana: University of Illinois Press, 1981), 345.

preserving the economic balance of the world, *The Daily Record,* Baltimore, 2/16/1935, 3.

so it will cause no more trouble, BCCC #2, docket A-579, 1934, 285.

possession itself is sometimes a strong factor, *The Daily Record,* Baltimore, 2/16/1935, 3.

planned to consult with Perry W. Fuller, Letter from Benjamin Bratton to W.H. Moran, January 3, 1935. U.S. National Archives, Record Group 87, closed investigations file C-11369. The report indicates that Fuller consulted a 1935 copy of Wayte Raymond's *Standard Catalog of United States Coins and Currency.* Raymond's *Catalog,* commencing in 1934, was one of the first annual guides to rare coin values.

all parties involved to settle out of court, *Baltimore Sun,* 1/27/1935, 6, also *Baltimore Evening Sun,* 2/9/1935, 18.

offered the Findlay-French team twenty-five percent, *Baltimore Evening Sun,* 2/16/1935, 1.

the journalistic atmosphere with which it has been surrounded, appellant's brief to the Maryland Court of Appeals, April 1935, docket #35, 5.

she had lost any legal standing, Courts are split on the question of whether the ground rent owner or the homeowner has the right to items found. The opinion in Rofrano v. Duffy, 291 F. 2d 848, 850 (2d Cir. 1961), authored by the eminent judge Charles Clark, would support the Schapiro position. The author is grateful to John Kleeberg for this citation.

Chapter 12. Judge O'Dunne and the Saulsbury Claim (pp. 69–73)

XXVIII

the court in session on Saturdays, *Baltimore Evening Sun,* 1/16/1935, 4. Also
BCCC #2, docket A-579, 1934, 349.

lasted five hours, *The Daily Record,* Baltimore, 2/11/1935, 3. No transcripts or
notes of the attorney's oral arguments are known, their only surviving record is in the opinion of Judge O'Dunne, as published in the *Daily Record.*

gold pieces stolen from the New Orleans mint, "The Numismatist," 9/1994,
1263–69, and "The Numismatist," 3/2000, 263–64.

produced a one-dollar gold piece dated 1859, BCCC #2, docket A-579, 1934,
244. This coin remains in the Saulsbury family today.

A closer examination of the one-dollar gold pieces, author's analysis. There
is no surviving record that O'Dunne or the attorneys considered the mintage distribution. The point may have been raised in the oral arguments by
opposing counsel.

their original mintages, R. S. Yeoman, *A Guide Book of United States Coins*
(Atlanta: Whitman Publishing, 2004), 201–202.

Chapter 13. The Findlay-French Claims (pp. 74–80)

XXIX

submitted a thirty page brief, *The Daily Record,* Baltimore, 2/11/1935, 3. This
document, as well as the competing brief from Levin, has been lost. However, much of the material was almost certainly recycled in the briefs to
the Maryland Court of Appeals (April 1935, docket #35). Judge O'Dunne's
opinion, published in the *Daily Record,* gives many indications of what was
contained in the Levin and Niles briefs.

an attorney named Sigmund Levin, the exact relationship of Sigmund and
Harry O. Levin is unclear. Sigmund, known as "Siggy," was likely a cousin or
second cousin. Interview with Harriet Berkis (daughter of Harry O. Levin),
2/9/2005.

Louisiana, heavily influenced by the French. *New Orleans Times Picayune,*
10/29/1982, 1. A nineteenth-century hoard uncovered at a downtown New
Orleans construction site in 1982 suggested that the truly operative law in
Louisiana was one of finder's keepers, as two hundred bystanders, many
dressed in business attire, descended into the pit and grabbed whatever
could be had.

He mounted the door with hinges and added a padlock, BCCC #2, docket
A-579, 1934, 125.

but under questioning from O'Dunne, BCCC #2, docket A-579, 1934, 129–
31.

Fleetwood testified that the door was always kept locked, BCCC #2, docket
A-579, 1934, 143.

The Kalis plumber, Robert King, testified likewise, BCCC #2, docket A-579, 1934, 147–49.

Harry Fleischer, a tenant in the second floor front apartment, BCCC #2, docket A-579, 1934, 252–63.

photographs of the cellar, French Exhibit A, Maryland Court of Appeals records and briefs, April 1935, docket #35.

Julia D'Alesandro, living in the first floor rear apartment, BCCC #2, docket A-579, 1934, 314–20.

Bessie Jones, Theodore's mother, no doubt understanding the import of the moment, BCCC #2, docket A-579, 1934, 334–38.

The records Kalis kept didn't help much, BCCC #2, docket A-579, 1934, 331.

a receipt from a local hardware store, French Exhibits B and C, Maryland Court of Appeals records and briefs, April 1935, docket #35, contain a copy of the Kalis work ledger.

Kalis couldn't say for sure what the new lock was for, BCCC #2, docket A-579, 1934, 362.

XXX

When there was no war going on, he declared one, *Baltimore Evening Sun*, 7/8/1981.

Good copy could always be found in his courtroom, Report of the Mid-Winter Meeting and 65th Annual Meeting of the Maryland State Bar Association, 1960, 18.

sending more than one man to the whipping post for wife-beating, *Baltimore Sun*, 10/31/1959, 13. See Also Gilbert Sandler, *Small Town Baltimore: An Album of Memories* (Baltimore: The Johns Hopkins University Press, 2002), 19.

a parody opinion written on the occasion of O'Dunne's retirement, Proceedings At Testimonial Dinner On The Retirement Of Hon. Eugene O'Dunne As Member Of The Supreme Bench, 6/25/1945, 9–13, also reprinted in the *Daily Record*, 11/5/1945.

Suppose the boys had been hunting rabbits in a public field, *Daily Record*, Baltimore, 2/16/1935, 4.

I'm going to get my mother a home out Canton way, *Baltimore Evening Sun*, 2/16/1935, 1.

talked about reuniting their families, *Baltimore News and Post*, 2/16/1935, 2.

Theodore had some concerns, *Baltimore News and Post*, 2/16/1935, 2.

The two boys made an appearance on local radio, *Baltimore Sun*, 2/17/1935, 15.

a remarkably similar tale of interred gold, Secret Service gold investigation files, 8/5/1941, U.S. National Archives, record group 87, entry 29.

Part 4 (pp. 81–97)

Chapter 14. Perry Fuller, Stamp and Coin Dealer (pp. 83–89)

XXXI

A washing machine for his mother, *Baltimore News,* 9/1/1934, 3, also *Baltimore American,* 9/2/1934, L3.

an electric washing machine showed up in her apartment, *Washington Post* 9/2/1934, M1, and BCCC #2, docket A-579, 1934, 336. Also *Baltimore News,* 9/1/1934, 3.

I think it caused trouble in the family, recollection of discussion with author's grandmother Lillie Augsburger, c. 1995.

doubled to a dollar and twenty cents in November, BCCC #2, docket A-579, 1934, 345–46.

Residential electric service, as late as 1930 only 70% of U.S. homes had electric service, David E. Nye, *Electrifying America* (Cambridge, MA: The MIT Press, 1990), 261.

not everyone on their block owned a radio, the 1930 census noted which residences had a radio set. U.S. Census 1930, Baltimore City, enumeration district #37, 22–3.

Ruth's Tavern on the ground floor of her apartment, *Baltimore Sun,* 2/17/1935. Also 1930 census (Baltimore City, enumeration district 30, 12A).

borrowed from Harry O. Levin, Statement of Ruth Grob to Secret Service Agent George Almoney, taken 9/9/1935. U.S. National Archives, Record Group 87, closed investigations file C-11369.

forced to devise a secret signal, *Baltimore News and Post,* 2/16/1935, 2.

believed that the government would not seize the gold coins, *Baltimore Sun,* 9/2/1934, 3.

found himself going bankrupt, Baltimore City Circuit Court #2, case 20020, 1935.

Perry was a southern boy, Fuller Family Archive, a selection of news clippings, and written recollections of Julia Fuller (Fuller's second wife), supplied to the author by Priscilla Menzies (Fuller's daughter).

He became a full time collectibles dealer around 1925, *Baltimore Sun,* 7/17/1979, Perry Fuller obituary.

in a house valued at twenty thousand dollars, U. S. Bureau of the Census 1930, Baltimore City, district #520, 12A.

XXXII

both announced the same day, *Baltimore Evening Sun,* 2/16/1935, 1.

I'm only a stoplight on the way, *Baltimore Sun,* 10/31/1959, 13.

The feds ultimately had to admit, *Baltimore Evening Sun,* 2/21/1935, 10.

would auction for around thirty thousand dollars, *Baltimore Evening Sun,* 2/21/1935, 14.

choice was probably made by Charles A. McNabb and Harry O. Levin, *Baltimore Evening Sun,* 3/7/1935, 13.

was an avid stamp collector and client, *Baltimore Sun Magazine,* 5/2/1954, detailed H. Findlay French's activity as a stamp collector. Also interview with G. Ross French (son of H. Findlay French), 1/5/2004.

Fuller and Mary Findlay had joined the Society on the very same day, *Maryland Historical Magazine,* 1930 (vol. 25), 83.

H. Findlay French wrote book reviews, for example, *Maryland Historical Magazine,* 1945 (vol. 40), 166.

one of them had represented one of Fuller's creditors, Isaac Lobe Straus represented a party who had consigned paintings to Fuller. Baltimore City Circuit Court #2 file 20020, 1935.

there was some thought to having the sale in New York, *Baltimore Evening Sun,* 2/21/1935, 14.

Fuller advertised the sale in New York, *New York Times Book Review,* 4/28/1935, 26.

won its fair share of free publicity in the newspapers, for example, *New York Times* 4/30/1935, 16.

consulted with his dentist, Fuller Family Archive, newspaper clipping from January, 1976.

They're not polished, *Baltimore Evening Sun,* 4/18/1935, 8.

Fuller got the number down to thirty-nine, Perry Fuller auction catalog, 5/2/1935, lot 438.

Chapter 15. The Findlay-French Appeal (pp. 90–92)

XXXIII

most of the value was in the one-dollar and twenty dollar pieces, the count here is the author's analysis of the auction catalog. Slightly differing tallies appeared in press and court records; see "Rare Coin Review," November 2002, 35–43 for further detail.

was probably thirty or less, present catalogers suggest that twenty or less exist today. For example, Sotheby's/Stack's Dallas Bank Collection, 10/29/2001, lot 16. This particular example realized ninety-two thousand dollars.

matchless uncirculated gems, recollections of Thomas Elder in *Hobbies Magazine,* March 1939, 88.

Many appear never to have been in circulation, *Baltimore Evening Sun,* 4/18/1935, 8.

a five dollar gold piece was worth five dollars and thirty cents, Q. David Bowers, *United States Gold Coins: An Illustrated History,* (Los Angeles: Bowers and Ruddy Galleries, 1982), 206.

lesser sized Civil War era hoard, Secret Service gold investigation files, U.S.

National Archives, record group 87, entry 29. This gold was discovered by workers on the farm of A.L. Bain in Kerens, Texas. The Secret Service, in consultation with the U.S. Mint, determined the gold coins to be of numismatic value, and Mr. Bain was permitted to sell the coins as such. Also see the *Corsicana Daily Sun*, April 16, 1947. The author is indebted to David Ginsburg for locating the contemporary press reference.

not a single mintmark was noted, the total coinage of one-dollar gold pieces from their inception in 1849 until 1856 was sixteen million, of which seven percent were struck at branch mints.

would arrange for the boys to get a coin or two, *Baltimore News*, 5/3/1935, 4.

XXXIV

have always felt a definite moral obligation, Maryland Court of Appeals, Records and Briefs, April 1935, cases 35–36, French brief, 5–6.

a condition of Levin agreeing to the public sale, Maryland Court of Appeals, Records and Briefs, April 1935, cases 35–36, French brief, 5. The brief refers to a separate written agreement between Levin and the Findlay-French ladies. A copy of this document has not been found.

seafaring associates who had left the treasure behind, Maryland Court of Appeals, Records and Briefs, April 1935, cases 35–36, Saulsbury brief, 29–35.

what the Court conceived to be equity and fairness to poor boys, Maryland Court of Appeals, Records and Briefs, April 1935, cases 35–36, French brief, 18.

treasure trove should be thought of as mislaid property, Maryland Court of Appeals, Records and Briefs, April 1935, cases 35–36, French brief, 25.

a similar case only one month previous, *Groover v. Tippins,* 179 S.E. 634.

Hard cases make bad law, Maryland Court of Appeals, Records and Briefs, April 1935, cases 35–36, French brief, 45–6.

Chapter 16. Trespassers or Discoverers? (pp. 93–97)

XXXV

learned Chancellor, Levin brief, 6.

work done on the house prior to their moving in, Elizabeth Saulsbury Audoun, BCCC2, 179.

didn't even purchase the property until June, 1865, Maryland Court of Appeals, Records and Briefs, April 1935, cases 35–36, French brief, 93.

Reuben Foster had produced a gold dollar dated 1859, Maryland Court of Appeals, Records and Briefs, April 1935, cases 35–36, Levin brief, 12.

whether American treasure trove was to be treated as lost property or mislaid property, Ibid., Maryland Court of Appeals, Records and Briefs, April 1935, cases 35–36, Levin brief, 47.

XXXVI

printed three thousand catalogs, *Baltimore Sun,* 4/28/1935, 13.

Fuller's office on 9 East Hamilton Street, *New York Times Book Review,* 4/28/1935, 26.

predicted the hoard would net twenty-five thousand dollars, *Baltimore Sun,* 4/30/1935, 5.

exhibiting the coins by appointment, *Baltimore Sun,* 4/30/1935, 5.

under police guard, *Baltimore Evening Sun,* 5/2/1935, 40.

underneath the glass chandeliers, *Baltimore Sun,* 5/3/1935, 26.

one hundred in attendance, *Baltimore Sun,* 5/3/1935, 26.

some dealers, some collectors, and some mere spectators. Edward L. Weikert Jr., "Numismatic Scrapbook Magazine, "November 1953, 1038, indicates that most were collectors, while another source indicates that most were dealers (*Baltimore Sun,* 5/3/1935, 15). Weikert, a long-time coin collector, would be the more reliable source.

mail bids had been received for every lot, *Baltimore News,* 5/2/1935, 21.

gifting a Thomas Jefferson letter to the Maryland Historical Society, *Maryland Historical Magazine,* volume 38 (1943), 96.

a spirited bidder who won other lots, *Baltimore Sun,* 5/3/1935, 15.

a Samuel Glenn of Boydton, Virginia, Ibid.

being approved for membership, "The Numismatist," 6/1935, 389.

John Zug, a fellow member, "The Numismatist," 6/1935, 383, 389.

A friend of Zug's, The Numismatist, 12/1949, 730–31.

romance of Civil War era gold, "The Numismatist," 5/1943, 356.

came to the auction late by one account, Edward L. Weikert Jr. "Numismatic Scrapbook Magazine," November 1953, 1037–38.

left early by another, *Baltimore Evening Sun,* May 3, 1935, 26.

I know but look at that, *Baltimore Sun,* 5/3/1935, 15.

folding it in half before he even left, *Baltimore News,* 9/3/1935, 2. This photograph, depicting Henry and Theodore in suits, was likely taken at the May auction sale. It shows Theodore holding a creased paper object, likely the same creased catalog that remains in the Sines family today.

The auction realized almost twenty thousand dollars, *Baltimore Sun,* 4/23/1936, 26. The exact figure reported to Judge O'Dunne was $19746.15. The prices realized list from the auction suggests a figure one hundred dollars lower. Combined with the fact the auction catalog describes 3,508 coins, whereas previous press accounts gave the figure of 3,558, this author theorizes that Fuller held out fifty one-dollar gold pieces for personal use and paid for them at two dollars each (a generous price as most in the auction sold for twenty or thirty cents less). These were possibly distributed to persons associated with the hoard as souvenirs, or sold later by Fuller.

XXXVII

The Court being equally divided, *Daily Record,* 7/6/1935, 7.

filed a motion for reargument, *Findlay vs. Jones* Chronology, found in BCCC #2, file 21483A.

under the control of Charles A. McNabb, *Baltimore Sun,* 7/4/1935, 17.

Perry Fuller presented a bill, *Baltimore Sun,* 4/23/1936, 26.

would park a Chevrolet sedan far down the street, BCCC #2, 9/20/1935, 76.

drove over to the Henry Grob residence, BCCC #2, 9/20/1935, 232.

often times Theodore was at the wheel, BCCC #2, 9/20/1935, 74.

XXXVIII

Bessie had been photographed in the papers, *Baltimore Evening Sun,* 9/1/1934, 3, also *Baltimore Evening Sun,* 2/16/1935, 1.

Rummel, a World War I veteran, City of Baltimore Health Department, Death Certificate #F-75884, 12/26/1940.

self described all-around man, Testimony of Philip Rummel, BCCC #2, case 20345.5, 43.

in bed for most of that year, Testimony of Frances Rummel, BCCC #2, case 20345.5, 252.

the family had gone out that evening, *Baltimore Evening Sun,* 9/3/1935, 40.

a house they wanted to buy in Overlea, *Baltimore News,* 9/3/1935, 2.

trudged over to the Eastern Police Station, Testimony of Philip Rummel, BCCC #2, 9/20/1935, 44.

their apartment had been ransacked, *Baltimore Evening Sun,* 9/3/1935, 40.

knives scattered on the floor, *Baltimore News,* 9/3/1935, 2.

thirty one hundred dollars in cash and five hundred dollars in gold, Testimony of Philip Rummel, BCCC #2, 9/20/1935, 49–50.

Part V (pp. 99–121)

Chapter 17. A New Turn of Events (pp. 101–107)

XXXIX

later explained the situation in court, BCCC #2, 9/20/1935, 46–8.

the next story from the family, *Baltimore Evening Sun,* 9/3/1935, 40.

Theodore summed it up, *Baltimore News,* 9/3/1935, 2.

the lieutenant later testified, BCCC #2, 9/20/1935, 19–20.

now the curse is on me, *Baltimore News,* 9/3/1935, 2.

hit him over the head, *Baltimore Evening Sun,* 9/3/1935, 40.

surprised to hear the family had any money, *Baltimore Evening Sun,* 9/3/1935, 8.

XL

fantastic tale of a second find, *Washington Post*, 10/3/1935, 11.

someone went through there with a plough, BCCC #2, 9/20/1935, 226.

dug up thoroughly after the first find, *Baltimore Sun*, 9/4/1935, 4.

Opinion is about evenly divided, letter from Secret Service operative Benjamin Bratton to Secret Service Chief W. H. Moran, undated but almost certainly September 1935. U.S. National Archives, Record Group 87, closed investigations file C-11369.

he also ordered that no coins, *Baltimore Evening Sun*, 9/17/1935, 11.

engaging a private detective, letter from Secret Service operative Benjamin Bratton to Secret Service Chief W. H. Moran, undated but almost certainly September 1935. U.S. National Archives, Record Group 87, closed investigations file C-11369.

I know nothing about it, *Baltimore Evening Sun*, 9/3/1935, 8.

Judge O'Dunne allowed a statement from Levin, BCCC #2, 9/20/1935, 3.

conducted without even stopping for lunch, Judge Eugene O'Dunne opinion, published in the *Daily Record*, Baltimore, 10/5/1935, 3.

XLI

we was digging around, BCCC #2, 9/20/1935, 150.

I can't tell you what Theodore said, BCCC #2, 9/20/1935, 222.

about in May, BCCC #2, 9/20/1935, 207.

Chapter 18. The Families Celebrate (pp. 108–111)

XLII

You don't know me and I don't know you, BCCC #2 9/20/1935, 196.

she took a beating, *Washington Post*, 9/4/1935, 3.

deposits starting June 10th, Ruth Grob deposited one thousand dollars at the Canton National Bank and twelve hundred dollars at the Equitable Trust company. The remainder of the original thirty-four hundred was used as pocket money. The bank records were presented at the trial. BCCC #2, 9/20/1935, 191–92.

close the place and lock the door, BCCC #2, 9/20/1935, 198. Also statement of Ruth Grob to Secret Service Agent George Almoney, taken 9/9/1935. U.S. National Archives, Record Group 87, closed investigations file C-11369.

moved out of their Caroline Street apartment, BCCC #2, 9/20/1935, 189. The new address was 1212 S. Highland Avenue (the court transcription incorrectly states "1212 S. Collington" in some places).

1929 Ford coupe, 1932 Ford V-8, BCCC #2, 9/20/1935, 214–15.

getting some dental gold work, BCCC #2 9/20/1935, 193. Also interview with G. Ross French (grandson of Elizabeth French, co-owner of 132 S. Eden), 1/5/2004, who stated that one of the boys' mothers had her teeth pulled and filled in with gold replacements.

XLIII

negotiated a price of twelve hundred and fifty, BCCC #2, 9/20/1935, 113.

bought an old Ford, BCCC #2, 9/20/1935, 105, 158.

broke down at least once, BCCC #2, 9/20/1935, 176.

new and unblemished 1935 Plymouth, BCCC #2, 9/20/1935, 159.

you are all right, you are my father, BCCC #2, 9/20/1935, 73.

hadn't seen my brother and sister, BCCC #2, 9/20/1935, 171.

large amount of cash and gold, Bessie Jones put the figure at $2,500 in currency and $2,000 in gold (BCCC #2, 9/20/1935, 100), conflicting with Rummel's testimony that it was $3,100 in currency only (BCCC #2, 9/20/1935, 62).

brother Eugene and sister Thelma, BCCC #2, 9/20/1935, 63, 97–8. Thelma's married name was Hallenbaugh.

I thought it was best to take it along, BCCC #2, 9/20/1935, 62–3.

currency in her daughter's safe deposit box, BCCC #2, 9/20/1935, 97.

no bank account in Baltimore, BCCC #2, 9/20/1935, 121.

sorry they did not leave it there, BCCC #2, 9/20/1935, 26.

older brother Eli, U.S. Bureau of the Census 1920, Baltimore City, district #203, 29. The last name is misspelled here as "Marill."

Chapter 19. The Merrill Brothers (pp. 112–116)

XLIV

display in a department store, BCCC #2, 9/20/1935, 249.

knocked on the door as 132 S. Eden, BCCC #2, 9/20/1935, 229.

Rummel explained it later, BCCC #2, 9/20/1935, 15, 55.

Eli doing the negotiating, BCCC #2, 9/20/1935, 231. Philip Rummel recalled a sales figure of $625 for the first batch, while the Merrill brothers independently put the number at $605.

taking care not to park in front of the building, BCCC #2, 9/20/1935, 76.

a lot of foolish and funny things, BCCC #2, 9/20/1935, 243.

don't pester me any more, BCCC #2, 9/20/1935, 59.

a person that gets a little excited, BCCC #2, 9/20/1935, 77.

she became very excited, BCCC #2, 9/20/1935, 233.

XLIV

The lawyers have them already, this quote appears in a press account, *Baltimore Sun*, 9/21/1935, 4, but not in the trial transcript. O'Dunne may have told the stenographer to leave it out of the record.

The police themselves had stolen the cash, Interview with Edward Sines (son of Theodore Jones), 3/14/2003.

We did not list the dates of the ones, BCCC #2, 9/20/1935, 235.

Merrill produced an inventory, BCCC #2, 9/20/1935, 250.

XLV

very seldom said anything, BCCC #2, 9/20/1935, 259.
the boy who found the gold, Interview with David R. Rummel, 5/18/2002.
in bed for six months, BCCC #2, 9/20/1935, 256.
he always talked in Jewish, BCCC #2, 9/20/1935, 84.
almost anybody would have been so tempted, Judge Eugene O'Dunne, *Daily Record*, Baltimore, 10/5/1935, 3.

Chapter 20. No Pot to be Found (pp. 117–121)

XLVI

according to Theodore, BCCC #2, 9/20/1935, 146–48.
Henry testified likewise, BCCC #2, 9/20/1935, 210–11.
used the word without being prompted, BCCC 9/20/1935, 117, 147.
moved out just a few days prior, BCCC #2, 9/20/1935, 138.
like it was nailed up, BCCC #2, 9/20/1935, 227.
still had the first pot in his safe, BCCC #2, 9/20/1935, 268.

XLVII

inspecting an electric pumping machine, *Baltimore Sun*, 9/5/1935, 24.
was given orally, *Daily Record*, Baltimore, 10/5/1935, 3.
cheated the ignorant, low-witted Jones tribe, *Daily Record*, Baltimore, 10/5/1935, 3. O'Dunne refers to this characterization in the opinion, but does not specify who made it, though it must have originated with the Findlay-French or Saulsbury team as Levin and Sobeloff had no motivation to argue accordingly.
maintained the injunction on all parties, "*French vs. Jones* Case Chronology," in file 21483A, BCCC #2. This occurred October 8, 1935.

Part 6 (pp. 123–139)

Chapter 21. Agent Benjamin Bratton (pp. 125–127)

XLVIII

his report to headquarters, letter from Benjamin Bratton to W. H. Moran, undated but almost certainly September, 1935. U.S. National Archives, Record Group 87, closed investigations file C-11369.
Bratton wrote in his report on the matter, U.S. National Archives, Record Group 87, Secret Service Daily Agent Reports, for 9/7/1935.
The Rummels and the Jones boy are all morons, letter from Benjamin Bratton to W. H. Moran, 9/7/1935. U.S. National Archives, Record Group 87, closed investigations file C-11369.
I did not turn over the new find of gold, statement of Ruth Grob Fisher, Sep-

tember 9, 1935. U.S. National Archives, Record Group 87, closed investigations file C-11369.

Bratton met with the Merrill brothers, letter from Benjamin Bratton to W. H. Moran, undated but almost certainly September, 1935. U.S. National Archives, Record Group 87, closed investigations file C-11369.

it is the opinion of this writer that they were speculating, letter from Benjamin Bratton to W. H. Moran, 9/20/1935. U.S. National Archives, Record Group 87, closed investigations file C-11369.

Chapter 22. Strategy in the Appellate Court (pp. 128–136)

XLIX
single case which was heard in the January, 1936 session, 170 Md. 318.

high public interest in preserving the finality of judgments, Simon Sobeloff & Wilfred T. McQuaid brief on behalf of Yale Merrill and Eli H. Merrill, 170 Md. 318, 6.

substantially benefited by such new evidence, Harry O. Levin & Sigmund Levin brief, 170 Md. 318, 6.

a re-argument should be granted, C. Arthur Eby & Emory H. Niles brief, 170 Md. 318, 13.

Boston University and Georgetown law reviews, *Boston University Law Review,* June 1935, 656–60, *Georgetown Law Journal* 23, 559–61.

L
first appearance in traffic court, *Baltimore Evening Sun,* 1/31/1936, 42.

he will have to serve a term, BCCC #2, 9/20/1935, 74.

You have had one chance here, *Baltimore Evening Sun,* 1/31/1936, 39.

found himself a free man, *Baltimore Sun,* 5/10/1936, 20.

LI
socializing course, *Baltimore Sun,* 4/16/1936, 4.

a different right and liability, 170 Md. 318.

entitled to a one-third share, *Baltimore Sun,* 4/23/1936, 26. The exact amount was $6224.86.

start it all over again with the second pot, *Baltimore Evening Sun,* 4/25/1936, 1.

LII
waited until June 30, 1936, BCCC #2, file 21483A.

settled out of court, *Baltimore Sun,* 10/2/1936, 4.

we read the gold clause act, BCCC #2, 9/20/1935, 230.

a pot to piss on, Interview with G. Ross French, 1/5/2004. Conversely, in 1936, the Findlay-French sisters signed court documents notarized in Atlantic County, New Jersey, where the two were apparently vacationing.

first graduating class of 1903, *Baltimore Sun*, 9/14/1980 (H. Findlay French obituary).

a son speculated, Interview with Michael Merrill (son of Yale Merrill), 11/8/2002.

the fellow that started out in this wanted more, BCCC #2 9/20/1935, 78.

LIII

driving without a license, *Baltimore Sun*, 10/8/1936, 28.

three months in jail, *Baltimore Sun*, 10/9/1936, 37.

lasting between nine and twelve months, *Baltimore Sun*, 4/16/1936, 4.

denied in April, 1937, *New York Times*, 4/18/1937, 27.

trickled in over the summer, BCCC #2, file 21483. The Hochman response is dated 8/26/1937.

LIV

hoards of a whole lifetime, Jacob Riis, *How the Other Half Lives* (New York: Charles Scribner's Sons, 1890), chapter 14.

working in the mayonnaise department, *Baltimore Evening Sun*, 8/25/1937, 32.

Panzer packing plant, City of Baltimore Health Department, Death Certificate #F38553, 8/26/1937.

sixteen dollars a week, *Baltimore News*, 8/25/1937, 15.

a plain dwelling in a none-too-affluent neighborhood, *Baltimore Sun*, 8/25/1937, 4.

quiet, reliable, well-behaved youth, *Baltimore Sun*, 8/25/1937, 22.

a swim in the Boston Street Harbor, Interview with John Grob Jr. (nephew of Henry Grob), 3/26/2002.

the hospital bill being only nineteen dollars, BCCC #2, file 22629. This file contains the Henry Grob probate material.

pallbearers included Henry's friends, *Baltimore Evening Sun*, 9/26/1937, 36.

thought all the gold had brought nothing but bad luck, Interview with Larry Zalenski (son of Lawrence), 11/4/05.

close friendship of the boys, statement of Ruth Grob to Secret Service Agent George Almoney, taken 9/9/1935. U.S. National Archives, Record Group 87, closed investigations file C-11369.

about all poor Henry ever got out of it, *Baltimore Sun*, 8/25/1937, 4.

Chapter 23. The Court Decides (pp. 137–139)

LV

I told him I have trouble with my meters, BCCC #2, 12/11/1934, 258.

folly, inexperience, extravagance and theft, Judge Samuel K. Dennis opinion, BCCC #2, equity file 21483, 12/28/1937.

a copy for the files in Washington, U.S National Archives, Secret Service closed investigation #C-11369, record group 87, entry 41.

LVI

free to settle her son Henry's estate, the Grob probate papers are located in the BCCC #2 equity files, #22629.

fought by able, resourceful people, Samuel K. Dennis opinion, BCCC #2 equity file #21483.

Part 7 (pp. 141–150)

Chapter 24. Treasure Trove Law (pp. 143–145)

LVII

England reformed its treasure trove laws, Roger Bland, Treasure Trove and the Case for Reform, *Antiquity and Law*, February 1996, 11–26. See also "Treasure Act 1996," http://www.hmso.gov.uk/acts/acts1996/1996024.htm.

fifteen hundred bronze coins dating to the fourth century, Bland, 17–18.

this pot has now gone missing, Interview with Edward Sines, 3/14/2003. Edward indicated that the original pot was on display for many years at the Star-Spangled Banner Flag House in Baltimore. The current curators have no knowledge of it. The Flag House was the residence of Mary Pickersgill, who wove the flag that flew above nearby Fort McHenry in the War of 1812.

more than ten million dollars today, while most of the coins in the hoard were not numismatically rare, there has been an explosion in the valuation of high-grade coins since the time of the hoard. An uncirculated gold dollar that sold for two dollars in the 1930s could fetch two thousand dollars today. This current value of the coins intensifies the extent of the damage done to the hoard by the finders and the local police officers.

Supreme Court of Texas, in 1955, *Schley v. Couch*, 284 S.W. 2d 333.

Tennessee followed suit in a 1985 case, *Morgan v. Wiser*, 711 S.W. 2d 220.

contradicted a Georgia decision, Groover v. Tippins, 179 S.E. 634.

half the states have enacted statutes, John M. Kleeberg, "The Law and Practice Regarding Coin Finds," *Commission Internationale de Numismatique, Compte rendu 53*, 2006. The author is grateful to John Kleeberg for pointing out this source.

and an Illinois case in 1992, 586N.E.2d, 826, 832–33. The author is grateful to John Kleeberg for providing this citation.

Chapter 25. The Coins are Dispersed (pp. 146–150)

LVIII

Walter Breen, a prominent numismatic author, Walter Breen, *Walter Breen's Complete Encyclopedia of U.S. and Colonial Coins,* (New York: Doubleday, 1988), 562. Since Breen's writing, numerous high-grade double eagles from the 1850s, recovered during the recent S.S. Central America salvage, have appeared on the market.

gave each a dollar from the hoard, Interview with C. Arthur Eby, Jr., 2/3/2003.

An experienced stamp collector, *Baltimore Sunday Sun Magazine,* 5/2/1954.

also acquired several Baltimore hoard coins, Interview with G. Ross French, 1/5/2004.

Eli Merrill's employer, Ike Berman, letter from Secret Service operative Benjamin Bratton to Secret Service Chief W. H. Moran, undated but almost certainly September 1935. U.S. National Archives, Record Group 87, closed investigations file C-11369.

one of the original organizers of the Baltimore Coin Club, "The Numismatist," 4/1935, 230.

formed one of the greatest American coin collections ever assembled, *Life Magazine* 4/1953.

might have been represented by John Zug, Q. David Bowers, *Louis E. Eliasberg Sr.: King of Coins,* (Wolfeboro, NH: Bowers and Merena Galleries, 1996), 35.

handled at least three hundred pieces, *Hobbies Magazine,* 3/1941, 96.

probably came directly from the Merrill brothers, statement of Bessie Rummel to Secret Service agent Benjamin Bratton, 9/6/1935. U.S. National Archives, Record Group 87, closed investigations file C-11369.

most brilliant lot of dollars we have ever offered, Thomas Elder auction catalog, 6/22/1935, 40.

inside connections at the United States mint, Roger W. Burdette, *Renaissance of American Coinage, 1905–1908,* (Great Falls, VA: Seneca Mill Press, 2006), 175.

Well- known northeastern numismatist, Letter to the author, 6/20/2005.

matchless uncirculated gems, *Hobbies Magazine,* 3/1939, 88.

LIX

damned nonsense, Proceedings at Testimonial Dinner on the Retirement of Hon. Eugene O'Dunne as Member of Supreme Bench, 6/25/1945, 8.

sold the 132 S. Eden property in 1939, Baltimore Superior Court Land Records, SCL #5974, folio 507. The property was sold to one Bertha Snousky on 11/7/1939.

might have ruled in favor of the ladies, Interview with G. Ross French, 1/5/2004.

falling down drunk, *Baltimore Sun,* 12/27/1940, 9; Email from David R. Rummel Sr. (nephew of Philip) to the author, 5/18/2002.

lost his brother Eugene, Interview with Edward Sines, 3/14/2003. The exact date of Eugene's death is unknown but was likely in the early 1940s.

suffered from extreme obesity, City of Baltimore Health Department, Death Certificate #9173, 10/7/1956, also interview with John Grob Jr., 3/26/2002. Emma died at 41.

she herself passed away the following year, Ruth Grob is buried in Oak Lawn Cemetery with a headstone indicating her death in 1957.

poisoned by individuals who he was investigating, letter from James Almoney (son of George Almoney) to the author, February 2006.

awarded a series of political appointments, *Baltimore Sun,* 1/5/1966 (Harry O. Levin obituary).

members of the Baltimore Jewish community, Correspondence, email from Robert Levin (grandson) to the author, 7/12/2004.

LX

using his legal name on his marriage certificate, Baltimore City marriage license #22575, 3/3/1938.

Periodic retrospectives in area newspapers, *Baltimore News-Post,* 5/23/1961, also *Baltimore News American,* 1/7/1981.

began collecting interest payments, BCCC #2 equity docket 43A, folio 720. The actual papers requesting and awarding the payments are missing in Maryland State Archives. However, the docket index summarizes and confirms their content.

Theodore's final payday, BCCC #2, equity docket 43A, folio 803, dated 5/19/1939.

brief stint in the army, letter from the National Archives and Records Administration to the author, 2/7/2006, in response to an FOIA request regarding Theodore Sines' military service.

remembered him as a good provider for his family, Interview with Edward Sines (son of Theodore Sines), 12/7/2005.

diagnosed with cancer in 1977, State of Maryland Certificate of Death 77-19600, 8/28/1977. Bessie Rummel, Theodore's mother, died 1/7/1971, City of Baltimore Health Department, Death Certificate # 71-0137.

ruled against asbestos manufacturers, *Washington Post,* 2/5/2004, B05 (Marshall A. Levin obituary).

Epilogue. 132 S. Eden Street Today (pp. 151–153)

LXI

razed around 1980, tax assessments for 132 S. Eden note "improvements" in 1977, and no "improvements" starting in 1979. The situation is identical for all the lots on Eden Street from 122 S. Eden to 136 S. Eden. However,

Robert Eagan, current owner of the property, believes that all these houses were razed in the mid-1980s.

second oldest park in Baltimore, *Baltimore Evening Sun,* 4/12/1939.

last of the Mohicans, Interview with Robert Eagan, 12/4/2003.

INDEX

Page numbers in italics refer to illustrations.

INDEX

F

Findlay, Charles, 7

Findlay, Mary Pillar Boyd, 7–8, 157

Findlay-French claim,
and civil suit, 104, 117; court
settlement declined, 68; and
English Common Law, 74, 92;
legal strategy of, 90–92, 97, 132;
and Maryland State Court of
Appeals, 85

Fleetwood, Charles, 6, 76, 157

Fleischer, Harry, testimony of, 4,
76–77, 95

Foster, Reuben
as legal representative to
Saulsbury estate, 48, 157; retains
Charles F. Stein Jr. for counsel, 48;
testimony for Saulsbury claim,
63–65; testimony of, 61

French, Elizabeth, 7–8, 9, 157

French, Henry Findlay (son of
Elizabeth), 8, 9, 157

Fuller, Perry
assesses coin value for catalog, 87;
and coin auction, 86, 86–87, 95,
97, 158; examines hoarded coins,
86; inventory for part one of
hoard, 164–166; regarding Gold
Act, 35; as stamp and coin dealer,
84

G

Gamerman, Harry, 12–13, 158

German, Fred, 158

gold coins, 99; first minted by U.S.
government, 24; and rare coin
collectors, 14

gold hoard
condition and value assessed, 87–
89; and Gold Act exemption, 35;
initial discovery of, 22–24; initial
plans for, 27; location in cellar, 56,
59, 60; noticed by numismatists,
35; police response to discovery,
32–33; preparation for auction,
87; and speculation as to origin,
72; theories of gold's source, 32

gold hoard, second, 101–107;
attempts to conceal, 133; found by
Henry and Theodore, 103; theft
of, 101, 102

gold recall
order by Franklin D. Roosevelt,
13–14; exceptions to, 14, 16, 126;
and Federal Reserve Bank, 13; and
hoarding of coins, 15

Grob, Gertrude, 158

Grob, Henry
and civil suit hearing, 106–107,
118; and coin auction, 81, 96;
estate of, 161–163; and first
discovery of buried coins, 22–24,
25, 28; and house at Eden Street,
17, 19–21; initial plans for the
coins, 27–29; legal ownership of
coins awarded to, 79; and Ruth
Grob, 36; testimony of, 56–57;
and Theodore Jones, 33, 34, 38

Grob, John [father], 17, 18, 158

Grob, John H. [brother], 19, 103,
104, 158

Grob, Ruth, 18–19, 36, 158;
approached by Merrills, 113–
114; and first encounter with
discovered coins, 27; and Joe
Fisher, 19; and Joseph Dragon,
19; and Ruth's Tavern, 19, 83–84;
and sale of coins, 108–109; and
settlement of Henry Grob estate,
162, 163; and work for canning
company, 19

Guerry, John Benjamin; and
romance of discovered gold, 39

H

Hendler, L. Manuel, 95

204